Monody in Euripides

The solo singer takes center stage in Euripides' late tragedies. Solo song – what the ancient Greeks called monody – is a true dramatic innovation, combining and transcending the traditional poetic forms of Greek tragedy. At the same time, Euripides uses solo song to explore the realm of the interior and the personal in an expanded expressive range. Contributing to the current scholarly debate on music, emotion, and characterization in Greek drama, this book presents a new vision for the role of monody in the musical design of *Ion*, *Iphigenia among the Taurians*, *Phoenician Women*, and *Orestes*. Drawing on her practical experience in the theater, Catenaccio establishes the central importance of monody in Euripides' art.

CLAIRE CATENACCIO is a scholar of ancient Greek literature and its modern reception. As a dramaturge and director, she has worked extensively with contemporary productions of ancient plays. She is a member of the faculty of Classics at Georgetown University.

Monody in Euripides

Character and the Liberation of Form
in Late Greek Tragedy

CLAIRE CATENACCIO

Georgetown University

Shaftesbury Road, Cambridge CB2 8EA, United Kingdom

One Liberty Plaza, 20th Floor, New York, NY 10006, USA

477 Williamstown Road, Port Melbourne, VIC 3207, Australia

314–321, 3rd Floor, Plot 3, Splendor Forum, Jasola District Centre, New Delhi – 110025, India

103 Penang Road, #05–06/07, Visioncrest Commercial, Singapore 238467

Cambridge University Press is part of Cambridge University Press & Assessment, a department of the University of Cambridge.

We share the University's mission to contribute to society through the pursuit of education, learning and research at the highest international levels of excellence.

www.cambridge.org
Information on this title: www.cambridge.org/9781009300131

DOI: 10.1017/9781009300179

© Claire Catenaccio 2023

This publication is in copyright. Subject to statutory exception and to the provisions of relevant collective licensing agreements, no reproduction of any part may take place without the written permission of Cambridge University Press & Assessment.

First published 2023
First paperback edition 2025

A catalogue record for this publication is available from the British Library

ISBN 978-1-009-30012-4 Hardback
ISBN 978-1-009-30013-1 Paperback

Cambridge University Press & Assessment has no responsibility for the persistence or accuracy of URLs for external or third-party internet websites referred to in this publication and does not guarantee that any content on such websites is, or will remain, accurate or appropriate.

for my parents

Contents

Acknowledgments [*page* viii]
Note on Editions and Translations [x]

Introduction: The Song at Work [1]

1 *Ion*: Monody As *Agōn* [41]

2 *Iphigenia among the Taurians*: Memory and Movement [82]

3 *Phoenician Women*: The Lyric Voice of a Shattered House [112]

4 *Orestes*: Monody As Messenger Speech [157]

Conclusion: Freedom and Form [187]

Appendix Actor's Song in the Extant Plays of Aeschylus, Sophocles, and Euripides [190]
References [192]
Index [214]

Acknowledgments

The idea of writing a book on singing actors in Greek tragedy arose from my work as a performer, director, and dramaturge. Staging plays for a live audience inspired me to concentrate on those elements of ancient drama that are not always obvious from the text as printed on the page, above all on the role of music. I therefore thank all those who have collaborated with me to make theater over the past two decades.

My scholarly and personal debts are many. This book began its life as a dissertation submitted to Columbia University in 2017. My utmost gratitude is due to Helene Foley for her wise and generous guidance as my *Doktormutter*. At the other end of the process, it was a pleasure to work with Michael Sharp as an editor and with Katie Idle at Cambridge University Press. I benefited from the suggestions of two anonymous readers who posed questions that led me to rethink aspects of my approach at a crucial stage. I have been fortunate in my colleagues and students at Georgetown University, who supported this project's development. I thank the mentors and colleagues who have encouraged me to become a better reader and writer as I moved from student to scholar: Jed Atkins, Tolly Boatwright, Peter Burian, Chris Celenza, Julie Crawford, Casey Dué, Marcus Folch, Justin Haynes, William Johnson, Cathy Keesling, Zoie Lafis, Catherine Langlois, Charles McNelis, Bridget Murnaghan, Greg Nagy, Marden Nichols, Josiah Osgood, Vicki Pedrick, Timothy Power, Elizabeth Scharffenberger, Mark Shiefsky, Alex Sens, Josh Sosin, Katharina Volk, Gareth Williams, and Nancy Worman.

Many of my friends are themselves scholars and artists. I thank Tori Akin, Charles Bartlett, Joshua Billings, Kate Meng Brassel, Fred Brown, Molly Borowitz, Lara Bryfonski, Ryan Campbell, Eva and Grace Catenaccio, Daniel Flanigan, Amy Garland, Roseen Giles, Richard Hutchins, Lucy Jackson, Evan Jewell, Cat Lambert, Rachel Lesser, Joe McDonough, Charles McNamara, Zachary Roberts, Henry Walters, Erika Weiberg, Leah Whittington, and Tom Zanker, who kept me company at different stages of the writing process. The inimitable Garett Albert translated all of Euripides' oeuvre with me over five years of weekly meetings, for which I am deeply grateful. I first studied Greek tragedy with the late Albert Henrichs, whose Dionysian passion inspired me. Finally, this book is dedicated to my parents, who taught me to love songs and stories.

Note on Editions and Translations

I have used the following editions for the Greek works discussed in this book. The lyric portions of tragedy present some textual difficulties. For monodies in Euripides, I generally follow the text and line numbers of de Poli (2011), substituting iota subscript for adscript, and rely on Diggle (1981) and Mastronarde (1994) for other portions of the plays. Translations are my own unless otherwise indicated and aim for clarity.

Battezzato, L. 2018. *Euripides:* Hecuba. Cambridge: Cambridge University Press.
De Poli, M. 2011. *Le Monodie Di Euripide: Note Di Critica Testuale e Analisi Metrica*. Padua: S.A.R.G.O.N.
Diggle, J. 1981. *Studies on the Text of Euripides:* Supplices, Electra, Heracles, Troades, Iphigenia in Tauris, Ion. Oxford: Oxford University Press.
Finglass, P. 2011. *Sophocles:* Ajax. Cambridge: Cambridge University Press.
Garvie, A. F. 2009. *Aeschylus:* Persae. Oxford: Oxford University Press.
Kassel, R. 1976. *Aristotelis* Ars Rhetorica. Berlin: De Gruyter.
Kassel, R. and C. Austin. 1983–2001. *Poetae Comici Graeci*. Berlin: De Gruyter.
Mastronarde, D. L. 1994. *Euripides:* Phoenissae. Cambridge: Cambridge University Press.
Page, D. L. 1972. *Aeschyli:* Septem Quae Supersunt Tragoedias. Oxford: Oxford University Press.

Introduction

The Song at Work

> She was the single artificer of the world
> In which she sang. And when she sang, the sea,
> Whatever self it had, became the self
> That was her song, for she was the maker.
>   Wallace Stevens, "The Idea of Order at Key West" (1934)

In Wallace Stevens' poem "The Idea of Order at Key West," two men stand by the sea and listen to a woman sing. Through her song the woman becomes the maker of her own world. She binds the disparate elements of emotion and sensation together in a formal composition. This anonymous, unaccompanied singer shapes, orders, enlarges, and even creates experience not only for herself but also for those who hear her.

Why does the individual voice raised in song move us so powerfully? To explain why song functions as it does is necessarily speculative. For the purposes of this project, the question may be considered from both linguistic and aesthetic perspectives. As an adaptive strategy for communication, song is a concentration of those elements of human speech that are heightened when emotion itself is high: variations in pitch and volume, rhythmical emphasis, and the repetition of sounds and syntactical units. From the standpoint of aesthetics, song draws upon a set of conventions and variations. Every song arises within a particular tradition and is heard by its audience based on prior encounters and expectations. This inevitably conditioned reception is notably prominent in the case of Greek tragedy, a stylized genre built up of a set of recognizable conventions, performed before an audience highly attuned to these conventions.

This book reveals Euripides' groundbreaking use of monody, or solo actor's song, in his late plays: in his hands, it is shaped into a potent and flexible instrument for establishing new narrative and thematic structures. At the same time, Euripides uses solo song to explore the realm of the interior and the personal in an expanded expressive range. Contributing to the current scholarly debate on music, emotion, and characterization in Greek tragedy, I examine the role of monody in the musical design of four plays of Euripides, all produced in the last decade of his career, between 415 BCE and his death in 406 BCE: *Ion, Iphigenia among the Taurians,*

Phoenician Women, and *Orestes*. These plays are marked by the increased presence of solo actor's song in proportion to choral song. The lyric voice of the individual takes on an unprecedented prominence with far-reaching implications for the structure and impact of each play. The monodies of Euripides are a true dramatic innovation: in addition to creating an effect of heightened emotion, monody is used to develop character and shape plot. These singing actors become the "artificers," to borrow Wallace Stevens' word, of the world in which they sing.

In *Ion*, *Iphigenia among the Taurians*, *Phoenician Women*, and *Orestes*, Euripides experiments against the backdrop of monody's traditional connection with lament. In contrast to the work of Aeschylus and Sophocles, where solo actor's song is predominantly connected with grief and pain, in these four plays monody conveys varied moods and states of mind. Although resonances of lament may still be present, monody in the late plays of Euripides can also express joy, hope, anxiety, bewilderment, accusation, and deliberation. Often, and simultaneously, it moves forward narrative exposition. As the scope of monody grows, its forms and dramatic functions change: passages of actor's lyric become longer, more metrically complex, more detached from the other characters onstage, and more intensely focused on the internal, emotional experience of the singer. In the four plays under discussion, we see a steadily increasing refinement and expansion of monody as a form, a development that rests upon changes in the style and function of contemporary music in the late fifth century.

My argument stands at the crossroads of two paths of inquiry: the study of dramatic form, on the one hand, and, on the other, the synthesis of affect, emotion, and character. These terms require some clarification. In modern literary criticism of Greek drama, "form" is employed in a number of different ways: to refer to the structural units of a play (e.g., ode or episode), or to the typical elements that recur from play to play (e.g., the *agōn*), or more broadly to the overall construction of the dramatic plot in a sequence of scenes.[1] Recent scholarship has emphasized the relationship between aesthetic form and politics and the cross-fertilization between the artistic structures of Greek tragedy and historical reality.[2] Victoria Wohl, in particular, has explored the ways in which the formal structures of Euripides' plays exert a "psychagogic force" on the audience, prompting emotional engagement with the dilemmas and contradictions of life in the

---

[1] Rutherford 2012: 7; Dubischar 2017.
[2] Vernant 1988; Zeitlin 1990; Rose 1992; Griffith 1995; Hall 1997; Wohl 2015; Levine 2015.

democratic *polis*.³ In all of these senses, Euripides has a highly developed and sophisticated sense of form. Although I will at times discuss the political and social context of Athens in the late fifth century, in this book I will principally be concerned with form as it functions within the plays themselves, focusing on the typical elements, such as the *agōn*, iambic *rhesis*, stichomythic exchange, messenger speech, and monody, which appear in combinations and re-combinations from play to play. By 415 BCE, these formal features of tragedy had become highly conventionalized and determined a set of expectations in the contemporary audience. As I hope to show, monody in the late plays of Euripides is always placed in self-conscious relation to these other formal elements of Attic tragedy.

Turning to the second set of terms, I argue that monody in the late plays of Euripides does represent a qualitative shift in concepts of individual emotion, sensation, causation, and subjectivity in tragedy, a new set of representations of what we might tentatively call "character." This is an especially fraught term in critical discourse. The ancient Greeks referred to the *dramatis personae* of a play as *prosopa* (πρόσωπα, "masks"), emphasizing outward appearance and presentation rather than an inner stamp. In recent work on characterization in Greek tragedy, scholars have discussed the difficulty of defining or evaluating character and the artificiality of divorcing it from other aspects of a literary work.⁴ Figures in Greek tragedy are idealized and fictionalized constructs, distinct from "real-life" people; the vision of the playwright is at all times shaped by social, cultural, and literary conventions.

In what follows, I adopt the inclusive definition of characterization put forward by Koen de Temmerman and Evert van Emde Boas, which includes the ascription not only of psychological and social traits but also outward appearance and physiology, habitual actions, circumstances, and relationships.⁵ I do not intend the word "character" to convey the modern Western notion of a consistent, lifelong pattern of reactivity and of moral stature that above all constitutes the essence of a specific human being. Nonetheless, Euripides does seem particularly interested in exploring conflict *within* the *dramatis personae* of his plays, and in staging the conflicts, decisions, and reversals that take place in

---

³ Wohl 2015.
⁴ Easterling 1973, 1990; Gould 1978; Gill 1986; Pelling 1990; McClure 1995; Worman 2002; Budelmann and Easterling 2010; de Temmerman and van Emde Boas 2018.
⁵ De Temmerman and van Emde Boas 2018: 2–3.

their interior worlds. Within this broader context, I propose that monody allows what is most distinctive about the singer at that moment to be brought out with particular strength and clarity of outline. Through solo song, Euripides reveals the inner state of the figure onstage and gives to it a place of central interest and importance.

Monody, like choral song and dance, takes Greek drama beyond storytelling and expands the art into a multimodal and multidimensional space. In the case of Euripides' musical craft, we are fortunate to have the comprehensive study of Naomi Weiss, who examines the role of *mousikē* (music, song, and dance) and *choreia* (choral song and dance) in four plays from the last fifteen years of Euripides' career: *Electra*, *Trojan Women*, *Helen*, and *Iphigenia in Aulis*.[6] Weiss demonstrates that Euripides combines contemporary musical innovations with the styles and motifs of traditional lyric poetry and contends that this mix of old and new is a central element of the poet's experimentation with the language and performance of *mousikē*. I share Weiss' interest in musical innovation in the late plays of Euripides and employ a similar methodology of close textual and metrical analysis. Yet there is almost no overlap in the material we consider or in the direction of our arguments. Weiss examines plays where most song is choral and discusses tragic choral poetry in reference to other, nondramatic genres. My own project, by contrast, focuses on plays where music is significantly the province of actors and puts monody in conversation with the other structural forms *within* Greek tragedy such as the *agōn* and the messenger speech.

Indeed, no single published work discusses monody in Euripides from a literary standpoint, although there do exist stimulating discussions of the monodies in individual plays. As in the case of formalism and characterization, this book draws together several strands of analysis. The philological tradition has produced important books about the metrical and structural elements of tragedy.[7] Other scholars have approached the role of lyric in drama from a variety of critical perspectives that consider its language and imagery, its links to established poetic and philosophical traditions, and its resonances with the political, social, and cultural developments of the Athenian *polis*; their writing on the songs of tragedy has focused on issues of gender, group identity,

---

[6] Weiss 2018a.
[7] Discussed further in the next section; compare Jens 1971. Work on lyric includes Kranz 1933; Conomis 1964; Dale 1968; Nordheider 1980; West 1982; Hose 1990; Lourenço 2011. De Oliveira Pulquério 1967–8, Brown 1972, and de Poli 2011 and 2012 deal specifically with meter in Euripidean monody.

democracy, religion, and myth.[8] Finally, recent work on music has enhanced our understanding of the style and ideological implications of the "New Music" – the catchall term used by modern scholars to describe the changes in musical style, language, and performance in the fifth and fourth centuries – for which Euripides was both celebrated and criticized by his contemporaries.[9] Drawing on these quite different schools of criticism, what I offer here is an integrated study of the aesthetic qualities of monody: how actor's song contributes to the unity of each play as a self-contained and self-referential dramatic work. Attention to such elements as prosody, meter, diction, syntax, setting, wordplay, imagery, and theme as well as to the more advanced techniques of irony, ambiguity, and internal tension can make available to us a richer set of readings – and of stagings – for a particular text. For a full appreciation of their complex role in Euripides' dramatic art, monodies must be considered both as formal poetic compositions and as expressive vehicles for emotion and character.

Monody, by its synthesis of lyrical structure and emotional expression, brings together the formal and affective dimensions of tragedy. As Eugenie Brinkema has written, "The turning to affect in the humanities does not obliterate the problem of form and representation."[10] Scholars have discussed the radical nature of Euripides' formal experimentation; they have also remarked on the complexity of the figures, particularly female ones, in his plays.[11] These are not separate assessments, but need to be taken together. As in all art, form and content shape each other. Euripides' use of monody in his late plays provides a means to the creation of more complex characters; and his desire to dramatize the internal emotional states of these characters in turn drives him to expand the boundaries of monody as a dramatic form.

---

[8] The bibliography is of course vast, and I mention here only works that I have found particularly stimulating: on myth, Conacher 1967; March 1987; on religion, Foley 1985; Mikalson 1991; Lefkowitz 2016; on gender and society, Zeitlin 1996; Foley 2001; Chong-Gossard 2008; Olsen and Telò 2022; on civic ideology, Goldhill 1986; Hall 1989; on social context, Winkler and Zeitlin 1990; Hall 2006; on Euripides' allusions to earlier works of literature, Torrance 2013; and on performance culture, Silk 1996; Wiles 1997; Goldhill and Osborne 1999; Easterling and Hall 2002; Peponi 2012; Butler 2015; Gurd 2016; Franklin 2016.

[9] This area is rich in recent studies, all of which include earlier bibliography; compare Pintacuda 1978; Murray and Wilson 2004; d'Angour 2006; Budelmann 2009; Levin 2009; Csapo 2010; Hagel 2010; Power 2010; Swift 2010; LeVen 2014, 2021; Weiss 2018a; Lynch and Rocconi 2020. The subfield now has a dedicated journal, established in 2013: *Greek and Roman Musical Studies*.

[10] Brinkema 2014: xiv. On the interdependence of affect and form, see further Gregg and Seigworth 2010.

[11] Foley 1981, 2001; Zeitlin 1996; Rabinowitz 1993; Blok 2001; Mossman 2005; Karanika 2014.

Monody and Dramatic Form

Every artistic tradition develops its own set patterns of repetition and variation and generates expectations built upon them. From cave-painting to the contemporary pop song, an art form is a specialized language with its own rules and regularities. A language depends for its intelligibility on its grammar – that is, on predictable morphology and on rules for the arrangement of units of signification. In particular, as Eduard Fraenkel writes in his commentary on Aeschylus' *Agamemnon*, "For Greek tragedy there exists also something like a grammar of dramatic technique."[12] Every Greek tragedy is constructed of discrete parts differentiated in form and style, which follow one another in a regular order. Innovation, modification, even subversion of these conventions are all possible; Greek tragedy was by its very nature a hybrid genre, which included and appropriated a wide variety of nondramatic subgenres from lyric poetry to forensic oratory and integrated them within a dramatic narrative.[13] But there is always a consciousness, shared between the artist and the audience, of the tragic theatrical tradition and its formal expectations.

The Greeks did not have a comprehensive general term for the different poetic forms of tragedy, which Aristotle in the *Poetics* names only as "parts" (τὰ μέρη).[14] In modern scholarship they are usually referred to by the German word *Bauform* (plural: *Bauformen*), a structural "building block"; the metaphor, drawn from architecture, imagines tragedy as a grand edifice built up of smaller units. The German philological tradition has generated valuable criticism of these *Bauformen*, with statistical detail and documentation. Much of this work is synthesized in the collection *Die Bauformen der griechischen Tragödie*, edited by W. Jens and published in 1971, which remains a valuable reference book.[15] The *Bauformen* recognized by Jens and his collaborators include the prologue, *parodos*, episode, choral ode, stichomythic exchange, messenger speech, *agōn*, *rhesis*, monody, supplication scene, and *exodos*.

This work is ongoing. Since the publication of Jens' collection, many of these individual *Bauformen* have been the subject of articles and monographs, while additional type scenes in tragedy, such as the *deus ex machina*, have been identified and studied. For example, the messenger speech has proven particularly fruitful, inspiring three books in as many

---

[12] Fraenkel 1950: ad 613. [13] Swift 2010; Weiss 2018a, 2019.
[14] Aristotle, *Poetics* 12.1452b.14–25. [15] Jens 1971.

decades, by Irene de Jong, James Barrett, and Margaret Dickin, respectively.[16] The choral ode – obviously of great interest for our study of monody, as the dominant musical *Bauform* of tragedy – has also received extended treatment for all three tragedians.[17] Useful synthetic works include a chapter on tragedy as a genre by Donald Mastronarde as well as a monograph on tragic style by Richard Rutherford, who discusses the varied handling of spoken dialogue and lyric song alongside topics such as vocabulary, rhetoric, and imagery, with illustrations from a broad range of plays.[18]

Nor is analysis of the formal structure of tragedy a phenomenon of modern times alone. The names of the different parts of tragedy seem to have been established already by the mid-fifth century. We can gather as much from the tragedies themselves, which sometimes explicitly display an awareness of their own preeminent patterns and governing rules. For instance, in Aeschylus' *Eumenides*, produced in 458 BCE, the chorus of Furies introduce the scene of stichomythic dialogue about to commence, enjoining their opponent Orestes to "exchange line for line, in alternation" (ἔπος δ' ἀμείβου πρὸς ἔπος ἐν μέρει, 585–586). In Euripides' *Medea*, produced in 431 BCE, Medea refers to the *agōn* in process as a "conflict of words" (ἅμιλλαν λόγων, 546). Likewise, in Euripides' *Suppliant Women*, produced in 423 BCE, at the beginning of the *agōn* scene Theseus accuses the Theban Herald of "contending in this contest" against him (ἐπεὶ δ' ἀγῶνα καὶ σὺ τόνδ' ἠγωνίσω, 427) and of entering into a "conflict of words" (ἅμιλλαν λόγων, 428).[19] And by the time of Plato a generation later, the phrase "a god from the machine" had become a proverb, reflecting the conventional scene that ends more than half of Euripides' extant plays.[20]

But by far the most important evidence for the conventional building blocks of tragedy comes from Aristophanes, especially his comedy *Frogs*, produced in 405 BCE, one year after the death of Euripides. It was because of his deep appreciation for tragic poetry that Aristophanes could be so sharp and witty a satirist. In *Frogs*, the god Dionysus journeys to the Underworld to resurrect a tragic playwright and save the city of Athens. While in Hades, Dionysus agrees to judge a contest of poetic excellence

---

[16] De Jong 1991; Barrett 2002; Dickin 2009.
[17] Foley 2003; Kowalzig 2007; Swift 2010; Billings, Budelmann, and Macintosh 2013; Gagné and Hopman 2013; Andújar, Coward, and Hadjimichael 2018; Weiss 2018a; Steiner 2021; Andújar forthcoming.
[18] Mastronarde 2010: 44–62; Rutherford 2012.
[19] This self-referential agonistic language also appears in the *Ion*, as we shall see in Chapter 1.
[20] Plato, *Cratylus* 425d, *Clitophon* 407a.

between the ghosts of Aeschylus and Euripides. The play culminates in a long and brilliant showdown between the two dead playwrights, who vehemently disagree on issues of language, character, and theme as well as on more technical matters such as how to compose music for the stage.[21] First Euripides performs a parody of Aeschylus' choral songs, lambasting their repetitive rhythms and ponderous language; then Aeschylus brings out the younger poet's "Muse" and proceeds to mock his choral lyrics and then his monodies.[22] Comic exaggeration and distortion notwithstanding, this presentation of the rival tragedians must bear some relation to the experience of the audience. Aristophanes displays a sophisticated awareness of critical terminology: he differentiates between prologue (πρόλογος, 1119), *rhesis* (ῥῆσις, 151), and monody (μονῳδία, 944). In other passages, Aristophanes uses the names of specific poetic meters such as iambics, anapests, and tetrameter.[23] We may conclude that at least some of Aristophanes' original audience would have been familiar with the chief characteristics and even the names of the constituent parts of tragedy and would have been able to distinguish between them in performance. Greek drama aimed to please both *hoi polloi* and the *cognoscenti*.

To summarize the discussion thus far, the Greek tragedians were professional artists working in a highly regulated and conventional medium. Many aspects of each play were already set: the number and gender of actors, the use of masks, the series of entrances and exits, the portrayal of violence onstage, and the mythological stories from which the plot could be drawn. In addition, the audience would have come to the theater with expectations about the *Bauformen* from which the play was composed. They would have expected an alternation of spoken scenes and scenes set to music, with a singing and dancing chorus; in addition, a play might or might not include an *agōn*, a deliberative *rhesis*, a messenger speech, or a monody delivered by an actor. Within these constraints, poets could exercise tremendous creativity. In the late work of Euripides, one aspect of this creativity consisted of playing with the expectations of the audience by unexpected and unusual combinations of different *Bauformen*.

In the tragedies of Aeschylus and Sophocles, *Bauformen* tend to follow one another in an ordered sequence without combination or overlap. In Aeschylus' *Agamemnon*, for instance, produced in 458 BCE, the play moves relentlessly forward to its denouement: a watchman hints at the dark truths within the palace in a prologue *rhesis*, the chorus explore the mythological

---

[21] On the contest, compare Hunter 2009: 10–54; Halliwell 2011: 93–154; Weiss 2018a: 3–14.
[22] Aristophanes, *Frogs* 1329–1363. On the parody of monody, compare de Poli 2012: 11–15.
[23] Aristophanes, *Frogs* 1204; *Acharnians* 627; *Clouds* 642, 645.

past of the house in their majestic *parodos*, a messenger delivers news of what has happened offstage, Clytemnestra and Agamemnon debate his decision to tread the crimson carpet in a taut, highly charged stichomythic exchange. Such a tightly organized structure, with a single rhythm of rise and fall, gives the impression of totality and unity. The late plays of Euripides are very different. They rarely proceed in a predictable linear fashion. Instead, these late plays spiral outward, following multiple plot threads and privileging the perspectives of multiple agents.

Here Donald Mastronarde's distinction between "closed" and "open" forms in tragedy may be useful.[24] A "closed" form depends on overt causal connections and focuses narrowly on a few main figures. In an "open" form, by contrast, some or all connections must be supplied by the audience of the play. The "open" form allows for the development of alternate structures of relatedness both formal and personal. As Mastronarde writes,

> Event (what happens because of outside forces) becomes as prominent as, or more prominent than, action (what occurs because of the deliberate choice of a figure). The number of figures involved in the action is increased and their separate influence on the course of events reduced. The rhythm of complication and resolution is varied and multiplied. The interconnection of the acts or scenes is to be understood by an inductive movement that notes juxtapositions and implicit parallels and contrasts rather than by a deductive movement that recognizes a causal connection in terms of "probability or necessity."[25]

As Mastronarde emphasizes, "the open structure is not to be viewed as a failed effort at closed structure, but rather as a divergent choice that consciously plays against the world-view of closure and simple order."[26]

Euripides is a master of the open form: his late plays demand interpretive effort from the audience. Like his predecessors, Euripides takes advantage of the all-encompassing capacity of tragedy to embrace, combine, and transform multiple genres and forms.[27] Rather than employing each *Bauform* as an element standing distinct and separate from what precedes and follows, Euripides creates composite orders. This drive toward formal experimentation is especially apparent in Euripides' novel use of monody in his late plays. In addition to strongly expressing a specific state of mind through song, a monody may simultaneously serve as part of an *agōn*, or as a deliberative *rhesis*, or as a messenger speech. In the plays I discuss,

---

[24] Mastronarde 2010: 63–87.　[25] Mastronarde 2010: 64.　[26] Mastronarde 2010: 64.
[27] Weiss 2019.

Euripides combines monody with other *Bauformen* to create hybrid structures, just as a collapsing telescope can be expanded or contracted, its parts nestled within each other. This is not a collapse into chaos, but a more concentrated order. One might also call the procedure Euripides employs in his monodies a liberation of form, as when the few simple shapes in a kaleidoscope are repositioned and reflected, such that while the individual elements are still recognizable, even disarmingly familiar at first glance, they transform into patterns wholly new.

The Emergence of Monody

The term "monody" in its etymological sense – "solo song," from μόνος and ᾠδή – refers only to a mode of vocal delivery and is not restricted to tragedy. The word was occasionally used in this wider sense in antiquity. For instance, Plato, in a passage from the *Laws*, discusses the regulation of musical contests in the education of children; in this section he also examines μονῳδία and χορῳδία, "solo performance" and "choral performance," without making any explicit connection to tragedy or even to theater.[28] But monody became over the course of the fifth century BCE a specialized technical term for one of the constituent *Bauformen* of Greek tragedy, indicating an extended song delivered by an actor, as opposed to by a collective chorus.

Today solo song is ubiquitous in musical drama. Works of musical theater aimed at a wide audience – from opera to Broadway musicals to Disney movies – are based around the showstopping arias of individual singers.[29] These solo songs are often the most popular and memorable parts of the dramas from which they are drawn. But this was not always the case. Greek tragedy emerged in the late sixth century; one of its sources was group songs associated with the dithyramb, a ritual musical celebration in honor of the god Dionysus.[30] Choral lyric was thus central to early tragedy. Tragic songs were predominantly composed for performance by a group of twelve or perhaps fifteen adult male Athenian citizens who sang and danced in unison.[31] A chorus might rehearse for weeks or months before the premiere, but the individual members probably continued their other, usual trades during this period.[32] As we know from the surviving plays of Aeschylus,

---

[28] Plato, *Laws* 764d; compare 765a.
[29] For a comparison of American musical theater and Greek drama, see Moore 2022.
[30] For ancient sources, see Csapo and Slater 1994: 89–101.
[31] On the size of the chorus, see Sansone 2016.   [32] Wilson 2000.

tragic odes from the early fifth century could be rich in imagery and dense with dramatic meaning, with metrical patterns of astonishing complexity; yet these songs were nevertheless constrained by the limits of amateur performance.[33]

Over the first half of the fifth century, tragedy developed its own particular musical conventions. Tragic choral odes, for example, came to be formed on the principle of strophic response, with each successive pair of stanzas introducing a new and distinct pattern. A strophic pair – a strophe and matching antistrophe – correspond in meter, music, and choreography. Strophic odes in tragedy thus have the structure AA BB CC, a structure distinct from lyric in other, nontheatrical genres of Greek poetry. The compositional technique of strophic response meant that tragedians could introduce tremendous metrical, musical, and choreographic variety into their compositions.[34] Variation was possible not only from ode to ode over the course of a given tragedy but also within each individual ode as it moved from one strophic pair to the next. In order to compose music to fit the dramatic situation, tragedians could draw inspiration from the wide repertoire of existing styles and traditions of Greek poetry including prayers, laments, wedding songs, magic spells, lullabies, and hymns.[35]

By the middle of the fifth century, tragedy had outgrown its local origins.[36] What had begun in Athens as a religious and civic ritual, integrating aspects of earlier epic and choral traditions became a unique art form with mass cultural appeal. The annual performance at the City Dionysia in Athens, which coincided with the beginning of the sailing season in the early spring, drew foreigners from across the Mediterranean world. Other powerful and wealthy cities soon built theaters of their own and commissioned poets, actors, and musicians to perform in them.[37] Aeschylus died in Gela in 456 BCE, as a guest at the court of the local tyrant Hieron, still writing and producing plays.[38] A generation later, Euripides and his fellow tragic poet Agathon both sojourned in Macedon at the invitation of King Archelaus.[39] By the end of the fourth century, tragedy was performed in theaters, some of them seating more than 10,000 people, all over the Greek world, from southern Spain to Sicily to modern Afghanistan.[40] This tremendous popularity was already well underway by the late fifth century.

---

[33] On music in Aeschylus, see Scott 1984; Bélis 2001; Gurd 2016: 58–96; Conser 2020.
[34] Battezzato 2009.   [35] Swift 2010.   [36] Revermann 2016.   [37] Bosher 2012.
[38] Smith 2018.   [39] Revermann 1999–2000; Duncan 2011.
[40] Bosher 2012. An interactive online map of ancient theaters is maintained by Whitman College.

Despite its status as religious ritual, tragedy had always been art for profit.[41] An increasingly sophisticated audience demanded novelty and skill in their entertainment, and the competitive nature of the festivals in Athens encouraged originality as well. Success was measured by the satisfaction of the spectators, who judged the performance. For the purposes of our interest in monody, the constant drive for innovation in tragedy manifested in two ways: the increasing prominence of music made by professional actors and *aulos* players rather than by the amateur citizen chorus, and the nature and sophistication of that music.

The late fifth century witnessed a tremendous increase in the extent and complexity of actors' roles in tragedy.[42] In the 440s BCE a separate prize for best actor was instituted at the City Dionysia in Athens.[43] Traditionally the art of acting, like that of dramatic composition, had been the province of well-connected, aristocratic families whose business was the theater. Aeschylus is said to have acted in his own tragedies, and his sons and nephews produced plays after his death. But by law actors at the City Dionysia and other dramatic festivals in Attica were not bound by the same restrictions of citizenship as choral performers. There arose a class of highly trained and highly paid professional actors from across the Mediterranean, who also specialized in the techniques of gestural, masked acting.[44] We know of one, Hegelochus, who acted as the protagonist in the original production of Euripides' *Orestes* in 408 BCE and whose unlucky mispronunciation of a key line cost him his career; he would have acted alongside a deuteragonist who played the demanding singing roles of Electra and the Phrygian.[45] Evidence of these developments in the professionalization of tragic performance can be detected quite clearly in Euripides' late plays, where many of his most striking, distinctive, and virtuosic musical passages take the form of monodies for the solo voice rather than choral songs.

The instrumental accompaniment for tragic songs changed as well. Archeologists and music historians have traced a progression during the later fifth century in the construction and capability of the *aulos*, the double-reed pipe used to accompany performances of Greek tragedy and comedy.[46] Technical advancements at this time made it easier for an *aulos* player to use a variety of scales, styles, and modulations while playing. New

---

[41] Wilson 2008.   [42] Slater 1990; Easterling and Hall 2002; Easterling 2002; Csapo 2010.
[43] Csapo and Slater 1994: 221–255.
[44] On acting techniques, see Csapo 2002; Green 2002; on vocal techniques, see Melidis 2020.
[45] Farmer 2016: 31–34.
[46] Martin 2003; Wilson 1999; LeVen 2010, 2014; Power 2010; Holzman 2016.

modes, harmonies, and tunings were also introduced in tandem with developments in Greek musical theory. By the end of the fifth century, there was a high demand at dithyrambic and dramatic competitions for star *aulos* players who were both expert and distinctive in their musical style. Already by 430 BCE, these *aulos* players had a reputation as predominantly non-aristocratic and non-Athenian. One such was the famous musician Pronomos from Thebes, whose name and image grace a large, richly detailed vase, now in Naples, depicting the actors of a victorious tragedy.[47]

Euripides was a central and pioneering figure in the musical revolution that swept through Athens during the later fifth century. Modern scholars often use the label "New Music" for this movement, but the Greeks themselves referred to it as "theater music" since it found its fullest expression in the genres of dithyramb, tragedy, comedy, and satyr-drama, all musical forms associated with theatrical performance in honor of Dionysus.[48] The chief characteristics of this new musical style in theater were multiplicity, complexity, ornamentation, and versatility. In the time of Aeschylus, the melody of a tragic song was expected to respect both metrical quantity and natural pitch accent.[49] But starting around 430 BCE, the composers associated with the New Music, among them Cinesias, Melanippes, Phrynis, Philoxenus, Telestes, and Timotheus abandoned this older style in favor of greater expressivity and spectacular effects.[50] Ancient sources depict these artists as having introduced a series of tonal, instrumental, and formal innovations in dithyrambs and nomes as well as in drama.[51] Star musicians dazzled audiences with performances not only on the *aulos* but also on the *kithara*, a type of concert lyre.[52] This expanded mimetic range was made possible by the professionalism and virtuosity of both composers and performers.

The New Musical revolution is one of the most widely discussed cultural events of antiquity. It sparked great controversy. Modern historians have examined comic parody, historical anecdotes, and musicological commentaries to reflect on the social and political dimensions of this change in musical style.[53] Ancient critics connected the New Music with democratic

---

[47] An entire volume has been devoted to this important work of art; see Taplin and Wyles 2010.
[48] On the term "New Music," see d'Angour 2006 and 2017. The ancient Greeks used the adjectives σκηνική or θεατρική; compare Aristotle, *Politics* 8.1342a17–21.
[49] Bélis 2001; Conser 2020.
[50] Yet revolutions in musical style were ongoing throughout the fifth century; compare LeVen 2014: 77–83.
[51] LeVen 2014: 71–112.   [52] Power 2010; Kárpáti 2012; Franklin 2016.
[53] See Michaelides 1978; Landels 1999; Murray and Wilson 2004; d'Angour 2006; Levin 2009; Csapo 2010; LeVen 2010, 2014; Power 2010.

mob culture and vulgar taste. Their accounts frequently employ metaphors of looseness, laxness, slackness, and softness, adding a moral dimension to their assault on the sound of the New Music. Others reviled it as barbarous, servile, anarchic, uncontrolled, and effeminate.[54] Plato dismissed it as musical "theatrocracy."[55] But these dissenting voices were predominantly drawn from the conservative elite. New Music was popular music, and all the surviving evidence suggests that it was embraced with enthusiasm by the mass theatrical audiences of the time, no doubt in part because of its opposition to conservative and aristocratic values.

Sadly, almost all the dramatic music from this period has been lost. Two fragments on papyrus from the Hellenistic period, amounting to several bars of music, can tentatively be connected to the choral odes of Euripidean plays.[56] These papyri show musically notated lyrics to choral passages from *Iphigenia in Aulis* and *Orestes*. The fragments are too short to give us much of an idea of overall musical composition, although they do indicate that the composer (perhaps Euripides, perhaps a later artist who restaged his plays) experimented with various metrical effects. There are no surviving musical fragments of Euripidean monody. But that is not to say we know nothing about the music of these compositions. The rhythms of the songs are reflected in the metrical patterns of the verses; some information about the musical system, including how the scales were conceived, survives in the works of Greek musical theorists; and musicologists can make inferences about the *aulos* based on fragments of ancient instruments, depictions on vases and wall paintings, literary descriptions, and cross-cultural comparisons. Most importantly, we have the words themselves from which much can be extrapolated about style and delivery. This evidence does not allow us to reconstruct the original musical performance of any tragedy but it does allow us to draw some tentative conclusions.

Even without musical notation, we can see that the influence of the New Music on the late plays of Euripides is showcased in his monodies, which demand and display the utmost skill of a professional singing actor and *aulos* player. In these compositions, Euripides often abandons the old rhythmic patterns of choral song with their more regular meters and strophic response in favor of free, nonstrophic stanzas of varying

---

[54] Ancient testimonia are collected in Barker 1984; Csapo and Slater 1994: 331–348.
[55] Plato, *Laws* 701a.
[56] On these papyri, see West 1992: 284–287; Pöhlmann and West 2001: 12–21. For a recent attempt to recreate the melody from *Orestes*, see d'Angour 2021. Based on the rhythms of Euripides' Greek text, Franklin 2019 describes his composition of "new ancient music" for a recent production of *Helen*.

meters. He introduces bravura effects such as repeated single words and unusual metrical resolutions. He also employs melisma – the extension of a single verbal syllable over several different notes – as attested both by the parody of his lyrics in Aristophanes' *Frogs* and by the few scraps of Euripidean text that preserve ancient musical notation, described earlier.[57] Another characteristic of this period of musical innovation seems to have been experimentation with the mixing of genres. Although such generic hybridity was by no means confined to Euripides' work or even to the theater in the late fifth century, Euripides in his late plays appropriates, transforms, and combines genres with particular self-consciousness and flair.[58]

Additional evidence for the growing popularity of tragic monody over the course of the fifth century comes from comedy.[59] The first use of the term "monody" in extant Greek literature comes from the *Horai* of the comic poet Cratinus, dated to the mid-420s BCE.[60] Two lines, transmitted as one fragment, twice mention monody: βούλει μονῳδήσωμεν αὐτοῖς ἕν γέ τι, "Do you want us to sing just one monody for them?" and οὐκ ἂν μονῳδήσειεν ἐκπεπληγμένος, "He could not sing a monody while struck out of his wits." Because of the lack of surrounding context, it is not entirely clear where the joke lies; the word ἐκπεπληγμένος, "struck out of his wits," could indicate suffering or, perhaps, extreme inebriation. In the plays of Aristophanes a generation later, the terms μονῳδία and μονῳδεῖν always refer unambiguously to tragedy.[61] As we have already seen, in *Frogs* monody is a central part of the competition between the ghosts of Aeschylus and Euripides in Hades; once he has mocked the choral odes of Euripides, Aeschylus parodies the style of his rival's monodies, specifically designating them as such (τὸν τῶν μονῳδιῶν τρόπον).[62] These references in the comic dramatists constitute our only fifth-century instances of the term μονῳδία and its cognates. Although many monodies in tragedy are self-referential, the tragic poets do not use the words μονῳδία or μονῳδεῖν.

---

[57] Aristophanes, *Frogs* 1314, 1349. [58] Weiss 2019.
[59] For comedy as a mirror of tragedy in the late fifth century, see Farmer 2016.
[60] Kassel and Austin 1983: fr. 270 PCG; Storey 2011: fr. 270. Aristophanes, *Peace* 770–705, dated to 421 BCE, describes Cratinus as already dead. Aristophanes has taken some comic license with his account: he claims that Cratinus died during the last Spartan invasion, outraged by the smashing of a full wine jar. The Spartan invasion took place in 425 BCE, and the last recorded victory of Cratinus was in 423 BCE, so the chronology cannot be quite correct, but probably gives a good estimate; see Sommerstein 1985: 165–166.
[61] Aristophanes, *Peace* 1012 (421 BCE): εἶτα μονῳδεῖν ἐκ Μηδείας; *Thesmophoriazousai* 1077 (411 BCE): ὦγάθ' ἔασόν με μονῳδῆσαι; *Gerytades* fr. 162 PCG (c. 408 BCE): θεράπευε καὶ χόρταζε τῶν μονῳδιῶν. See Kassel and Austin (1983–): fr. 162 PCG.
[62] Aristophanes, *Frogs* 1330.

Aristotle in the *Poetics* speaks only of monody to classify it under the heading of τὰ ἀπὸ τῆς σκηνῆς, "what comes from the stage," which is contrasted with music from the chorus.[63] Based on this evidence, it seems that μονῳδία and μονῳδεῖν emerged as technical terms for solo actor's song in tragedy over the course of the late fifth century. This dating coincides with the period in which Euripides composed his most daring and inventive monodies.

For our purposes, monody will be defined as a passage of solo actor's lyric of at least ten lines, which is either uninterrupted or only briefly interrupted by the chorus or by other actors.[64] Monody stands in contrast to other musical arrangements in tragedy, where voices alternate more frequently and the individual sections by each participant are shorter. Such arrangements, which I generally refer to as a "lyric dialogue," may take the form of an *amoibaion* (ἀμοιβαῖον), where one actor sings in alternation with another singing actor or the chorus, or an *epirrhema* (ἐπίρρημα), where an actor sings in alternation with a speaking actor or the chorus. The formal distinction in most cases corresponds to one of function: in a lyric dialogue, the focus is on communication, even if that communication is frustrated or incomplete, while in monody the emphasis is on the isolation and self-absorption of the singer. By these criteria, I have cataloged the passages of solo actor's song in the complete extant plays of Aeschylus, Sophocles, and Euripides in the Appendix.[65] As can be seen at a glance, actor's song occurs in nearly every play that has come down to us. In Aeschylus, each individual passage of actor's song is brief; an actor rarely sings for more than five consecutive lines without interaction from another actor or the chorus. But in the works of Sophocles and even more so in those of Euripides, actor's songs of ten lines or more – true monodies – take on a role of greater importance. Over time, these monodies increase in both length and frequency, especially after 415 BCE.

With this chart before us, we may pause to consider two suggestive accounts of monody: those of Eric Csapo and Edith Hall. Csapo's article

---

[63] Aristotle, *Poetics* 1452b.
[64] Barner 1971: 279 proposes that monody is "eine vom Schauspieler gesungene ('lyrische' oder 'melische') Partie von größerem Umfang und relativer Eigenständigkeit," which we may translate as "a portion sung by an actor (whether lyric or melic) of great extent and relative independence." The terms "Umfang" and "Eigenständigkeit," literally "extent" and "independence," obviously leave some room for interpretation.
[65] The dates are in most cases are approximate. My final count of monodies differs slightly from those of Barner 1971; Pöhlmann and Heldmann 2008: 255–256; and de Poli 2011: 4–5. When an actor sings two passages of lyric within a single continuous musical composition – as, for instance, in the *parodos* of Euripides' *Hecuba* – I have included both passages on the same line of the chart.

"Later Euripidean Music" synthesizes large amounts of data to demonstrate that over the course of his career Euripides shifted the musical burden of his plays from the chorus to the actors.[66] In plays produced before the mid-420s BCE (*Alcestis, Medea, Heracles,* and *Hippolytus*), actors deliver on average 13.3 percent of all song; most music comes from the chorus. In the following decade (*Andromache, Hecuba, Suppliant Women, Electra,* and *Heracles*), the portion of song presented by actors is significantly higher than in the early plays, constituting on average 37 percent of song in each tragedy.[67] In the late plays (*Ion, Trojan Women, Iphigenia among the Taurians, Helen, Phoenician Women,* and *Orestes*), the actors deliver on average 47.1 percent of all song. Csapo's research makes clear that the overall percentage of music to speech in each play remains relatively constant, and that the chorus continue to play a prominent part, especially in Euripides' posthumous plays *Bacchae* and *Iphigenia in Aulis*. Nevertheless, over the forty years of Euripides' career, the percentage of song delivered by actors as monody rises from about one eighth of the music in each play to almost half.

This quantitative increase, Csapo posits, responds to a desire on the part of playwrights, musicians, and actors to display a musical range and virtuosity beyond the reach of the amateur chorus and developed together with the increasing professionalization of actors and musicians in the fifth century. He suggests that the increased prominence of solo song in late Euripides is, in part, a function of the exigencies of dramatic competition. In the chapters that follow, I offer a complementary explanation: that the music of actor's monody matched the sorts of plays that Euripides wanted to write. Monody in particular was uniquely suited to conveying emotion, especially the intense and highly volatile emotions of an individual in extreme circumstances.

Turning to Edith Hall, we find the argument that social distinctions within tragedy were reflected in different modes of musical expression.[68] In Euripides, Hall proposes, monody is a marker of high social status, indeed almost always of royalty inherited by blood. When enslaved characters sing, it is usually the case that they are members of the aristocracy who have fallen upon hard times, as in the cases of Hecuba, Andromache, and

---

[66] Csapo 1999–2000. For the continued relevance of the chorus in this period, compare Weiss 2018a; Jackson 2020.
[67] Three plays written before 415 BCE have no monody: *Medea, Children of Heracles,* and *Heracles*. Medea sings in anapests before she comes onstage (96–98, 111–114, 144–147, 160–167), but never delivers a full monody; see Mastronarde 2002: ad 96–130. Hall 1999: 116 attributes this lack of song to Medea's being a "manly" woman.
[68] Hall 1999, expanded in Hall 2006: 288–320 and 2012.

Electra. Those born into slavery – with the exception of the Phrygian in Euripides' *Orestes* – do not use lyric. But it is not all aristocrats who sing: Hall concludes that "singing in Euripides seems to be a female (and barbarian) prerogative," and that, although some males in Euripides do sing, singers in Euripides are generally "the 'others' of the free Greek man in his prime."[69] Yet, looking at our chart of extant monodies, we notice that men do sing in a fair number of plays. Hall concedes that, among men, barbarians can sing (Polymestor in *Hecuba*, the Phrygian in *Orestes*); so may old men (Theseus in *Hippolytus*), immature young men (Ion in *Ion*), and men who have been driven to utter humiliation and agony (Philoctetes in *Philoctetes*, Heracles in *Trachiniae*). While Hall's thesis seems broadly correct, then, these partial exceptions to her rule deserve further exploration: many of the monodies I consider challenge the expectation of a lament by a royal, barbarian woman and innovate against this expected backdrop.

Emotion, Subjectivity, and Song

The nature of the connection between music and the emotions is notoriously difficult to define. Some fundamental questions lie at the heart of most inquiries, ancient and modern. Most relevant to our investigation of monody, we might ask how solo song in drama functions as a means of self-expression, and how it creates a sense of subjectivity different from that created by speech. These questions are complicated by the fact that we have lost virtually all the music of fifth-century tragedy. In the parallel case of ancient dance, Sarah Olsen has proposed a methodology that foregrounds the tension between the embodied ephemerality of performance and the fixity of the written word.[70] The idea that ancient music and dance are somehow "beyond words" makes them challenging subjects for scholarly interpretation. However, these challenges should not deter us completely.

Poetic representations of the emotional effects of music in ancient Greek literature are rich and varied.[71] In the *Odyssey*, we find examples of music making the listener feel melancholy, as when Penelope hears the song of the bard Phemius; or making the listener cry, as when Odysseus weeps at the performance of Demodocus at the Phaeacian court.[72] On the other hand, in

---

[69] Hall 1999: 112.   [70] Olsen 2021.
[71] For these examples I draw on LeVen 2021: 168–205 and Griffith 2021.
[72] Homer, *Odyssey* 1.325–327, 8.256–531.

Hesiod's *Theogony*, the Muses remind us that music can make its hearers forget their ills and may bring them respite from worries.[73] In Euripides' *Bacchae*, the music of Dionysus is capable of inducing states of joy, ecstasy, and even madness.[74] In Aristophanes' *Birds*, the song of the nightingale enchants its hearers and pauses all strife.[75] In ancient philosophy, too, music is assumed to work forcefully upon the emotions. Plato writes that music imposes order on the soul, and that training in certain kinds of rhythm and harmony produces men who are temperate, courageous, and good.[76] Aristotle reasons that music can be used for amusement, entertainment, and education since "song is man's sweetest joy."[77] Yet if music is consumed in inappropriate ways, both philosophers think it can throw the soul into disorder and even corrupt whole cities.[78]

Modern approaches lend support to these ancient ideas about the varied emotional power of music. The field of music psychology seeks to explain the connection between music and the emotions using the broader collection of approaches known as cognitive science. The cognitive science of music integrates ideas from philosophy, music theory, neuroscience, anthropology, ethology, and computer modeling to answer questions about music's role in human lives. Research in these fields has established some basic facts about music.[79] For instance, across the world, music occurs in contexts of ritual and play, and people experience music much more frequently in groups than they do alone. Many cultures recognize the capacity of music to induce particular states of mind, and it is often perceived as expressive in ways that go beyond language. Musicologist Ian Cross has described this quality as "floating intentionality" – the sense that music means something, but something that cannot be pinned down precisely.[80] Cross hypothesizes that "floating intentionality" allows for large groups of people listening to music to experience the pleasure of a shared communicative experience even though the specific details of their understanding might differ profoundly. Indeed, the sense of being transported beyond oneself is a hallmark of musical listening around the world. This experience has variously been referred to in terms of a surplus of affect or a heightened state of arousal.

---

[73] Hesiod, *Theogony* 55.   [74] Euripides, *Bacchae* 576–603.   [75] Aristophanes, *Birds* 209–222.
[76] Plato, *Laws* 659d–660a8. On references to dance and music in this work, see Peponi 2013 and Folch 2016.
[77] Aristotle, *Politics* 1339b10–1340b19.   [78] Plato, *Laws* 700a7–701b4.
[79] Here I summarize some of the findings presented in Sacks 2007; Bicknell 2009; Koelsch 2012; Thompson 2014; Margulis 2019.
[80] Cross 1999.

This heightened state of arousal seems to be particularly focused in the case of solo song. Solo song is what ethologists call a "super-normal stimulus."[81] In social species, like humans, the expression of strong emotion in another member of the group is a signal of a situation that most likely calls for a response such as fight, flight, or nurturance. Emotions are coded into language first and foremost at the level of prosody.[82] When humans experience emotion in response to events of high importance in order to signal it to others we vary the speed, volume, and pitch of our voices. Song is an exaggeration and a formalization of such signaling. A single voice raised in song sends a cue that something vital is being communicated and concentrates the attention of the listeners on that individual.

Yet the issue is more complicated than this, for emotions are conditioned by the social world in which they operate, and classical views of the emotions differed from our own. The Greeks of Euripides' age conceived of emotions not as spontaneous, irrational, or purely internal phenomena, as we tend to do today; rather, the ancient view of emotions included a necessary component of evaluation and reference to the outside world.[83] Aristotle, in the second book of the *Rhetoric* (2.1, 137a20–23), defines emotion (πάθος) in terms of its effects on judgment:

> ἔστι δὲ τὰ πάθη δι' ὅσα μεταβάλλοντες διαφέρουσι πρὸς τὰς κρίσεις, οἷς ἕπεται λύπη καὶ ἡδονή, οἷον ὀργὴ ἔλεος φόβος καὶ ὅσα ἄλλα τοιαῦτα, καὶ τὰ τούτοις ἐναντία.
>
> Let the emotions be all those things on account of which people change and differ in regard to their judgments, and upon which attend pain and pleasure, for example anger, pity, fear, and all other such things, as well as their opposites.

Aristotle's definition emphasizes the central role of cognition in emotion. For example, an emotion such as anger depends on the subject's judgment of what counts as an offense, and what counts as an offense depends on the other parties involved and on prevailing cultural norms.

Aristotle, then, seems to have understood emotions as arising primarily in and from social interactions. This is a useful data point for any discussion of emotion in Greek tragedy, as on the stage figures are almost always presented in dynamic relationship to one another. Aristotle wrote several generations

---

[81] Barrett 2010, building on the foundational work of von Frisch, Lorenz, and Tinbergen.
[82] Margulis 2019: 34–48.
[83] For the culturally specific dynamics of emotion in ancient Greece, compare Nussbaum 2001; Konstan 2006; Cairns 2019.

after Euripides; in the decades that separate the two authors, ways of depicting emotion in literature and drama had changed considerably, in no small measure due to the influence of Euripides and his fellow playwrights. In the chapters that follow, I will examine moments in Euripides' plays when figures use song to reflect on their emotions: that is, on human relationships, and on the feelings and evaluative judgments that arise from them. For instance, in the tragedy *Ion*, the subject of Chapter 1, the Athenian queen Creusa contemplates breaking years of silence to accuse the god Apollo of once violating her. She sings, "My soul, how can I be silent?" (ὦ ψυχά, πῶς σιγάσω; 859). In this monody, Euripides explicitly dramatizes a conversation between a woman and her own emotion, drawing attention to the high stakes of this conversation by his marked use of solo song.

The contrast between speech and song is central to the expressive potential of tragedy. With the varieties of song, a greater range of attitudes becomes available to the personages of the drama: states of passionate intensity find their full voice. As Richard Rutherford has written: "Fundamental is the principle that sung verse gives more scope to emotion expressed through extravagant phrasing and wild exclamation: song is less controlled and rational than spoken verse. That is not to say that reason is alien to lyric, but it is conjoined with intensity of passion or at least powerful commitment."[84] Most likely there was always song, as well as dance, fully integrated into Greek theatrical performance; certainly it is present as far back as we can trace. There were clearly good reasons for dramatists to hold onto the tradition of song, and to develop it to their ends. Thus, if the monodies in Euripides' late plays stand out in contrast to passages of actor's lyric in earlier tragedy, it is not because the mode itself is new.[85] Rather, as I hope to show, the poet has taken a familiar form, expanded its range, and turned it to new purpose.

Monody and Lamentation in Aeschylus, Sophocles, and Euripides before 415 BCE

Singing actors feature in almost all the tragedies that have come down to us from antiquity, but they are employed very differently, both in form and dramatic function. The greatest common thread before 415 BCE is the connection of actor's song with lamentation. In the ancient literary critics,

---

[84] Rutherford 2012: 246.
[85] On the comparable repurposing of older meta-musical forms in the choral odes of tragedy, see Weiss 2018a: 23–58.

we find monody classified as a *threnos* (θρῆνος), an individual lament, and distinguished from a *kommos* (κομμός), a lament shared between an actor and the chorus.[86] The relationship between lamentation in Greek tragedy and actual death rites in Attica in the fifthcentury BCE is neither straightforward nor entirely clear; nevertheless, drawing on evidence from archeology, vase paintings, and literature, we may sketch out some relevant features of contemporary funeral practice.[87] Aristocratic funerals were grand public events. Despite periodic attempts to limit display through legislation, funerals were occasions for wealthy families to demonstrate their power and influence. Lamentation played a prominent role at every stage of the funeral: at the wake (πρόθεσις), during the procession when the body was carried by chariot to the gravesite (ἐκφορά), and at the gravesite itself. These lamentations often involved not only family members but also hired mourners, usually unrelated women over sixty years old, who were known for their skill in inducing grief.[88] Lamentation in Greek culture was largely the province of women, especially the wives, mothers, and sisters of the deceased.[89] Funerals thus provided a remarkable opportunity for female voices to be heard publicly in a culture that usually enjoined silence upon them. Although in tragedy a monody of lament may be sung by a male or female character, as we shall see, issues of gender are always in play.

An important commonality between early monody and lamentation is the use of song to underscore the connection between the individual actor and the collective chorus. An antiphonal or shared "call and response" structure is a standard feature of actual Greek laments, ancient and modern.[90] Usual *topoi* include the expression of grief and loss, a contrast between past and present, praise for the dead, and anger and a desire for vengeance at those responsible for the death, as well as the desire of the mourner to die, and a description of the mourning rites offered for the deceased.[91] Certain stylistic features are also prominent: anaphora, anadiplosis, polyptoton, repetition, direct address to the dead, and inarticulate

---

[86] On monody and lamentation in Aristotle and ancient lexicography, see de Poli 2012: 14–20. He cites the scholiast to verse 113 of Euripides' *Andromache*, who equates monody and lamentation entirely: "monody is a song by a single lamenting character" (μονῳδία ἐστὶν ᾠδὴ ἑνὸς προσώπου θρηνοῦντος).

[87] On lamentation in Greek culture and tragedy, see Alexiou 1974; Loraux 1987: 45–49, [1999] 2002; Hall 1989: 83–84, 121–133; Foley 1993, 2001: 21–29; Segal 1993; Sultan 1993; McClure 1999; Murnaghan 1999; Suter 2003, 2008; Dué 2006: 30–56; Swift 2010: 298–367; Nooter 2011; Weiss 2017; Curtis and Weiss 2021: 261–310.

[88] Foley 2001: 26. [89] Swift 2010: 304–310. [90] Alexiou 1974: 131–160; Tsagalis 2004: 48–50.

[91] Dué 2006: 30–56.

cries of grief. This musical heritage is strongly felt in early monody. Before 415 BCE, almost every composition for a singing actor in tragedy involves a musical part for the chorus as well, and much of the dramatic interest derives from their interplay.

Notably, there are no full-fledged monodies in the six certainly genuine and complete plays of Aeschylus – that is, there are no passages of actor's lyric longer than ten lines that are not interrupted by the chorus or another actor.[92] In general, actor's lyric is much less common than in the work of Sophocles and Euripides. Rather, the musical contribution of the chorus is central to the thematic and imagistic coherence of each drama: in Aeschylus' *Suppliant Women*, for example, the chorus sing and dance for more than half of the play; in *Agamemnon* and *Choephoroi* for just under half.[93] *Prometheus Bound* presents a more complicated case. The play contains two showstopping monodies: the lament of the Titan Prometheus and the maddened song of Io, the former lover of Zeus who is now pursued across the world by a stinging gadfly.[94] As Sarah Olsen has explored, the monody of Io uses an extreme variety of music and meters to accentuate its central theme: Io's failure to conform to a standard Greek model of maidenhood, with its rituals of orderly dance, song, and controlled sexual initiation.[95] Io's plight takes the form of a never-resting journey, captured by her agitated, erratic song and dance in the theater.[96] Certainly, both Io's monody and the lament of Prometheus are unlike anything in the other six plays attributed to Aeschylus and seem closer to the techniques of Sophocles and especially of Euripides. Unfortunately, both the authorship and date of *Prometheus Bound* are uncertain, which makes it difficult to draw conclusions from it about Aeschylean practice or even practice that necessarily influenced Euripides.[97] It is likewise challenging to generalize from the evidence of Aeschylus' fragmentary plays: it seems probable that the character of Orpheus sang in

---

[92] In *Seven against Thebes*, first produced in 467 BCE, it is possible that Antigone and Ismene appear in the last scene and may have joined in song with the chorus in their final lines, but I do not accept this passage as original. On the ending of this play, compare Dawe 1967; Flintoff 1980; Orwin 1980; Torrance 2007: 19–20, 108–120.

[93] Scott 1984.   [94] See Appendix.   [95] Olsen 2021: 52–72.

[96] See Taplin 1977: 265–267 on Io's movements and Nooter 2017: 62–63 on the sonic register of her song.

[97] For the question of the play's authenticity, see Griffith 1977, [1983] 2000; Bees 1993; Podlecki 2005: 195–200. Yoon 2016 argues that it was produced separately from *Prometheus Unbound*, which weighs in favor of a later date. My own opinion is that *Prometheus Bound* was composed in the last third of the fifth century by an author who was familiar with the tragedies – and the monodies – of Euripides.

Bassarides, part of a lost Lycurgus trilogy, and several fragmentary lines of lyric hexameters have plausibly been attributed to the disguised goddess Hera in either *Semele* or *Water Bearers*.[98] Yet in these cases too, insofar as we can judge, passages of solo lyric seem to have been relatively brief and closely integrated with music from the chorus.

More about the origins of monody can be gleaned from Aeschylus' other plays. Aeschylus composed three powerfully effective scenes where singing actors interact with a speaking or singing chorus: the lamentation of Xerxes in *Persians*, the Cassandra scene in *Agamemnon*, and the exchange of Orestes and Electra in *Choephoroi*.[99] The highly emotional content of these scenes anticipates the subject matter of later monodies: Xerxes mourns his fall from glory; Cassandra communicates fantastic sights visible to no one else and predicts her own death; Orestes and Electra grieve for their dead father and make ready their plan for revenge. Yet Aeschylus' lyric dialogues differ from later monody because of the integral and expansive role of the chorus, who in each case respond to the solo singer and shape the movement of the scene. The focus in these exchanges is on communication, or, in Cassandra's case, on frustrated communication, rather than on the experience of the individual in isolation.

While Sophocles makes greater use of solo song in his plays than Aeschylus, actor's lyric nevertheless remains tied to lamentation. No hero in the extant plays of Sophocles is restricted to purely iambic lines: Ajax, Oedipus, Antigone, Creon, Electra, and Heracles all sing in lyric.[100] Fragmentary plays hint at even more singing roles; for instance, as a young man Sophocles himself was supposed to have sung and played the *kithara* onstage in the title role of his lost tragedy *Thamyris*, about the human poet who boasted he could defeat the Muses in song.[101] The ubiquity of such "singing heroes" in Sophocles' plays has been explored by Sarah Nooter, who proposes that Sophocles has his central characters appropriate the language of lyric poetry in order to create an authoritative identity as poets and prophets, inspired by the gods.[102] Song confers power. Indeed, as Nooter states, "an ancient audience would recognize the hero in a Sophoclean play partly by his

---

[98] On Aeschylus' *Bassarides*, see West 1990: 26–50 and Watson 2015; on the hymn of Hera, see Prodi 2022.
[99] See Appendix.
[100] See Appendix. Electra's song comes closest to the type of monody we see in Euripides; compare Nooter 2011 and 2012: 101–123.
[101] Wilson 2009.   [102] Nooter 2012.

capacity to slide from spoken lines into song."[103] Drawing on the work of Bernard Knox, Nooter further suggests that the lyrics of the hero express a radical isolation from the other figures on the stage.[104] Yet there exists a tension between heroic isolation and the effect that the intransigence of the hero has on the community. Solo song in Sophocles is always embedded in a larger musical part that includes exchange with the chorus or with other actors, even if the soloist temporarily ignores them.[105]

Even more than Aeschylus and Sophocles, Euripides seems to have been fascinated by the potential of monody from his earliest plays. Taken as a group, Euripides' plays composed before 415 BCE bear out Edith Hall's thesis that monody is primarily a mode of expression for royal women, and that the songs are strongly connected with lament.[106] These early monodies cluster in three main positions: before the *parodos*, in the first or second episode in pairing with another monody, or in the final scenes of the play.[107] Female singers outnumber male singers, and the positioning of monody seems to be affected by gender as well: women tend to sing earlier in the play, while men's songs are reserved for the end. Monodies are usually sung in situations of loss and grief, as in Aeschylus and Sophocles, and frequently employ dochmiacs and anapests. There is movement over time toward greater length, more astrophic form, and more varied meter.

The evidence of lost and fragmentary plays from all stages of Euripides' career corroborates these general trends. It is tantalizing to speculate, for instance, about the monody that began *Andromeda*, probably produced alongside *Helen* in 412 BCE; the heroine's lament in lyric anapests, delivered by an actor chained to a rock and interacting with the echo of her own voice, presented such a striking and memorable musical scene that it formed the subject of an extended parody in Aristophanes' comedy *Thesmophoriazousai* the following year.[108] *Antiope*, produced within a few years of *Andromeda*, also contained a monody early in the play,

---

[103] Nooter 2012: 10–11.
[104] A Sophoclean "hero" as defined by Knox 1964 denotes a character central to the action of the play, who is fierce, unyielding, unteachable, and unwilling to accept the limitations of the human situation.
[105] See Barner 1971: 313–320; Csapo 1999–2000: 407.   [106] Hall 1999.
[107] Beverley 1997: 24–26.
[108] On *Andromeda*, see Klimek-Winter 1993; Gibert 1999–2000; Kannicht 2004: 233–260; Phillips 2015. In *Andromeda*, perhaps, part of Euripides' innovation was to combine a monody of lamentation with an expository prologue *rhesis*, a *Bauform* familiar from his other tragedies; see Schmidt 1971: 34–44.

delivered by the musician Amphion and possibly dealing with the creation of the cosmos and the history of the lyre.[109] Fragments from Euripides' *Hypsipyle*, performed around 410 BCE, preserve verses from a monody sung by Hypsipyle, once queen of Lemnos and now enslaved as a wet nurse to the infant Opheltes in Nemea; the extant lines suggest that the monody drew on various traditional forms of women's song, including lullaby and weaving chant, as well as on lament.[110] Much exciting work remains to be done connecting the tragic fragments with larger trends in Euripides' practice as a composer.

In order to compare the ways in which the individual tragedians compose lyric for solo voice, it may be helpful to consider specific examples. In the readings that follow, I draw attention to some relevant characteristics of three solo songs, one from Aeschylus, one from Sophocles, and one from an early play of Euripides, in such a way as to show both commonalities and changes in practice over time. These three songs will provide a backdrop against which we may more clearly discern the innovations of Euripides in his late plays.

(A) Our first example comes from the earliest extant tragedy, Aeschylus' *Persians*, produced in 472 BCE. The Persian king Xerxes, who dominates the last part of the play, does not utter a single line of spoken verse in iambic trimeter: his entire part is lyric.[111] His long-delayed entry marks the dramatic climax to which the whole tragedy, with its anxious search for news of the battle of Salamis, has been leading.

Xerxes' language characterizes him as barbaric, luxurious, effeminate, and above all defeated. His lyrics are marked by frequent cries of grief and distress, as he indulges in lamentation and self-pity. But he is not alone in his suffering, as a later monodist might be. After the opening in anapests – a meter generally associated with the entrance of a new character in tragedy – the king is joined by the chorus of Persian elders in a shared strophic composition.[112] The scene includes seven strophic pairs in responsion as well as an epode. From line 1002 onward Xerxes and the chorus alternate individual lines, further binding together the king and his people. The immoderate grief of the Persians is thus contained in a tight, regular, and predictable musical form. This lyric

---

[109] On *Antiope*, see Kambitsis 1972; Wilson 1999–2000; Kannicht 2004; 283–291; Natanblut 2009; Billings 2021: 170–186.

[110] On *Hypsipyle*, see Cropp 2004; Chong-Gossard 2008: 75–79, 96–98; Tsolakidou 2012: 98–152; Simone 2020.

[111] Hall 2006: 290–295.

[112] On this scene, see Hall 1996: ad 908–1078; Rosenbloom 2006: 122–138; Garvie 2009: ad 908–1077; Swift 2010: 326–335; Gurd 2016: 68–73; Nooter 2017: 115–121.

exchange reinforces the condemnation of Xerxes' decadent folly as expressed elsewhere in the play, but also unites the shattered kingdom in sorrow. Here is the anapestic opening, followed by the first strophe-antistrophe pair:

Ξέρξης	ἰώ,	
	δύστηνος ἐγὼ στυγερᾶς μοίρας	
	τῆσδε κυρήσας ἀτεκμαρτοτάτης,	
	ὡς ὠμοφρόνως δαίμων ἐνέβη	
	Περσῶν γενεᾷ· τί πάθω τλήμων;	910
	λέλυται γὰρ ἐμοὶ γυίων ῥώμη	
	τήνδ' ἡλικίαν ἐσιδόντ' ἀστῶν·	
	εἴθ' ὄφελε Ζεῦ, κἀμὲ μετ' ἀνδρῶν	
	τῶν οἰχομένων	
	θανάτου κατὰ μοῖρα καλύψαι.	915
Χορός	ὀτοτοῖ, βασιλεῦ, στρατιᾶς ἀγαθῆς	
	καὶ περσονόμου τιμῆς μεγάλης,	
	κόσμου τ' ἀνδρῶν,	
	οὓς νῦν δαίμων ἐπέκειρεν.	
	γᾶ δ' αἰάζει τὰν ἐγγαίαν	920
	ἥβαν Ξέρξᾳ κταμέναν, Ἅιδου	
	σάκτορι Περσᾶν· † ἀγδαβάται † γὰρ	
	πολλοὶ φῶτες, χώρας ἄνθος,	
	τοξοδάμαντες, πάνυ ταρφύς τις	
	μυριὰς ἀνδρῶν, ἐξέφθινται.	925
	αἰαῖ αἰαῖ κεδνᾶς ἀλκᾶς.	
	Ἀσία δὲ χθών, βασιλεῦ γαίας,	
	αἰνῶς αἰνῶς ἐπὶ γόνυ κέκλιται.	930
Ξέρξης	ὅδ' ἐγὼν οἰοῖ αἰακτός·	[στρ. α
	μέλεος γέννᾳ γᾷ τε πατρῴᾳ	
	κακὸν ἄρ' ἐγενόμαν.	
Χορός	πρόσφθογγόν σοι † νόστου τὰν †	
	κακοφάτιδα βοάν, κακομέλετον ἰὰν	
	Μαριανδυνοῦ θρηνητῆρος	935
	πέμψω πέμψω πολύδακρυν [ἰαχάν].	
Ξέρξης	ἵετ' αἰανῆ [καὶ] πάνδυρτον	[ἀντ. α
	δύσθροον αὐδάν· δαίμων γὰρ ὅδ' αὖ	940
	μετάτροπος ἐπ' ἐμοί.	

Χορός	ἥσω τοι † τὰν πάνδυρτον λαοπαθῆ (τε) σεβίζων ἀλίτυπά τε βάρη πόλεως γέννας † πενθητῆρος· κλάγξω δ'αὖ γόον ἀρίδακρυν. (907–945)	945

XERXES Ah! Miserable am I,
since I met with this hateful, most unexpected fate.
How savagely a god has trampled upon
the Persian race. Wretched, what shall I suffer?
For the strength of my knees is loosened
as I look upon the aged men of the city.
Zeus, if only the doom of death
had hidden me as well
among the ranks of men who are gone!

CHORUS Alas, our king, for our noble army
and for the high honor of Persian rule,
for the splendor of the men,
whom now the god has cut down.
The land bewails the youth she raised,
killed for Xerxes, who glutted Hades with Persians.
Many men, the country's flower,
bows in hand, a dense multitude of soldiers,
have utterly perished.
Alas, alas for our trusted might!
The land of Asia, king of the earth,
terribly, terribly,
has been bent over double on its knees.

XERXES Behold me – woe! – the object of
your lamentation; to my nation,
My fatherland, I am a source of evil.

CHORUS As a greeting to welcome you home
I shall send, I shall send
an ill-omened shout, an accursed cry,
from a Mariandynian mourner,
a wail choked with sobbing.

XERXES   Go on, raise a discordant cry
         brimming with woes and tears, for the god
         has turned against me.

CHORUS   I will utter the song of lamentation
         to commemorate your suffering,
         and our sea-beaten ships,
         from a city in mourning for its children.
         I will wail, I will wail
         with a tearful song of grief.

Several characteristic features of lament are immediately apparent. Both Xerxes and the chorus punctuate their lyrics with inarticulate, ritualized cries of grief (ἰώ, 908; ὀτοτοῖ, 919; αἰαῖ αἰαῖ, 928). Almost every line of the exchange includes explicit vocabulary of mourning and misfortune (δύστηνος, 909; τλήμων, 912; αἰάζει, 922; αἰακτός, 931; μέλεος, 932; θρηνητῆρος, 939). The chorus identify their outburst in the strophe as a "shout of lamentation" (πρόσφθογγόν ... κακοφάτιδα βοάν, κακομέλετον ἰάν, 935–936), and Xerxes encourages them to continue with their discordant cry, "brimming with woes and tears" (ἵετ' αἰανῆ [καὶ] πάνδυρτον δύσθροον αὐδάν, 941–942), to which they respond with another wail of grief (κλάγξω δ' αὖ γόον ἀρίδακρυν, 946–947). The relationship between the monarch and his people is emphasized by his use of an imperative verb and their immediate response to his command (ἵετ', 941). Later in the *kommos*, both parties use verbs that indicate that they are performing together the traditional, physical actions of lamentation, such as beating their breasts, tearing their hair, and rending their clothes (1046–1077).[113] The refrain "wail now in response to me" is repeated several times at the conclusion of the *kommos* as a demonstration of the unending antiphonal lament that will now occupy the Persians (βόα νυν ἀντίδουπά μοι, 1040, 1048, 1066). Each strophe is divided between Xerxes and the chorus, emphasizing the double tragedy of king and country.

Other features are typical of Aeschylus in his lyrics. The passage contains several unusual or compound adjectives (ἀτεκμαρτοτάτης, 910; τοξοδάμαντες, 926). Foreign loan-words and place-names lend an exotic flair (ἀγδαβάται, 924; Μαριανδυνοῦ, 937). Aeschylus' famous use of abstruse and abstract language is immediately apparent. For instance, the

---

[113] See Garvie 2009: ad 1054–1058.

downfall of Persia is couched in multivalent metaphors. The chorus lament for the noble army (στρατιᾶς ἀγαθῆς, 918) but also for the metonymical "high honor of Persian rule" (περσονόμου τιμῆς μεγάλης, 919). The soldiers who have died are bewailed not as individuals but as "the splendor" or "ordered beauty" of men (κόσμου τ' ἀνδρῶν, 920). An important image throughout the play has been that of the Persian youth as the "flower" of the nation, a precious growth now "plucked" or "cut" in death (χώρας ἄνθος, 925). Continuing this image, the chorus imagine an unnamed, vengeful deity as having "plucked" or "cut down" this flowering crop of youths (δαίμων ἐπέκειρεν, 921).

As the earliest surviving example of actor's song on the tragic stage, we may take this passage as a template for monody in subsequent decades, one that may be built upon and varied. The composition is explicitly one of mourning; it showcases elevated and abstract language, more similar to choral lyric than to iambic dialogue; and the antiphonal composition is carefully arranged to emphasize the bond between soloist and chorus.

(B) Our second example, from Sophocles' *Ajax*, demonstrates the increased range and complexity of actor's lyric a decade or two after Aeschylus' death. The date of *Ajax* is uncertain, but it probably belongs to the middle period of Sophocles' career, around the year 440 BCE.[114]

The first episode of the play shows us the hero at his nadir of humiliation. After his mad slaughter of the herds, when he realizes what he has done, Ajax appears singing on the *ekkyklema*, the wheeled platform that displays the interior of his tent (348–429). Some passages of this *kommos* anticipate the monodies of Euripides' early plays, for instance in their plangent grief and emphasis on Ajax's desolate state. But the differences in approach and effect are significant. In a scene of eighty lines, Ajax sings three strophic pairs, while his spear-bride Tecmessa and the chorus of Salaminian sailors seek to restrain him in lines of spoken iambic trimeter.[115] The exchange involves attempts at argument and response: the chorus console Ajax, warn against an excess of grief, caution and comfort him; Tecmessa urges him to think of her and of his own former strength. Ajax, meanwhile, ignores them almost completely.[116] As William

---

[114] On dating, see Finglass 2011: 1–11.

[115] On this scene, see Nooter 2012: 31–41. On the comparable case of Heracles in Sophocles' *Trachiniae*, who sings while all the other characters are restricted to iambic verse, see Butler 2015: 121–160 and Catenaccio 2017; on Heracles in Euripides, see Holmes 2008.

[116] See Nooter 2012: 39, who writes, "Sophocles shows Ajax becoming more isolated through sung lament, rather than using lamentation to connect to the chorus."

C. Scott writes, despite the interjections of Tecmessa and the chorus, Ajax "virtually sings one long lyric."[117] The variation in form – that is, sung lyrics for the hero versus spoken iambics for his wife and the chorus – emphasizes the lack of communication between the different parties.

The scene is dynamic rather than static: as the *kommos* progresses, the hero's isolation becomes more extreme. In his opening lines, Ajax calls for death, curses his enemies, and laments his own fall from fortune. He never addresses his speech to any human being actually present, but his words and sentiments are comprehensible to them. Increasingly Ajax withdraws into himself, invoking absent or nonhuman witnesses: the hated Odysseus (379–381), his forefather Zeus (387), the Underworld (394–395), and the Trojan landscape (412–413). Yet there is something about his withdrawal that is not quite "into himself"; or we might say that he withdraws into a very public vision of himself. Ajax projects himself as the center of an increasingly expansive, supernatural world. The effect is to dramatize his self-inflicted, self-willed isolation from those who love him most and would try to help him.

Throughout the *kommos*, Ajax's agitation is conveyed by apostrophe, impassioned repetition, and asyndeton. These poetic devices are brought to a climax in the final antistrophe:

ἰὼ	
πόροι ἁλίρροθοι	
πάραλά τ' ἄντρα καὶ νέμος ἐπάκτιον,	
πολὺν πολύν με δαρόν τε δὴ	
κατείχετ' ἀμφὶ Τροίαν χρόνον·	415
ἀλλ' οὐκέτι μ', οὐκέτ' ἀμπνοὰς	
ἔχοντα· τοῦτό τις φρονῶν ἴστω.	
ὦ Σκαμάνδριοι	
γείτονες ῥοαὶ	
εὔφρονες Ἀργείοις,	420
οὐκέτ' ἄνδρα μὴ	
τόνδ' ἴδητ' – ἔπος	
ἐξερῶ μέγα –	
οἷον οὔτινα	
Τροία στρατοῦ	
δέρχθη χθονὸς μολόντ' ἀπὸ	425
Ἑλλανίδος· τανῦν δ' ἄτι-	
μος ὧδε πρόκειμαι.	(412–427)

[117] Scott 1996: 76.

> Ah! Surging straits,
> caves by the shore, and pasture of the coast,
> you have held me at Troy
> for a long, long time.
> But no more, no more, when I have
> ceased to draw breath.
> Let any man who understands know it!
> O streams of Scamander,
> my neighbors,
> kind to the Argives,
> no longer shall you look upon
> this man – I will utter
> a mighty boast –
> such a man as no other
> that Troy has seen coming
> from the land of Hellas.
> But now I lie here thus,
> without honor.

The rhythm of the passage is almost entirely dochmiac, a tragic meter associated with excitement and emotional distress and particularly popular in later monodies.[118] The language is elevated, with resonances of epic and earlier tragedy. As Patrick Finglass comments, the range of vocabulary in this scene "simultaneously conveys the grandeur and bitterness of Ajax's suffering."[119] Ajax sings not to his onstage audience but to the impersonal caves and coastline that have witnessed his greatness as a warrior and now witness his shame.

This passage of Sophocles is very unlike the example from Aeschylus. Compared to the lyrics of Xerxes in Aeschylus' *Persians*, Ajax's song is less closely linked to the surrounding action. The poet pauses the plot to explore Ajax's reaction. The language, despite some unusual adjectives (e.g., ἁλίρροθοι, "surging"), is more condensed and clear, with shorter lines and stanzas, simpler syntax, and swifter transitions between ideas. Ajax's *kommos* is similar to the antiphonal lament of Xerxes and the chorus in *Persians* in that it dramatizes grief following a loss of honor, but the focus is radically different: in Aeschylus the emphasis was on the vengeance meted out by an implacable deity against the Persian people as a group, while here it is on the suffering of the hero in isolation. Both songs touch on themes of loss, personal responsibility, and the individual's relationship to the community, and both use the language of lamentation; but where

---

[118] On meter in this scene, see Scott 1996: 73–78; Finglass 2011: ad 348–429.
[119] Finglass 2011: ad 348–429.

Aeschylus' handling is repeated and general, Sophocles hews closely to one person and his immediate, pressing situation. In this and other passages of actor's lyric, Sophocles opens up new possibilities for characterization through the vivid portrayal of the turbulent inner state of an individual, a potentiality that will be developed further by Euripides.

(C) The two scenes we have analyzed thus far take us to the boundary of Edith Hall's thesis that actor's song in tragedy is the province of "royal women in extreme circumstances." Xerxes and Ajax are royal and *in extremis*, but neither is female. It is arguable that in both cases grief and defeat have feminized these men, and that Xerxes is already less than a man because of his luxury and his foreignness. Nonetheless, for the full expression of unambiguously female grief in monody we must turn to the early plays of Euripides. Consequently, our third example comes from Euripides' *Hecuba*, probably performed around 425 BCE.[120] As we shall see, in this play Euripides exploits the connection of monody with lamentation to emphasize Hecuba's apprehension, sorrow, and grief.

The prologue of the play is spoken by the ghost of Polydorus, the murdered son of Priam and Hecuba. After the ghost's departure, Hecuba enters along with the other Trojan women who are awaiting enslavement and deportation to Greece. Her first words are in marching anapests, probably chanted, but she soon transitions to lyric anapests. The chorus inform Hecuba that as a final act of brutality before the departure of the ships, the Greeks plan to sacrifice her daughter Polyxena on the tomb of Achilles. Hecuba's response gives full range to her distress:

>   οἲ ἐγὼ μελέα, τί ποτ' ἀπύσω;
> ποίαν ἀχώ, ποῖον ὀδυρμόν,   155
> δειλαία δειλαίου γήρως
> <καὶ> δουλείας τᾶς οὐ τλατᾶς,
>   τᾶς οὐ φερτᾶς; ὤμοι μοι.
> τίς ἀμύνει μοι; ποία γενεά,
> ποία δὲ πόλις; φροῦδος πρέσβυς,   160
> φροῦδοι παῖδες.
> ποίαν – ἢ ταύταν ἢ κείναν; –
> στείχω; ποῖ δὴ σωθῶ; ποῦ τις
> θεῶν ἢ δαίμων ἐπαρωγός;
> ὦ κάκ' ἐνεγκοῦσαι   165
> Τρωιάδες, ὦ κάκ' ἐνεγκοῦσαι

[120] On dating, see Collard 1991a; Gregory 1999: xii–xv; Battezzato 2018: 2–4.

πήματ', ἀπωλέσατ' ὠλέσατ'· οὐκέτι μοι
βίος ἀγαστὸς ἐν φάει. (154–168)

Ah, I am wretched – what shall I say?
What sound shall I utter, what cry of lamentation,
a woman wretched for wretched old age
and for slavery, unendurable, unbearable? Alas for me!
Who is my protector? What family,
what city? Gone is my aged husband,
gone my children.
What road shall I walk, this one or that?
Where indeed will I be safe?
Where is one of the gods or a divinity to help me?
O you who have suffered terrible things,
women of Troy, you who have suffered terrible pains,
you have destroyed me, wrecked me! No longer
does life in the light bring me joy.

Hecuba's monody contains many of the paradigmatic features of female lament in Greek culture.[121] The most marked is the insistent use of rhetorical questions that are posed and then either explicitly or implicitly rejected by the mourner. These questions are introduced by interrogative words, which cluster in remarkable concentration in this short section (τί, 154; ποίαν, 155; ποῖον, 155; τίς, 159; ποία, 159; ποία, 160; ποίαν, 162; ποῖ, 163; ποῦ, 163). Such repeated questions emphasize the mourner's distress and confusion. Hecuba cannot comprehend what has happened to her and does not know how to proceed. In addition to the use of rhetorical questions, lamentation is signaled by the adjective "gone," repeated in anaphora (φροῦδος, 160; φροῦδοι, 161). Finally, Hecuba expresses her longing for death by saying that life is no longer desirable for her (167–168). In this monody the plot comes entirely to a halt, while the emotions of Hecuba take center stage. In every sentence Hecuba focuses on herself, emphasized by the preponderance of first-person verbs (ἀπύσω, 154; ἀχώ, 155; στείχω, 163; σωθῶ, 164). When Hecuba mentions others, it is always in relation to herself: family, city, husband, and children have left her (159–161), no god will help or protect her (163–164), even the women of Troy who share her fate have destroyed her (165–167).

The language of the monody is highly charged throughout but straightforward in content and syntax. Euripides avoids the exotic adjectives of Aeschylus' *Persians* as well as the specific details of individual experience

[121] Suter 2003, 2008; Dué 2006: 117–135.

that we observed in Sophocles' *Ajax*. Rather, the power of the song comes primarily from sonic effects. The repetition and polyptoton of important words – ποίαν and ποῖον (155), δειλαία and δειλαίου (156), φροῦδος and φροῦδοι (160–161), ἀπωλέσατ' and ὠλέσατ' (167) – emphasize the obsessive nature of Hecuba's thoughts and feelings. Euripides also juxtaposes words with similar sounds; for example, ἀπύσω and ἀχώ (154–155), στείχω and σωθῶ (163). Surely the virtuosic performance of the singer playing Hecuba and the piper accompanying the song were essential in creating a pathetic and stirring effect.

We have seen that both Aeschylus and Sophocles, albeit in different ways, exploit the interplay between the soloist and other characters onstage. So too Euripides. Although in this passage Euripides has Hecuba dwell obsessively on her own suffering, she is soon joined by another singer: when Hecuba's daughter Polyxena emerges from the *skene*, her opening lyrics match Hecuba's in a shared strophic composition (154–176 = 197–215).[122] The music of lamentation unites mother and daughter. Music also brings together the royal family and the women of the chorus. Over the course of the play, the suffering of Hecuba as an individual is balanced against the suffering of the Trojan women as a collective.[123] Hecuba's monody thus shows her as extraordinary in what she has suffered, but fundamentally connected to the other female characters in the play.

All three of the passages of actor's lyric examined here have in common the expression of intense personal emotion, above all grief at loss and bereavement, anger, despair, and a desire for death. The connection between solo song and lamentation runs deep in Greek tragedy. All three tragedians draw heavily on the function of song in a largely oral culture to give ritualized expression to intense, conflicting emotions and to provide solace amid anxiety, loss, and confusion. As Charles Segal has shown, the traditional features of lamentation are both incorporated and transformed by tragedy. By absorbing inarticulate grief into formal lyric, as Segal writes, "the tragic poet is able to identify the emotional experience of suffering with the musical and rhythmic impulse of dance and song."[124]

As we have seen, Xerxes in *Persians* is formally restricted to sung verse, a limitation unique in extant tragedy; his lyrics emphasize his grief and utter defeat; and through lamentation he is bound together with the community represented by the chorus of Persian elders.

---

[122] On the arrangement and meter of this scene, see Battezzato 2018: ad 154–215.
[123] On the sympathy of Hecuba and the chorus, see Mossman 1995: 69–93.
[124] Segal 1993: 16.

Compared to Xerxes, Sophocles' Ajax displays a greater formal and emotive range, encompassing iambic dialogue and extended *rhesis* as well as song; song marks a moment of extreme distress, and emphasizes the isolation of the hero. Yet Sophocles resembles Aeschylus in that he embeds the actor's lyric within a larger exchange with Tecmessa and the chorus. The singing actor is chiefly conceived of in terms of his membership of or isolation from a group. Likewise, in Euripides' *Hecuba*, although Hecuba focuses almost exclusively on herself, she is later joined musically to both the chorus of Trojan women and to her daughter Polyxena. In all three cases, actor's song engages with the language, themes, and meters of lamentation and employs an antiphonal musical structure shared between soloist and chorus drawn from actual Greek songs of mourning.

Monody in the Late Plays of Euripides

The practices of Aeschylus and Sophocles, and also of Euripides in his earlier works, are in contrast to the innovative approach to monody taken by Euripides in his late plays. In the plays produced after 415 BCE – in particular *Ion, Iphigenia among the Taurians, Phoenician Women,* and *Orestes* – Euripides departs from the model of actor's lyric established by his predecessors and followed in his own previous work. In these later compositions, solo song is not restricted to women, to royalty, or to situations that call for lamentation; nor is the soloist necessarily closely tied to the chorus. Instead, the monodies of these four plays constitute a departure from tradition, both formally and in the information they convey about the singer.

First, a word on production dates. As always with Greek tragedy, this issue presents some difficulty. Not all extant plays are dated, and not all dates are secure. Very many more plays were produced than are extant, written by the three canonical Athenian playwrights and by many others. Of the seventeen surviving plays of Euripides (not including the probably spurious fourth-century *Rhesus* or the satyr-play *Cyclops*), we have fairly secure production dates for nine plays, based on the information recorded in ancient hypotheses and scholia. The remaining plays can be dated relative to these on stylistic grounds. From the evidence of the securely dated plays, scholars have concluded that as time went on Euripides introduced various modifications, in particular increasing the frequency of resolution (i.e., the substitution of two short syllables for a long) in his lines of iambic trimeter and making greater use of passages in trochaic tetrameter.[125] Although we cannot be sure in which year exactly a play was produced, the cumulative evidence allows us to divide Euripides' theatrical career into stages – early, middle, and late – with some confidence. In the last decade of Euripides life, five extant plays have certain dates: *Trojan Women* was produced in 415 BCE and won second prize; *Helen* was produced in 412 BCE, along with the fragmentary *Andromeda*; *Orestes* was produced in 408 BCE; and in 405 BCE, after Euripides' death, the poet's son (or perhaps nephew) mounted the late poet's three tragedies *Iphigenia in Aulis*, *Bacchae*, and the lost *Alcmaeon in Corinth*. The other plays I discuss in this book – *Ion*, *Iphigenia among the Taurians*, and *Phoenician Women* – were produced sometime during this final decade, and probably in this order, although the exact chronology is not crucial for my argument.

In each of the four chapters that follow, I discuss the monody or monodies in one play, looking at choice of singer, positioning, meter, strophic form, language, and imagery; I also offer an interpretation that locates monody in the larger design of the drama. In these four plays, Euripides successively redefines monody: each song takes over a traditional *Bauform* of tragedy and builds upon it. Monody becomes a site of formal innovation and experimentation. At the same time, it facilitates the creation of an individual voice of broad expressive range, a voice both internally coherent and distinct from all others.

The first chapter presents Euripides' use of monody to express a contest of ideas in *Ion*, produced around 414 BCE.[126] In this play there is no formal *agōn*, where two figures set forth arguments in a direct struggle for dominance. Nevertheless, in *Ion* the central conflict of the play does receive its most explicit expression through the diametrical opposition of passionately held views. These views are expressed at length, but in song and separately, in the monodies of Ion and Creusa. In the prologue, the orphan Ion sings a paean to Apollo, the transcendent god at whose temple he serves. Through his monody the young man manifests his devotion to Apollo, his concern with purity and propriety, and his position as an orphan. The Athenian queen Creusa has had

---

[125] For the metrical criteria used to date Euripides' plays, both surviving and fragmentary, see Cropp and Fick 1985; Stinton 1990: 349–350; Allan 2008: 1–4; Parker 2016: lxxvi–lxxx; Gibert 2019: 1–4.

[126] For dating, see Martin 2018: 24–32; Gibert 2019: 1–4.

a much more direct and troubled experience of Apollo, repeatedly alluded to in the opening scenes. At the pivotal moment of the play, she delivers a musical accusation against the god who once violated her and, as she believes, left their infant son to die. Is Apollo benevolent and bright, or violent and uncaring? Because the god himself never appears onstage, the incompatible perspectives of Ion and Creusa demand interpretive reconciliation in the mind of the audience. In the two monodies, Euripides brings together the legalistic exposition typical of agonistic *rhesis* and the emotionality of lyric song.

The second chapter takes up the idea of monody as a vehicle for character. In *Iphigenia among the Taurians*, produced around 414–412 BCE, Euripides composes two monodies that highlight two critical stages of the heroine's emotional journey from stasis to purposeful action.[127] The virgin Iphigenia, rescued from her father Agamemnon's attempt to sacrifice her and magically transported by the goddess Artemis to the distant realm of the Taurians, is held as a captive priestess, forced by the king to oversee human sacrifices. Her brother Orestes and his friend Pylades arrive by chance in the land of the Taurians; after recognizing each other by signs, Orestes and Iphigenia determine to escape. In her first monody, which opens the play, Iphigenia mourns the unfulfilled potential of her young life, where each status was canceled, each promised doing undone. This vivid portrait of Iphigenia's inner state creates context for the scenes that follow, where she hides her true feelings and narrowly avoids sacrificing her own brother. Iphigenia's second monody, delivered after the reunion scene with Orestes, marks a shift in her mind and a crisis in the plot. Here we see Euripides taking the traditional form and turning it to new and innovative purpose: monody becomes a site for deliberative thought and decisive action, acting as a *rhesis* wherein the heroine formulates a plan for the future. Iphigenia's resolve is expressed not through a reasoned weighing of options in iambic trimeter but through song. The heroine's second monody represents not only emotion but motion of the mind as well; a gathering for the leap forward and the leap itself. The two monodies in this play thus mark two points in the inflection of Iphigenia's character, as she leaves behind her status as a passive victim and finds her purpose as the functional head of her family.

---

[127] For dating, see Wright 2005; Kyriakou 2006: 39–41; Marshall 2009; Parker 2016: lxxvi–lxxx.

The third chapter explores *Phoenician Women*, produced around 410 BCE.[128] In this play actor's lyric takes on a role of unprecedented importance in the shaping of plot and in the development of character, counterposed to and to some extent replacing choral lyric. The Phoenician women who make up the chorus are outsiders to Thebes; by contrast, the three monodists stand at the very heart of the city, its inmost, incestuous natives. Antigone, Jocasta, and Oedipus – all singing characters – are inextricably bound up in the ruin of their house. Monody translates the dramatic movement of the play into something distinctively inward and personal: all action is concentrated into reaction. Framing the quarrel and combat of Polyneices and Eteocles, the four scenes of actor's lyric in the play vividly portray the effect of the catastrophe on the individual members of the family. Three of these four lyric scenes feature Antigone; through song Euripides traces her progression from a sheltered maiden to a distraught mourner and finally to a mature woman who takes charge of her own and her father's fate. As in the case of Iphigenia in *Iphigenia among the Taurians*, the multiple songs of this virginal heroine show a progression from powerlessness to agency. Euripides here experiments with monody not only as a structural device to shape plot and create meaning but also as a means for the development of a complex female figure through the presentation of her evolving emotional state.

In the fourth chapter I turn to *Orestes*, produced in 408 BCE, which stands as the culmination of a decade of experimentation with monody as a versatile dramatic form.[129] At the climax of the play, the disappearance of Helen is reported not by a messenger in an iambic *rhesis* but by an anonymous, enslaved Phrygian in a virtuosic monody that is twice as long as all the combined songs of the chorus. The tonal and rhetorical ambiguities in the Phrygian's song underscore the increasing fragmentation and chaos of the plot. This monody overturns the expectations of the audience through its combination of the traditionally antithetical genres of monody and messenger speech. The Phrygian is an unprecedented type of narrator in tragedy, offering instead of an objective reporting of events a "polyphonic" account that draws on a multiplicity of genres and styles.

In the last decade of his career, Euripides establishes monody as a dramatic form of considerable versatility and power. In examining

---

[128] For dating, see Craik 1988: 40–41; Mastronarde 1994: 11–14.
[129] For dating, see Willink 1986: xxii.

these four plays, I hope to show some of the various potentials of this new Euripidean music as a major structural element in tragic drama, insofar as it can heighten emphasis, allow for the development of emotional states both subtle and extreme, reveal and deepen character, and mirror thematic movements. The poetry is charged with increased affect and expressivity; at the same time, it articulates a new self-consciousness about the reciprocal capacities of form and content to shape one another. The playwright repeatedly reconfigures the relationship between form and content, expanding the range of what can happen onstage, of what can be said and sung. Here we may discern the shift of sensibility in Euripides' late work, which proceeds *pari passu* with an apparent loosening of structural demands, or what one with equal justice might recognize as an increase in degrees of freedom and a new conception of order: a liberation of form.

1 | Ion

Monody As *Agōn*

The god Apollo stands at the center of *Ion*. He has set the plot of the play in motion and directs its progress through his agents Hermes and Athena; his image is always before the audience in the form of his temple; and the men and women who occupy the stage repeatedly attempt to justify, criticize, or influence his actions. Yet, because Apollo himself never appears, he remains unknown and unknowable. Like his Homeric counterpart, he acts from afar. Mortals must puzzle out this complex, ambiguous god as best they can: is he a divine embodiment of purity and light or callous, cruel, ruled by all-too-human passions?[1]

The debate about the nature of Apollo is carried on primarily through the juxtaposition of competing accounts. *Ion* is unusual among the plays of Euripides in that it lacks a formal *agōn*, where opposing arguments may be brought into direct conflict.[2] Rather, the cases for and against the musical god are presented in musical form through the paired monodies of Ion and Creusa. The solo lyric mode of the two monodies demands that they be interpreted in apposition despite the scenes that separate them. Similarities of meter, diction, imagery, and theme focus attention on the disparity between the radically different points of view expressed by the singers. Ion's monody praises a benevolent god in a peaceful, ordered world. Creusa – although she has not heard Ion's monody – denies and contradicts this song of praise, offering in its place a vision of a pitiless deity and

---

[1] Modern scholars, too, are divided on the issue. Assessment of Apollo's morality has shifted over the course of the last century: earlier scholars tend to favor the view that Apollo is above blame, while more recent writing emphasizes ambiguity and the simultaneous existence of multiple perspectives. On the former view, compare Murray 1965 [1913] and Wasserman 1940: 589, who exonerates Apollo from guilt for the rape of Creusa because a god cannot be judged by human standards: "a strong virility is just one aspect of his epiphany." Spira 1960; Burnett 1962 and 1971: 127–129; Willetts 1973; Sinos 1982; Gellie 1984; Farrington 1991; and Rabinowitz 1993: 195–201 all agree that, within the framework of the play, Apollo's behavior presents little problem since Creusa indicts Apollo not for sexual misconduct but for neglecting the child that he sired, and the play shows this criticism to be misguided. Other critics consider both sides of the issue; compare Wolff 1965; Lloyd 1986; Giannopoulou 1999–2000; Swift 2008: 36–50; Mirto 2009: 49–53; and Martin 2018: 8–10.

[2] Lloyd 1992: 3 identifies thirteen explicitly marked *agōn* scenes in the extant corpus of Euripides. The other plays that lack an *agōn* scene are *Heracles*, *Iphigenia among the Taurians*, *Helen*, and *Bacchae*.

a world arbitrary and full of pain. The attitudes presented in the monodies are diametrically opposed; each singer offers a position that is absolute and internally consistent. In this way the two monodies create what amounts to an emotionally charged musical *agōn*, witnessed by the spectators if not recognized by the *dramatis personae*, uniquely suited to an argument over the morality of the musical god.

The *agōn* as a *Bauform* of tragedy is typically a set of paired speeches composed in iambic trimeter and delivered within a single scene.[3] The contrasting monodies of *Ion* are not contained within a single scene and in fact are separated by half the play; nonetheless, in what follows I draw upon the conventions of the *agōn* to shed light on the combative relationship between the two songs. The musical *agōn* of *Ion* characterizes the figures of Ion and Creusa through the competitive presentation of their worldviews. Any contest of arguments raises questions about the sufficiency of language and of human constructs within a given play; here the issue at stake is the ability of mortals to understand and to judge the actions of the god.[4]

Yet the *agōn* of Ion and Creusa is inconclusive, because both participants are arguing from a partial understanding of events and their consequences. Michael Lloyd draws a distinction between the *agōnes* of Euripides' early and late plays: in the earlier plays, "it is obvious which side is in the right, and tension derives from uncertainty about whether an obviously sympathetic character will win his or her case."[5] In the late plays, by contrast, there are usually good arguments on both sides, and interest is focused more on the conflicting ideas and their articulate expression. The *agōn* scenes of Euripides' late plays depict a central conflict in a vivid and compelling manner and offer the fullest and subtlest possible account of two contrasting points of view. It is exactly this depiction and account that the monodies of *Ion* set out to achieve. The further action of the play is built upon the confrontation of these two stark attempts to define the nature of Apollo; the logical tension between the attitudes of Ion and Creusa demands some degree of resolution. Only after the exchange of songs can the characters, and the audience, come to an understanding that incorporates both the beauty and the harshness of the god.

The conflict over divine morality is not confined to the lyric portions of the play. Hermes in the prologue presents one view of Ion's birth and nurture; his narrative will be called into question by the human characters who later appear. Ion and Creusa come together onstage in two scenes to

---

[3] On the *agōn* in Euripides, see Duchemin 1968 [1945]; Collard 1975; Conacher 1981; Lloyd 1992; Dubischar 2001; Mastronarde 2010: 222–245; and Billings 2021: 159–222.
[4] Foucault 2001: 27–74. [5] Lloyd 1992: 131.

debate and discuss the god's actions, in the first episode (236–451) and in the *exodos* (1250–1548). In these scenes the argument is carried forward through rapid stichomythic exchange as well as longer speeches in iambic trimeter. The forum is public, even legalistic: Ion and Creusa respond to one another and to the interjections of the chorus. In the final scene, Athena in her epiphany seems to remove the impasse by confirming Ion's divine parentage, but her *ex machina* pronouncement cannot completely expunge the questions that have been raised by earlier scenes.[6] Ultimately, no account of Ion's conception, birth, and nurture emerges as truer than any other; throughout these iambic scenes, various versions of the story coexist, collaborate, and compete for authority.

The two monodies, by contrast, focus on private, subjective experience and emphasize the emotions of the individual singers. Ion's monody is delivered in complete solitude; Creusa in her violent outburst of song seems to have temporarily forgotten the other characters onstage and addresses Apollo directly. Each character is, for the duration of the monody, alone with the god. The language of the songs appeals to the imagination rather than the intellect and makes use of a wide imagistic repertoire: metaphor and extended simile; compound adjectives; an abundance of vocabulary that draws attention to sound, sight, and movement; and the jarring juxtaposition of pictorial elements. This wealth of sensory detail gives the monodies a dream-like immediacy. Ion's song wells up from him spontaneously as an expression of his quiet joy in serving the god. When Creusa finally breaks her long silence, she not only remembers the pain of the rape and of abandoning her child but also relives it, excruciatingly.

The contrasting songs also create a complex web of meta-poetic allusion. Monody connects mother and son to each other but also to Apollo in his role as the god of music. The privileged connections that both Ion and Creusa have to Apollo are underscored by the very act of singing. As scholars have noted, both monodies formally resemble the paean, Apollo's particular genre; the refrain of Ion's monody explicitly invokes Apollo by his cult title Paean (Παιάν, 125–128 = 141–143), while Creusa employs the traditional structures of a praise hymn ironically to set off her scathing indictment of the god.[7] Monody allows Ion and Creusa to approach the god of song directly through his own preferred modality.

---

[6] On the *deus ex machina* in this play, see Wildberg 1999–2000.

[7] Discussed further in Section 1.3. Compare Owen 2003 [1939]: 78; LaRue 1963; Furley 1999–2000: 188; Rutherford 1994–1995 and 2001: 111–112; Swift 2010: 61–103; and Olsen 2021: 73–99.

This chapter falls into four sections. In the first, I explore Ion's monody, which presents the god as unequivocally glorious but at the same time hints at the limitations of the young man's life. Then, in the second section, I discuss the first episode, in which Ion and Creusa seek to apply human moral standards to Apollo's conduct. The necessity, and the impossibility, of reconciling the human demand for justice with the opaque morality of the gods have long been recognized as a core concern of Euripides' work.[8] In this instance, Ion and Creusa deploy the terms of "justice" and "injustice" in debate, at once intellectual and impassioned; this exploration will be counterposed to the emotional expressivity of the monodies. In the third section of the chapter, I examine Creusa's monody, in which she first debates with herself about whether to speak out and then lays her grievance at the foot of the god. The final section deals with the *exodos*, where the conflict is first heightened and then, after the recognition of mother and son, reconciled within a larger gratitude.

1.1 Ion's Monody (82–183): Worshipping Alone

The monody of Ion is highly unusual in position, content, and form. In extant tragedy this is the only full-fledged male monody before the *parodos*.[9] The subject matter of Ion's song – contentment in his work and calm contemplation of a benevolent deity – is likewise unique.[10] The song continues for 100

---

[8] Many scholars have written about the depiction of the gods in Euripides, and the discussion continues in lively fashion. I have found particularly helpful Vellacott 1975; Hartigan 1991; Mikalson 1991; Giannopoulou 1999–2000; Wildberg 1999–2000; and Lefkowitz 2016.

[9] *Contra* Gibert 2019: ad 82–183, who comments that "singing by a character alone on stage before the arrival of the chorus is common" – only for female singers! Two other examples exist of men singing early in their respective plays, both of which highlight the unique nature of Ion's song. In *Prometheus Bound*, immediately after the opening scene with Hephaestus, Bia, and Kratos, the first utterance of Prometheus is a mixture of iambics and lyrics (88–127) and leads directly into a lyric *amoibaion* with the chorus of Oceanids (128–192). As I discuss in the Introduction, the authorship and date of this play have been so much disputed that it cannot be seen as a clear predecessor to *Ion*; indeed, the author of *Prometheus Bound* seems, in my opinion, to have been familiar with Euripides and even to have imitated his use of monody. In *Hippolytus* (428 BCE), Hippolytus upon his entrance directly sings three lines of lyric (58–60) in praise of Artemis and then joins the secondary chorus of youths in a hymn (61–72). Hippolytus' solo is very short, but the parallel with *Ion* is significant: in both cases the play opens with the young man's lyric praise of the deity that he especially worships; as the play progresses, the morality of that god is called into question.

[10] The remarkable features of Ion's song may be seen more strongly in contrast with the monody of Hecuba in *Trojan Women* (415 BCE), which also comes before the *parodos* and opens with recitative anapests. The effect in both cases is to isolate the solo voice as the center of interest and then to deepen and develop the themes introduced in the monody through interaction with

lines, quite long for a monody, and has a clear metrical structure. Several explanations have been offered for the atypical nature of the song, all of which emphasize the creation of dramatic irony and foreshadowing. Ion sings of being Apollo's son; he is in fact Apollo's son, more truly than he knows. The monody shows us what Ion's life has been like up to this point by opening a window on his past existence. It gives us, as Anne Burnett observes, "the closing moments of [Ion's] enchanted childhood."[11] K. H. Lee writes that there is in Ion's song "a sense of complete immersion in the present, with the contentment that that brings."[12] The song evokes the serenity and solitude of Ion's life, while also recognizing the outside forces that will soon disrupt it. Soon his history and future prospects will occupy Ion's mind. Hermes in the prologue has informed the audience that on this day Ion's time as a servant in the temple of Apollo will come to an end. The tragedy portrays a young man on the brink of manhood and dramatizes his transition into the adult world, whose complications and moral ambiguities will shake his pure and simple faith.[13]

Despite its calm tone, I would argue that the monody is in fact quite nuanced in its presentation of Ion's inner state. He is not as tranquil as he appears: underneath his pious calm we may discern a preoccupation with his unknown parents, with the trauma of his early life, and with his own identity and status.[14] Formally, the monody combines elements of a paean, the solemn choral hymn to Apollo, and a solitary work song, especially in Ion's address to his broom and the description of his daily activities.[15] Movement and gesture were an integral component both of paeans and of many work songs, and we may imagine that in this scene Ion's solo song was accompanied by solo dance. As Sarah Olsen has suggested, Ion's performance as a solo

---

the chorus. Hecuba's monody is an impassioned lament, signaled by the opening words, "Up, wretched woman!" (98), entirely different in tone from Ion's reverent address to the sun.

[11] Burnett 1971: 104. Hunter 2011: 21 sees the monody as the "Apolline high point" of the play.

[12] Lee 1996: 88.

[13] Compare Beverly 1997: 81. The figure of the young man on the edge of manhood is frequent in tragedy, exemplified by Hippolytus, Neoptolemus, and Orestes in all of his appearances. Rynearson 2014 discusses Ion's connection to these other characters, focusing on the parallels with Orestes in the *Oresteia*. Some scholars connect this phenomenon to the annual ceremony of the *ephebeia* and the formation of Athenian ideology; compare Goldhill 1987 and Winkler 1990. For the connection in *Ion* between generational passage and civic myth, see Segal 1999.

[14] As noted by Pedrick 2007: 89, who comments that Ion "has no relationship to his origins in the past" and is an "artifact of abandonment," eager to set off on a quest for his true identity. Hoffer 1996: 291 discusses Ion's attitude to his status as a temple slave, which combines "naïve contentment with wistful longing."

[15] On the paean as a genre, see Käppel 1992: 32–86; Rutherford 1994–5 and 2001: 3–136; and Swift 2010: 61–103. On work songs, see Karanika 2014: 136–159 and Olsen 2021: 73–94.

male dancer is a mark of his liminal status in this opening scene, poised between his servile past and the elevated authority of his future.[16] As a solo singer, Ion is likewise remarkable; in the fifth century, the paean was primarily associated with the creation of a sense of community and solidarity and was almost always performed by a chorus of young men.[17] The choreutes of a paean were thought to represent the *polis* as a whole approaching the god Apollo to ask for healing in a time of crisis or to offer praise and celebration when that crisis was averted.[18] Ion worships alone. As a dancer and singer not joined by a chorus, Ion is singled out in the prologue as a figure defined by his isolation from other people; one major theme of the play will be the young man's integration into the larger structures of family, community, and city.

On the surface, Ion's world is calm, precise, and predictable: the orderly progression of the monody matches its subject matter.[19] In contrast to many of the monodies in Euripides' late plays, which are astrophic and employ a wide variety of meters, here the poet offers a unified composition.[20] The monody falls naturally into three large metrical sections: it begins with recitative anapests (82–111); develops with a lyric strophe and antistrophe, punctuated by a short refrain, repeated twice (112–143); and finishes with an epode of lyric anapests that echoes the opening movement and brings the song to a close (144–183).[21] The two anapestic sections, one chanted, one sung, neatly frame the strophic pair and refrains. In the central strophic section, Ion reaches his greatest heights of expressivity and emotion, but even here the poetical flights are contained within the metrical systems of the rest of the monody, relying principally on spondaic anapests. There is evidence that spondaic meter was associated with the paean; in performance, it also has the effect of slowing the tempo of the song and enforcing a measured predictability.[22]

---

[16] Olsen 2021: 93–94.

[17] Swift 2010: 63–64. Compare Weiss 2018a: 104–116 on the analogous paradox of absent choral music in *Trojan Women*.

[18] Rutherford 2001: 7–9.

[19] The organized metrical structure of the monody is noted by Barlow 1971: 46–48; Beverley 1997: 80–95; de Poli 2012: 99–105; and Martin 2018: ad 82–183.

[20] The structure of the monody is thus in tension with the characteristics of late Euripidean music as identified by Csapo 2004: 228, including voluble rhythm and melody, strange vocabulary, and chaotic syntax. Certainly the effect here is not to create "a dizzying effect of giddiness, if not outright hysteria," as Csapo suggests. These generalizations may be truer of Creusa's monody, but, as we shall see, her emotionality is balanced by the forward thrust of a persuasive argument.

[21] Line-by-line metrical analyses can be found in Owen 2003 [1939]: 85–186; de Poli 2011: 175–187; Lourenço 2011: 258–261; Martin 2018: ad 82–183; and Gibert 2019: ad 82–183. For Euripides' use of lyric anapests, see Lourenço 2011: 45–52.

[22] Rutherford 1994–5.

Each metrical section has its own focus and primary topic; the musical structure of the song thus moves in tandem with its thematic development. Four subjects are addressed. In the first twenty-nine lines, Ion summarizes his status, in anapests (82–111). Then he moves to a section of elevated lyric, addressed, daringly, to his holy broom (strophe, 112–124), which concludes with a direct invocation of the god (125–127). He turns his attention to the sprinkling of water that purifies the steps of the temple (antistrophe, 128–140). The strophe-antistrophe pair is brought to a close by a repetition of the paeanic refrain (141–143). Finally, in a section of freer, astrophic lyric anapests, he wards off the birds that threaten to defile the temple with their droppings (154–181). At the end of each section there is a kind of σφραγίς, or poetic seal, which reinforces the divisions of meter and of theme, and stamps on Ion's work a sacral quality. The preoccupations and prejudices in Ion's conception of Apollo and, necessarily, in his conception of life are developed as the song proceeds.

The opening anapestic section, a self-contained movement both metrically and thematically, itself falls into four parts, each rounded off by a concluding paroemiac: a description of sunrise (82–88), the activity in the temple precinct (89–93), instructions to Ion's fellow attendants (94–101), and Ion's own tasks (102–111). The absence of Doric forms suggests that this part was not sung but delivered in recitative.[23] The sections increase in length and move from the outer fringes of Ion's perception to a contemplation of what is nearest to him, his own work and worship. Ion begins with a reverent depiction of the rising sun at Delphi:

> ἅρματα μὲν τάδε λαμπρὰ τεθρίππων
> Ἥλιος ἤδη λάμπει κατὰ γῆν,
> ἄστρα δὲ φεύγει πυρὶ τῷδ' αἰθέρος
> ἐς νύχθ' ἱεράν·
> Παρνησιάδες δ' ἄβατοι κορυφαὶ
> καταλαμπόμεναι τὴν ἡμερίαν
> ἁψῖδα βροτοῖσι δέχονται.   (82–88)

> This shining four-horsed chariot,
> Helios, already shines on the world,
> and at this celestial fire the stars flee
> into holy night.
> The peaks of Parnassus, untrodden,
> shining the day in reflection, receive
> the sun's wheel for mortal men.

[23] De Poli 2011: 175.

After evoking the vistas of heaven and Parnassus, he turns his focus to the familiar scene of the temple and its daily activities:

> σμύρνης δ' ἀνύδρου καπνὸς εἰς ὀρόφους
> Φοίβου πέταται.
> θάσσει δὲ γυνὴ τρίποδα ζάθεον
> Δελφίς, ἀείδουσ' Ἕλλησι βοάς,
> ἃς ἂν Ἀπόλλων κελαδήσῃ. (89–93)

> The smoke of myrrh, undiluted,
> floats upward to the peaks of Phoebus.
> The Delphian priestess sits on the sacred tripod,
> rendering sound into song for Greeks
> from the torrents Apollo utters.

Ion next addresses the attendants of the shrine, directing them to perform their ritual tasks. The idea of serving, both menial and exalted, will be developed throughout the four sections of the monody and constitutes one of its principal themes. Ion instructs the attendants to ready themselves for their work in the temple:

> ἀλλ', ὦ Φοίβου Δελφοὶ θέραπες,
> τὰς Κασταλίας ἀργυροειδεῖς
> βαίνετε δίνας, καθαραῖς δὲ δρόσοις
> ἀφυδρανάμενοι στείχετε ναούς·
> στόμα τ' εὔφημον φρουρεῖτ' ἀγαθόν,
> φήμας τ' ἀγαθὰς
> τοῖς ἐθέλουσιν μαντεύεσθαι
> γλώσσης ἰδίας ἀποφαίνειν. (94–101)

> But you Delphians who attend on Phoebus,
> go down to the silvery whirls of Castalia,
> and, cleansed in pure streams, go to the shrine.
> Take care that your mouth be well-omened and good,
> and that your tongue utter words that are good
> to those who arrive to consult the oracle.

As the address to Helios emphasized light, these lines introduce another image of central thematic importance: purity.[24] The waters of Castalia are "silvery" (ἀργυροειδεῖς) and its dews are "pure" (καθαραῖς). All words uttered in the presence of the god must be "well-omened"

---

[24] Compare Pellegrino 2004: ad 149–150 and Martin 2018: ad 94–101 on Ion's concern with purity.

(εὔφημον) and "good" (ἀγαθόν, ἀγαθάς), as exemplified by Ion's own monody, which he presents as an offering to Apollo. Through his own song, Ion gives an example to his fellow servants of how the god must be addressed.

Ion then summarizes his own threefold task: to sweep the floor, cleanse the temple with sacred water, and ward off the birds that threaten to defile the holy precinct:

> ἡμεῖς δέ, πόνους οὓς ἐκ παιδὸς
> μοχθοῦμεν ἀεί, πτόρθοισι δάφνης
> στέφεσίν θ' ἱεροῖς ἐσόδους Φοίβου
> καθαρὰς θήσομεν, ὑγραῖς τε πέδον
> ῥανίσιν νοτερόν· πτηνῶν τ' ἀγέλας,
> αἳ βλάπτουσιν σέμν' ἀναθήματα,
> τόξοισιν ἐμοῖς φυγάδας θήσομεν· (102–108)

> But for me, my work, from childhood on,
> I labor always: with laurel boughs
> and holy garlands to keep
> the entrances pure and the temple floor
> wet with cleansing water; and the flocks of birds
> that befoul the ritual offerings,
> with my arrows I frighten them into flight.

Each of these tasks will be further developed in its own section of the monody. The anapests conclude with a statement of Ion's status as an orphan and a servant of Apollo:

> ὡς γὰρ ἀμήτωρ ἀπάτωρ τε γεγὼς
> τοὺς θρέψαντας
> Φοίβου ναοὺς θεραπεύω. (109–111)

> Being motherless, fatherless, I care for
> this shrine of Phoebus
> which has nourished me.

The opening anapestic section of the monody thus introduces in light, impressionistic strokes the character of the young man – that is, what is most distinctive about him and his mindset at this initial moment of the play. Ion is devoted to Apollo; he rejoices in the beauty of the natural world; he is exacting, almost fastidious, in his quest for purity; he knows his duty to visitors and to the temple where he works; and he thinks of himself as motherless and fatherless, alone but for the protection of the god. These traits will be extended and expanded upon in the lyric strophe and antistrophe and in the final section of free lyric anapests.

When the other servants have left the stage, Ion is completely alone. Perhaps with a quickening of tempo, he moves from recitative into full lyrical song. The strophe and antistrophe are complementary in subject matter and develop Ion's tasks as introduced in the anapestic section. The strophe is a prolonged address to the broom that Ion uses to sweep the temple:

ἄγ', ὦ νεηθαλὲς ὦ
καλλίστας προπόλευμα δά-
φνας, ἃ τὰν Φοίβου θυμέλαν
σαίρεις ὑπὸ ναοῖς,
κήπων ἐξ ἀθανάτων,
ἵνα δρόσοι τέγγουσ' ἱεραί,
ῥοὰν ἀέναον
παγᾶν ἐκπροϊεῖσαι,
μυρσίνας ἱερὰν φόβαν·
ᾇ σαίρω δάπεδον θεοῦ
παναμέριος ἅμ' ἁλίου
πτέρυγι θοᾷ
λατρεύων τὸ κατ' ἦμαρ. (112–124)

Come, O you, bloom-fresh,
O you instrument of loveliest laurel,
who sweep this precinct of Phoebus
before the temple,
cut from undying gardens
where holy streams, sending forth
an unfailing flow, water
the holy locks of the myrtle.
With you I sweep
the threshold of the god,
day after day, when the swift wing
of the sun arrives, serving every day.

Ion's exhortation to his broom, introduced by an imperative and a vocative (ἄγ', ὦ νεηθαλὲς ὦ), signals the beginning of a work song.[25] The broom, an ordinary domestic object, is elevated to a holy status because it is associated, in Ion's eyes, with the service of Apollo; it becomes an extension of Ion

---

[25] Karanika 2014: 146–147.

himself, hard-working and humble.²⁶ The broom is made of laurel, Apollo's sacred tree, and grew beside the waters in the god's precinct, like Ion himself. It is "bloom-fresh" (νεηθαλές), a neologism that draws attention to its everlasting youth and remains close to divine immortality: it comes from undying gardens where fresh springs never fail.²⁷ We may picture the actor playing Ion holding the vertical line of the broom in parallel to his own body as he sings and dances.²⁸ The broom thus becomes what Shirley Barlow terms an "obsessive object," an article that acquires a significance beyond its immediate use as a stage prop because of the way it is described by its owner.²⁹ For Ion, the broom symbolizes the unity of worship and servitude in his daily life: just as the lowly broom can become holy through its service to the temple, so he, though a menial, glories in his work.

The refrain that joins strophe and antistrophe reestablishes the song's pious solemnity:

> ὦ Παιάν ὦ Παιάν,
> εὐαίων εὐαίων
> εἴης, ὦ Λατοῦς παῖ.   (125–127 = 141–143)
>
> O Paian, O Paian,
> goodly life and long
> be yours, O Leto's son!

This formal invocation of the god is less personal than the rest of the monody. The meter of the ephymnium is entirely spondaic, a slow, measured rhythm appropriate to worship. The repetition of ὦ Παιάν ὦ Παιάν explicitly links Ion's monody to the cult songs sung throughout the Greek world in honor of Apollo.³⁰ As we have seen, in fifth-century Greece, the paean would immediately evoke certain ideas, chief among them a sense of community and solidarity. The performance of the paean should be a collective, choral address to the god, thanking him for his aid or asking for salvation in a time of crisis.

---

²⁶ Hunter 2011: 24 notes that Ion projects his view of himself onto his broom. On the importance of the broom and other props in *Ion*, with a particular focus on the tokens that bring about the recognition, see Mueller 2016: 70–84.
²⁷ On νεηθαλές, see Liddell, Scott, Jones (LSJ) s.v.
²⁸ For the choreography of this solo dance, compare Olsen 2021: 84–94.
²⁹ Barlow 1971: 48. This seems to be a favorite technique of Euripides': Ion's broom may be compared to the torch carried by Cassandra in *Trojan Women* (308–341) or Electra's jug of water in *Electra* (140–143). The object in each case symbolizes and makes visible a major thematic concern of the speaker: servitude, marriage, poverty.
³⁰ On the paean, see Käppel 1992: 32–86; Rutherford 1994–5 and 2001: 3–136; and Swift 2010: 61–103. Metrically the refrain consists of *molossoi*, which are characteristic of hymns; compare Owen 2003 [1939]: ad 125–127; West 1982: 55–56.

Ion's solitary paean – and, later, Creusa's – is abnormal and places him beyond the normal religious rhythms of human society.

The antistrophe makes more specific Apollo's role as Ion's guardian:

> καλόν γε τὸν πόνον, ὦ
> Φοῖβε, σοὶ πρὸ δόμων λατρεύ-
> ω τιμῶν μαντεῖον ἕδραν·
> κλεινὸς δ' ὁ πόνος μοι
> θεοῖσιν δούλαν χέρ' ἔχειν
> οὐ θνατοῖς, ἀλλ' ἀθανάτοις·
> εὐφάμους δὲ πόνους
> μοχθεῖν οὐκ ἀποκάμνω.
> Φοῖβός μοι γενέτωρ πατήρ·
> τὸν βόσκοντα γὰρ εὐλογῶ,
> τὸ δ' ὠφέλιμον ἐμοὶ πατέρος
> ὄνομα λέγω
> Φοίβου τοῦ κατὰ ναόν. (128–140)

> Noble is the work, O
> Phoebus, serving you before your house,
> honoring your seat of prophecies;
> and glorious is my work, to pair
> these hands as slaves to the gods,
> no mortal masters, but deathless ones.
> Well-omened work, I never tire of labor.
> Phoebus is my maker, my father;
> for I praise the one who tends me,
> the one who helps me, and call him by the name
> of father, of Phoebus, all through his shrine.

The meter and music of the antistrophe match that of the preceding strophe to Ion's broom. Here words denoting labor and servitude again occur in a positive context: πόνον, λατρεύω, πόνος, δούλαν, πόνους, μοχθεῖν. The adjective κλεινός (glorious, 131) grants to Ion's work a glory that is both heroic and religious: Ion's service is an honor because of his bond with the god.

The repetition of the paeanic refrain closes the strophe and antistrophe pair, and introduces the final lyric section. Ion announces that he has finished his sweeping and will now move on to his second task, cleansing the floor of the temple with sacred water:

> ἀλλ' ἐκπαύσω γὰρ μόχθους
> δάφνας ὁλκοῖς,
> χρυσέων δ' ἐκ τευχέων ῥίψω

1.1 Ion's Monody (82–183)

γαίας παγάν,
ἃν ἀποχεύονται
Κασταλίας δῖναι,
νοτερὸν ὕδωρ βάλλων,
ὅσιος ἀπ' εὐνᾶς ὤν. (144–150)

But I will pause my labors
with the laurel boughs,
and from golden cups I will pour
the stream of the earth,
what the whirls of Castalia let flow,
casting down fresh water,
I, holy from my bed.

The emphasis again is on purity both of the water and of Ion himself. He has ordered the other temple attendants to bathe themselves in preparation for their service in the shrine, but he himself needs no such cleansing: he is holy "from his bed" (150). Ion spends all of his days in the temple precinct and sleeps there as well. The other temple attendants have contact with the outside world and so must purify themselves before they cross the boundary between secular and sacred to serve the god. Ion has no experience, no human relationships, outside the temple. Like the Pythia, Ion remains pure because he withdraws from the natural cycles of worldly life. He is also sexually pure, although not entirely naïve about the relations between men and women.[31] Ion equates his own purity with the purity of the shrine and of the god. The action of the play will demonstrate that he is purer than the god he serves, at least in human terms.

Ion now comes to the third and most elaborately presented of his tasks as he notices and reacts to the birds who threaten to defile the temple with their droppings. The structural break is signaled by the introduction of lyric anapests, a new meter that will make up the rest of the song, and by the *extra metrum* cry of ἔα ἔα (154). Although this section lacks strophic responsion, the lines are nevertheless clearly organized into thematic units. After an opening description, Ion addresses three birds in particular, each one carefully described through details that display both the wildness of the natural creature and its connection to divinity.[32] Until now, Apollo's temple has been a world unto itself. Here, for the first time, outside forces threaten to disrupt the serenity of the sacred precinct. Ion believes the intruders intend

---

[31] He questions Creusa about her "friend" in the first episode; after she has been revealed as his mother, he speculates that a mortal liaison, not a divine rape, led to the birth (341, 1523–1527).

[32] Giraud 1987.

violence, and he responds with violence. Just as Ion enforced silence and well-omened speech upon his fellow attendants, he now restricts access to the sacred space.[33] Purity must be maintained at all costs:

> ἔα ἔα·
> φοιτῶσ' ἤδη λείπουσίν τε
> πτανοὶ Παρνασοῦ κοίτας.
> αὐδῶ μὴ χρίμπτειν θριγκοῖς
> μηδ' ἐς χρυσήρεις οἴκους. (154–157)

> Ah! Ah!
> They have come, the birds of Parnassus,
> they have already left their nests,
> I give the warning: do not come near
> the cornice-stones and the golden temple.

The eagle, the first intruder, is marked for its physical power and its connection to Zeus. The second bird, a swan, is a singer, like Apollo:

> ὅδε πρὸς θυμέλας ἄλλος ἐρέσσει
> κύκνος· οὐκ ἄλλᾳ φοινικοφαῆ
> πόδα κινήσεις;
> οὐδέν σ' ἁ φόρμιγξ ἁ Φοίβου
> σύμμολπος τόξων ῥύσαιτ' ἄν.
> πάραγε πτέρυγας·
> λίμνας ἐπίβα τᾶς Δηλιάδος·
> αἱμάξεις, εἰ μὴ πείσῃ,
> τὰς καλλιφθόγγους ᾠδάς. (161–169)

> This other rows toward the precinct,
> a swan. Won't you ply to another place
> your bright red feet?
> Even Apollo's lyre
> as your accompaniment
> wouldn't save you from my bow.
> Avert your wings!
> Go to the shores of Delos;
> or if you disobey, you will bloody
> the lovely-sounding songs of yours.

---

[33] Hoffer 1996: 291 explores the themes of patriarchal oppression and ideology in the *Ion*, suggesting that Ion's monody emphasizes "the connection between purity and the domination by which purity is enforced."

Here Ion draws a contrast between the two stringed instruments of Apollo, the lyre and the bow. The syntax pits Apollo's lyre directly against Ion's bow. This puts Ion in the position of a *theomachos* (θεόμαχος), one who fights against a god: in his sung challenge, Ion approximates simultaneously both Apollo the musician and Apollo the archer. He urges the swan to leave Delphi and fly to Delos instead to avail himself of the temple and lake there; if he does not, Ion threatens him with death.[34] The blood that Ion envisions picks up the detail of the bird's red feet from several lines earlier.[35] The vivid image emphasizes the impiety of the bloodshed – impure within the space of the temple precinct – that Ion considers. The conflict between Ion and the swan thus suggests a conflict in Ion's conception of Apollo, where Apollo's purity exists in tension with the threat posed by the musical bird.

A repetition of the cry ἔα ἔα introduces the third and final attacker. The bird is left deliberately unspecified. Ion identifies it as καινός, "new," or even "strange," and supposes that its intent is to build a nest for its young within the temple precinct. The use of καινός, an adjective often applied to the daring flights of the New Music, may indicate a change in the accompaniment of the *aulos* or the vocal effects and choreography of the monody at this point.[36] In fact, the expressivity of dance in this scene is noted by the ancient literary critic Demetrius, a rare reference to *Ion* in performance from the Hellenistic period.[37] The movements of Ion and of the imagined birds could perhaps have been matched by mimetic effects on the pipes to emphasize Ion's mounting distress:

> ἔα ἔα·
> τίς ὅδ' ὀρνίθων καινὸς προσέβα;
> μῶν ὑπὸ θριγκοὺς εὐναίας
> καρφηρὰς θήσων τέκνοις;

---

[34] The manuscripts have αἱμάξεις, a reading defended by Lee 1969 and Gibert 2019. The emendation αἰάξεις, "you will cry out in pain," would enrich the musical imagery of the passage and is adopted by Diggle 1981: 97; Beverley 1997: 95; Pellegrino 2004; and Martin 2018. The swan changes its song to a cry of pain and lament. The possibilities are discussed by de Poli 2011: 186–187, who ultimately supports the manuscript reading.

[35] As pointed out by several commentators, actual swans have black feet and are mute. Euripides includes these details because they are traditional as well as sensually arresting. This image looks ahead to the bird that reveals in death the poison plot of Creusa (1205–1206). The threat that Ion poses to the bird at the beginning of the play will be resolved in the bird's sacrifice to save the young man's life; compare Elderkin 1940.

[36] Compare Csapo 2004 as well as Weiss 2018a: 9, on the musical resonance of words of spinning and whirling.

[37] Demetrius, *On Style* 195, who writes that the stage business with the birds furnishes wide scope for movement to the actor playing Ion (κινήσεις πολλὰς παρέχει τῷ ὑποκριτῇ). The work is of uncertain date, but was perhaps written c. 250 BCE. See Gibert 2019: ad 154–183 and Olsen 2021: 89–94 on dance in this scene.

ψαλμοί σ' εἴρξουσιν τόξων.
οὐ πείσῃ; χωρῶν δίναις
ταῖς Ἀλφειοῦ παιδούργει
ἢ νάπος Ἴσθμιον,
ὡς ἀναθήματα μὴ βλάπτηται
ναοί θ' οἱ Φοίβου.
κτείνειν δ' ὑμᾶς αἰδοῦμαι
τοὺς θεῶν ἀγγέλλοντας φήμας
θνατοῖς· (170–181)

Ah! Ah!
What is this strange new bird approaching?
Won't it set a woven nest
under the eaves for its young?
My singing bow will ward it off.
You won't obey? Go rear your family
by the whirls of Alpheus
or the Isthmian grove,
so the dedications remain unharmed,
and the temple of Phoebus.
But I feel shame to kill you,
who bear the prophecies of the gods
to humankind.

Ion engages with this third bird at greater length and with more emotion because the threat that it poses is more dangerous. It wants to make the temple its home to raise its chicks in the sacred space. This unknown bird is a maternal figure; the passionate force that Ion turns against the nesting bird prefigures his conflict with Creusa at the climax of the play.

We have seen that the monody presents what matters most to Ion at the opening of the play. First and foremost, the song conveys his devotion to Apollo. The god's name is invoked thirteen times, twelve times as Φοῖβος, once as Ἀπόλλων, while the cult title Παιάν and the matronymic Λατοῦς παῖ mark the refrain.[38] The repeated use of the god's name and titles gives the song the quality of a hymn. As William Furley has discussed, hymns in tragedy show the conception of divinity held by the singer; in this case the monody expresses Ion's special connection with the god.[39] He sees Apollo as exclusively benevolent, beautiful, and bright, a view not so much false as naïve and simplistic, and underscored by his desire for connection. Ion's solitude is emphasized by resonances of the paean, elsewhere a collective

---

[38] At lines 90, 93 (Ἀπόλλων), 94, 104, 111, 114, 129, 136, 140, 151, 164, 178, and 182.
[39] Furley 1999–2000.

1.1 Ion's Monody (82–183) 57

and choral form.⁴⁰ Yet in its exuberance, Ion's song nonetheless participates in the lyric vitality of the god.

Ion's second great theme is his own work. Words for labor and service occur throughout the monody: πόνους (103), μοχθοῦμεν (104), θεραπεύω (111), λατρεύων (123), πόνον (128), λατρεύω (130), πόνος (131), δούλαν (132), πόνους (134), μοχθεῖν (135), μόχθους (144), λατρεύων (152), μόχθοις (181), δουλεύω (182), and θεραπεύων (183). Ion's tasks are defined by adjectives such as καλόν (128), τιμῶν (130), κλεινός (131), and εὐφάμους (134). Although he is enslaved, Ion's servitude to him is not a lowly occupation; it is holy because of the god whose temple he tends. This attitude of pious humility will shortly be tested by argument and by event.

A third preoccupation, closely related to the theme of work, is sacred purity. Ion's three tasks – sweeping, washing, and guarding against the birds – emphasize cleanliness, organization, and exclusion. For Ion, order is associated with sanctity; hence the clustering of words such as σεμνός (107), ὅσιος (150), ζάθεος (91), and ἱερός (85, 104, 117, 120). The purity of the temple depends on the establishment of boundaries. The attendants must wash themselves before crossing into the precinct and must maintain ritual silence within its walls. Access is restricted not only for humans but for animals as well. The wildness and fertility of nature, represented by the birds, must be kept out – but no boundary can hold them. The paradox is irresolvable, for sacred purity cannot be permanently achieved. Ion's frustration at the birds is a preliminary and premonitory sign that his stance is not proof against all assaults.

Finally, Ion's song makes repeated reference to his status as an orphan and to the role of Apollo and the temple as foster parents. References to parentage conclude each of the three metrical sections of the monody. At the end of the opening anapestic section Ion describes himself as "motherless and fatherless" (ἀμήτωρ ἀπάτωρ, 109); later he declares that Phoebus is his parent (Φοῖβός μοι γενέτωρ πατήρ, 136; πατέρος ὄνομα λέγω, 139); and in the last lines of the song, he reiterates his devotion to serving the ones who have reared him (183). Presumably these references are meant metaphorically and are instances of dramatic irony. Yet, at the same time, parentage is a personal concern of Ion's as he tries to define his own identity in traditional terms. Ion begins the play with an idealized vision of Apollo as his sole parent; Creusa's allegations against the god strike at the heart of his faith. Of course, what he does not know is that, had there been

---

⁴⁰ See Hunter 2011: 21. Olsen 2021: 87 suggests that the audience might imagine Ion, future ruler of Athens, as a potential leader of the choral paean; his solo performance here rehearses the authoritative position foretold for him.

no divine violation, Ion himself would not exist. What is denied in Ion's mind has, at the outset, already been literally incorporated.

These four themes – the brilliance of Apollo, sacred purity, humble work, and the mystery of parentage – lay the groundwork for the drama as a whole. Over the course of the play, Ion must resolve the challenge that his birth poses to Apollo's purity. The song presents a state of idealization and serenity that cannot stand but that nonetheless defines an aim.

1.2 *Parodos* and First Episode: Connection and Complexity

The subsequent scenes set off by contrast the unique dramatic and poetic qualities of Ion's monody. In the *parodos*, the chorus complicate Ion's initial henotheistic vision and offer in its place a pantheon where Apollo is one god among many. In the first episode, the dialogue of Ion and Creusa prepares for the coming conflict; an agonistic element is introduced, but indirectly. Where the two monodies present fully realized visions of the god, the stichomythic exchange in the first episode introduces Ion and Creusa's opposing views through the exchange of stories. Ion's monologue, delivered after Creusa leaves the stage, shows how the young man's unquestioning adoration of Apollo has been challenged and changed by their interaction.

These three scenes stand out against Ion's monody formally as well as dramatically. On the level of poetic technique, the modes of choral song, dialogue, and monologue all lend themselves to different possibilities of expression from those inherent in solo song. Ion's monody, I have argued, is a lyrical outpouring of his state of mind. His preoccupations are introduced obliquely and through imagery rather than through exposition. The song of the chorus resembles the monody in its lyrical vocabulary and its sense of immediacy, but expresses collective rather than individual impressions. In Ion's dialogue with Creusa, the focus is on the interaction between the two characters; each line responds to the question or statement that it immediately follows. Although the monologue echoes the monody in its exploration of Ion's inner state, here Ion moves forward through logical reasoning rather than through free association. Comparison with these three scenes thus highlights the distinctive nature of the opening monody.

The final anapestic section of Ion's monody gives way directly to the entrance song of the chorus, which begins in the same meter. The entrance of multiple new arrivals has already been prefigured in the monody by Ion's distress at the birds who befoul the temple and seek to build their nests there; he cannot accept these other creatures who pose a challenge to the purity of Delphi and to his own solitary and special position there. In performance, the shift from a single voice to multiple voices would be strongly felt. The continuity provided by the anapestic meter allows differences of imagery and theme to emerge more strongly.

As we have seen, Ion's monody establishes the personal significance of Delphi for a servant who has grown up in its precinct. The visual elements of the temple are familiar to Ion, and for him call for no description; indeed, they are all he has ever known. The chorus, by contrast, judge the temple as outsiders, focusing on visual detail rather than religious experience and on collective appreciation rather than personal contemplation.[41] In the absence of elaborate set decoration, words are the essential vehicle of expression.[42] The women of the chorus encourage one another to "look" and "see" specific aspects of the temple and confirm that they too "behold" what is pictured (ἰδοὺ τάνδ, ἄθρησον, 190; ὁρῶ, 194; ἄθρησον, 201; σκέψαι, 206; δερκόμεσθα, 208; λεύσσεις, 209; λεύσσω, 211; ὁρῶ, 215). The vocabulary of vision punctuates short descriptions in the present tense of individual sculptural groups; the chorus describe the works of art as though the myths they represent are taking place before their eyes. Where Ion in his monody concentrates exclusively on Apollo, the attention of the chorus moves from one sculptural group to another: Heracles (190–193), Iolaus (194–200), Bellerophon (201–204), the rout of the Giants (205–207), Athena (205–211), Zeus (212–215), and Dionysus (216–218). Apollo, who surely was depicted on the temple, is conspicuous by his absence from their description.[43] Instead, the Athenian women of the chorus emphasize their relationship to Athena, "my goddess" (ἐμὰν θεόν, 211).[44] The polytheism of the chorus is a shift in perspective and proposes a corrective to Ion's exclusive dedication to Apollo.

In the first episode, Creusa's bitterness at the god opposes Ion's reverence even more starkly. This is the first scene of iambic dialogue in the play; the two mortal characters are shown in dynamic interaction with one another. Ion and Creusa are contrasted not only in their view of Apollo but also in their means of expression: Ion is consistently open and direct

---

[41] On the *parodos*, see Rosivach 1977; Zeitlin 1994; and Basta-Donzelli 2010.
[42] Scene painting became more elaborate over the course of the fifth century, but any visual details conveyed by the *skene* building itself, or by panels fixed to it, were likely missed by spectators sitting beyond the first few rows.
[43] See Mastronarde 1975; Emerson 2007: 39–42; and Stieber 2011: 284–302. The archeological hypothesis is that the eastern pediment of the temple showed Apollo mounted in his chariot as he arrived at Delphi.
[44] On Athenian perspectives in the play, see Zacharia 2003.

about his thoughts and feelings, while Creusa utilizes indirection and partial truth to move tentatively forward. A contrast therefore emerges between Ion's monody, with its apparent order and clarity, and the veiled nature of Creusa's speech. Solo song has already been established in the play as a mode through which a character expresses unfiltered emotion. Dialogue, with its structure of give and take between two characters, now emerges as an alternative form of communication.

For the audience, Ion is already a partially known entity, distinguished, as we have seen, by his devotion to Apollo, his concern with purity and propriety, and his position as an orphan. His emotional state is apparently calm and content but he has some doubts about his identity and his position in the world. Ion's interaction with Creusa fills out this portrait. He is sensitive to Creusa's distress and instantly sympathetic to her suffering (241–246, 307). He shows himself highly conscious of social distinctions and repeatedly comments on Creusa's nobility and status (236–240, 262–263, 293); he bluntly states his own position as a slave (τοῦ θεοῦ δοῦλος, 309). The meaning of "slave" has shifted since his monody: for Creusa, the term is clearly pejorative, and from her position of regal anger she cannot appreciate Ion's attitude of reverential "servitude" to Apollo. Her nobility confers an authority that Ion instantly notices and respects and must take into consideration. The dialogue, then, encourages Ion to review and ultimately to question his contentment with being a slave in the temple.

Creusa, by contrast, is mysterious. Her words suggest that she is both angry and afraid, but not until her monody will she express the extent of her rage and shame. In her opening lines, although preoccupied with her memory of the past, she is courteous to Ion and grateful for his care (246–251). She answers the young man's inquiries and expresses pride in her great lineage (260–261, 264). In turn she is curious about his background (309). Her deepest concerns are implicit in her statements and questions. Her most obvious preoccupation is with having a child; that is the overt motivation for her visit to the temple (304). Even before she reveals the reason that she seeks a prophecy, she repeatedly alludes to motherhood: she considers Ion's mother fortunate to have such a son (308) and, when she learns that he is an orphan, pities him as well as the mother who bore him (312, 324). The paternal longing that Ion expressed in the monody dovetails with the maternal longing felt by Creusa to create a strongly ironic effect.

Creusa's own thoughts incessantly return to the deep injustice of her impregnation, childbirth, supposed infanticide, and subsequent childlessness. The sight of the temple, the name of the Long Rocks, and the story of Ion's birth all remind her of her past and present sufferings (249–251, 286–

288, 306, 330).⁴⁵ Her pain and her yearning are expressed through ambiguous speech as again and again she begins to tell her story and then restrains herself.

The iambic interaction between Ion and Creusa in the first episode reinforces the conflict that the monodies will reveal in lyric form. The *agōn* is not between the characters themselves, who here establish a delicate sympathy. Rather, the account of Apollo put forth in Ion's monody is challenged by Creusa's story of the god's harsh neglect of her "friend." Yet Ion does not completely abandon his former reverence: although convinced by her account, he still scruples to accuse the god directly. He forestalls Creusa's desire to question and accuse the god: Apollo will not prophesy about a matter he wants concealed because the matter causes him shame (αἰσχύνεται τὸ πρᾶγμα, 365–367). Ion's rebuke to the god will not be public, but private.

After Xuthus and Creusa depart, Ion is left alone onstage. The ensuing monologue, like his monody, is delivered in part to himself and in part to the silent god.⁴⁶ The reverent tone of his monody may be contrasted with this speech in iambic trimeter. Here his central concern is not divine holiness but human concepts of wrongdoing and retribution. The conversation with Creusa has profoundly disrupted Ion's belief in Apollo's goodness; his monologue conveys the bewilderment, disbelief, disappointment, and anger he now feels. The young man's paean was calm, orderly, organized; now his speech is disjointed, and his words can barely keep pace with his rapidly changing feelings. Where the song emphasized light and visibility, here Ion wonders at Creusa's silence (σιγῶσ', 432) and her "hidden" words (κρυπτοῖσιν, 430). Instead of reverence, she offers "abuse" (λοιδοροῦσ', 430).

Ion pushes away these troubling thoughts. He resolves to return to his usual tasks, but cannot perform them with the same serenity as previously. Abruptly he breaks off – the caesura is strongly marked – to consider Apollo's conduct:

> νουθετητέος δέ μοι
> Φοῖβος, τί πάσχει· παρθένους βίᾳ γαμῶν
> προδίδωσι; παῖδας ἐκτεκνούμενος λάθρᾳ
> θνῄσκοντας ἀμελεῖ; μὴ σύ γ'· ἀλλ', ἐπεὶ κρατεῖς,
> ἀρετὰς δίωκε. (436–439)

---

⁴⁵ For psychoanalytical interpretations of this scene, see Pedrick 2007: 88–93 and Weiss 2008, who compares Creusa's preoccupation with the past to Freud's description of fixation to trauma.
⁴⁶ See Shadewalt 1926: 227–230 on the sense of alienation and estrangement in the monologue. The passage has long been a centerpiece in discussions of Euripides' supposed criticism of the gods; see Gibert 2019: ad 429–451.

> I must rebuke Phoebus – what is he doing?
> To force a girl to bed and then abandon her!
> To leave a child to die that has been born
> in secret! No, not you! But, since
> you have power, seek the virtuous path.

Ion does not speak in a high poetic register but addresses the god familiarly and almost as an equal. The verbal adjective νουθετητέος gives the sense of rebuke or scolding, as of a parent chiding a child.[47] The expression τί πάσχει and the imperative μὴ σύ γ' are colloquial, furthering the impression of a conversation between intimates.[48] The incredulous questions, short, asyndetic sentences, and strong sense pauses within individual lines convey Ion's agitation. The monologue thus shows Ion moving away from his own isolated world. Out of Creusa's hearing, Ion responds to her earlier charges against the god. He attempts to define and censure Apollo's misconduct in the idiom of human morality with terms such as "base" (κακός, 441), "punishment" (ζημιοῦσιν, 441), "just" (δίκαιον, 442), "laws" (τοὺς νόμους, 442), and "injustice" (ἀδικίας, 447). This legalistic language contrasts with the vocabulary of Ion's monody, where Apollo's goodness was expressed primarily through visual imagery and the phenomena of the natural world. The shift in register prepares for Creusa's monody, where the metaphor of accusation and defense will be taken to its extreme as the *agōn* is joined in earnest.

1.3 Creusa's Monody (859–922): A Voice of Challenge

Creusa's monody is the structural and emotional center of the play.[49] The song stands out so distinctly that it has often been discussed as a self-contained tour de force, admired for its lyrical intensity and for the

---

[47] As seems to be the case at *Bacchae* 1256; see Martin 2018: ad 436b–451 and Gibert 2019: ad 436–437.
[48] See Lee 1997: ad 436–439.
[49] The position of the monody, which bisects the play almost exactly at its midpoint, is unusual. The typical pattern in Euripides is for women to sing in the first third of the play and men to sing in later episodes; in *Ion* this pattern is reversed. See further Beverley 1997: 7–19, who notes that in the plays produced after 415 BCE it becomes much more common for women to sing in later episodes, for example Iphigenia in *Iphigenia among the Taurians* (869–899), Antigone in *Phoenician Women* (1485–1538), Electra in *Orestes* (982–1012), and Iphigenia in *Iphigenia at Aulis* (1279–1335, 1475–1499). The effect here is to mark through the change in mode a critical turning point in the action of the play.

concentrated beauty of its imagery.⁵⁰ More recently, scholars have appreciated the monody's realistic portrayal of Creusa's mental anguish as a victim of trauma.⁵¹ Formally, as Sarah Olsen has demonstrated, the monody invokes not only the paean to Apollo but also maiden choral songs associated with weddings throughout the Greek world; just as Ion's solo performance raises questions about his liminal status at the beginning of the play, Creusa's invocation of a marriage hymn prompts the audience to think about her forced and unhappy "marriage" to the god.⁵² Drawing on these different readings, I hope to show that Creusa's monody is enriched by competitive engagement with the monody of Ion; through the agonistic juxtaposition of the two songs Euripides focuses attention on the contradictory nature of Apollo.

The monody is the third and climactic telling of Creusa's rape by Apollo and of the birth and abandonment of their child. Hermes in the prologue gives a detached, third-person account: he states that Apollo "yoked Creusa by force" but does not speculate on the emotional consequences of the union (ἔζευξεν γάμοις βίᾳ, 10–11). In the first episode, Creusa offers a more detailed version of what happened, but displaced onto her "friend" (338–358). The monody provides the first direct, unrestrained access to Creusa's experience as she breaks her long silence in a supreme moment of agony. The monody is also a pivotal point in the action, marking Creusa's transition from passive victim to vengeful agent. The song is the culmination of her feelings of grief about the loss of her child; it is also the moment when her anger and her desire for revenge break forth and become a motivating force in the plot as she pivots from private anguish to declared *agōn*. As Creusa reveals the truth of her past, she sets herself against Apollo, Xuthus, and especially Ion as the agents of her pain and humiliation.

In the monody, in order for engagement to break through inaction, song must first break through silence.⁵³ Creusa's internal struggle is expressed through the formal arrangement of the monody. Her monody is more varied and extreme than Ion's in its metrical structure, as in its content. There is no strophic response and the divisions between thematic sections are not clearly marked by metrical shifts. Nevertheless, it does have an overall formal unity. As in Ion's monody, anapests are the dominant meter: Creusa's song is composed almost exclusively of anapests and paroemiacs

---

⁵⁰ Compare Imhof 1966; LaRue 1963; Barlow 1971: 45–50; Segal 1999; Furley 1999–2000; Rutherford 2012: 261–267; and Rynearson 2014.
⁵¹ Dunn 1990; Scafuro 1990; Weiss 2008; Kearns 2013.   ⁵² Olsen 2021: 94–98.
⁵³ The theme of speech, song, and silence is also explored through the figure of Apollo, the singing god who remains silent throughout the play; see Hartigan 1991.

with an occasional admixture of dochmiacs.[54] The anapestic meter both recalls the paean and emphasizes the connection between Creusa's song and Ion's. In Ion's monody, as we have seen, the predominance of long syllables reinforces the mood of measured calm, especially in the refrain invoking the god directly (125–127 = 141–143). When Creusa calls on the god, she too does so in entirely spondaic metra, as though parodying the traditional refrain of the paean (ὦ Λατοῦς παῖ, 885; ὠή, τὸν Λατοῦς αὐδῶ, 907).[55] In other parts of the song, Creusa's anapests are more heavily resolved. In the description of the rape, the runs of short syllables support a sense of agitation, even panic (e.g., the twelve consecutive short syllables in line 889 after the entirely spondaic lines 886–888). The greater variation and flexibility of the anapestic meter in Creusa's monody emphasize her labile emotional state.

Thematically, the monody falls into two unequal parts, delineated by a shift in meter: Creusa first makes up her mind to break her silence (859–880) and then, at greater length, delivers her charge against Apollo (881–922). In the first section, Creusa wavers between song and speech; this alternation of modes dramatizes the combat between her sense of shame (αἰδοῦς, 861) and her drive to reveal the truth. The movement from the hesitant first section to the more determined and hostile second section is underscored by the change from recitative to lyric anapests. Dochmiacs in the lyric section create variety at two moments of extreme agitation, the description of the rape and the direct invocation of the god that immediately follows this revelation (894–896, 906). The sections of the monody are also distinguished by a change in who is addressed: Creusa's inner struggle in the first section becomes an outward accusation against Apollo in the second.[56] As in Ion's monody, where his attention expands to include the temple servants and the birds that threaten the temple, Creusa moves from a contemplation of her own inner state to an active engagement with the outer world.

As we move through the monody, we may observe the ways in which Creusa defines her adversaries and sets herself against them. The song starts with a clarion call to battle, an apostrophe in sung lyrics.[57] By turning

---

[54] For metrical analyses, see Owen 2003 [1939]: 85–186; de Poli 2011: 187–196; Lourenço 2011: 267–269; Martin 2018: ad 859–922; and Gibert 2019: ad 859–922. On dochmiacs in Euripides, see Lourenço 2011: 30 and 53–64, who writes that this meter "invariably denotes a heightening of emotional tension."

[55] See Lourenço 2011: 31, who writes, "It is tempting to view the insistent use of anapestic phrases consisting mainly or entirely of long syllables ... as somehow indicative of a more contained level of grief than that expressed in dochmiac and iambo-trochaic."

[56] See Schadewalt 1926: 217–218.

[57] The Doric alpha in ψυχά suggests that these lines, as well as the following two lines of paroemiacs, were sung.

1.3 Creusa's Monody (859–922)

away from her onstage audience and speaking to her own soul, Creusa engages once again in the struggle that presumably has gone on for many years:

> ὦ ψυχά, πῶς σιγάσω;
> πῶς δὲ σκοτίας ἀναφήνω
> εὐνάς, αἰδοῦς δ'ἀπολειφθῶ;   (859–861)
>
> My soul, how can I be silent?
> Or how illumine the dark
> coupling, leave behind my shame?

The decision to speak out is fraught with anxiety and cannot be made lightly; the spondaic rhythm builds suspense. To tell her story, Creusa will abandon silence and darkness (σιγάσω, σκοτίας), which throughout the play have been set against truth and light.[58]

First and foremost, in this short lyric section Creusa is concerned for her sense of "shame" (αἰδώς), here connected with her strong inhibition against speaking out, even to herself, or to the god who knows all too well what has happened. The Greek term αἰδώς has a much broader and deeper acceptation than the English "shame": it includes "honor," a woman's chastity and loyalty, which depends upon her freedom from any imputation of sexual impropriety.[59] In a traditional patriarchy, if a woman engages in sexual relations, which she may have no power to refuse, her honor is regained or lost by what happens subsequently, specifically by what the man does; and its state of repair is evaluated by her family and society. Honor therefore is not a characteristic of an individual alone but of the individual within a social web of mutual obligations, extending into the community and backward and forward in time.

After this emotional beginning, only three lines long, Creusa pauses in her song – the next passage is delivered in recitative, not sung (862–880). The address to her soul seems to have been a false start. To leave shame behind is no easy matter. Before she can passionately denounce the god, must she not abandon her modesty as a wife and as a woman?

Creusa's struggle between silent shame and song is explicitly framed as an *agōn*, initiated with a series of rhetorical questions. Now that her

---

[58] As, for example, when Ion in his monologue suspects Creusa's silence (σιγῶσ', 432) and her "hidden" words (κρυπτοῖσιν, 430). See Chong-Gossard 2008: 146–147 on the imagery of silence.
[59] On *aidōs* in Euripides, see Cairns 1993: 265–342.

husband has become her betrayer, Creusa no longer must contend in a "contest of virtue" (ἀγῶνας ... ἀρετῆς):

> τί γὰρ ἐμπόδιον κώλυμ' ἔτι μοι;
> πρὸς τίν' ἀγῶνας τιθέμεσθ' ἀρετῆς;
> οὐ πόσις ἡμῶν προδότης γέγονεν; (862–864)
>
> What still blocks or hinders me?
> What contest of virtue is placed in my path?
> Has my husband not become my betrayer?

In what follows, Creusa sets herself against two adversaries. She names both Xuthus and Apollo as betrayers, using the same word, προδότης, to frame the recitative passage at 864 and 880.[60] Xuthus has violated his duty as husband by attempting to bring a bastard child into the house. Apollo has defeated her even more cruelly; Creusa later refers to the moment when the god raped her as a "terrible contest" (ἀγῶνα δεινόν, 939) where she "joined" or "grappled" with Phoebus (ξυνῆψ', 941).[61] In the scenes prior to the monody Creusa was willing to grant that Apollo could partially redeem himself (425–428); now that he has given a child to Xuthus, but not to her, the betrayal is complete and irremediable.

The audience recognizes that Creusa is more hobbled in this *agōn* than she knows. In fact, of course, neither Apollo nor Xuthus has betrayed her in the way she imagines. They are, indeed, not entirely blameless and could perhaps be convicted of lesser charges: Xuthus believes that Ion is his illegitimate son and plans to adopt him, and Apollo has caused Creusa years of suffering. But in her chief complaint Creusa is in error. By making her mistake the central theme of her song, the poet undercuts her argument in the *agōn*. Apollo has not abandoned his son and left him to die, and he has not granted to Xuthus the favor he denied Creusa. The tension between the factually flawed content of the monody and its intensely sympathetic tone raises questions about the adequacy of human constructs in understanding the ways of the gods.

Yet I would argue that in this scene the language of the *agōn* has both theatrical and metatheatrical significance.[62] As a monodist, Creusa is engaged in an agonistic contest against Apollo as a singer: in form as well

---

[60] For προδότης ("betrayer") used to refer to marital infidelity, compare *Medea* 206, *Alcestis* 180, and *Hippolytus* 590.

[61] See Pellegrino 2004: ad 863 on the athletic metaphor. Cassandra in *Agamemnon*, another victim of Apollo's lust, describes her struggle against the god's advances in terms of wrestling (*Ag.* 1202–1209).

[62] *Contra* Lee 1997: ad 863, who writes that "the metaphor from athletic competition is very common in Euripides ... and scarcely felt." Martin 2018: ad 863 suggests that Creusa's

as content, she opposes the unfeeling paean that she imagines Apollo playing on his lyre (905–906). As Jene LaRue has demonstrated, the power of Creusa's monody derives in part from the adaptation of the traditional hymnal style to express feelings of loss and anger.[63] This blasphemous inversion is more marked because Ion's monody has already demonstrated a pure, reverent paean. Thus Creusa's monody contradicts Ion's song of praise as well even though she herself has not heard it. Creusa is not aware of the *agōn*, which is nonetheless joined between the two paeans since it takes place in the space of the theater only. Her conflict with Apollo and his creature Ion will become more marked as the song continues.

Once the metaphor of the *agōn* has been introduced, Creusa lists her grievances:

> στέρομαι δ' οἴκων, στέρομαι παίδων,
> φροῦδαι δ' ἐλπίδες, ἅς διαθέσθαι
> χρῄζουσα καλῶς οὐκ ἐδυνήθην,
> σιγῶσα γάμους,
> σιγῶσα τόκους πολυκλαύτους. (865–869)

> I am stripped of my home, stripped of my children,
> all hopes abandoned, hopes that all might be well,
> that I couldn't fulfill, silencing the marriage,
> silencing the birth, full of wailing.

As in a legal proceeding, she invokes witnesses for her denunciation of Apollo:

> ἀλλ' οὐ τὸ Διὸς πολύαστρον ἕδος
> καὶ τὴν ἐπ' ἐμοῖς σκοπέλοισι θεὰν
> λίμνης τ' ἐνύδρου Τριτωνιάδος
> πότνιαν ἀκτήν,
> οὐκέτι κρύψω λέχος, ὡς στέρνων
> ἀπονησαμένη ῥᾴων ἔσομαι. (870–875)

> But no – by the star-studded seat of Zeus,
> and by the goddess who presides over my cliffs,
> and by her sacrosanct shore on the well-watered lake of Tritonis,
> I will no longer hide our shared bed,
> so that lifting the load
> from my heart, I will be healed.

antagonist in the *agōn* is "womanhood in Athens or in general," where the areas of competition are the production of children and maintenance of the household.

[63] LaRue 1963. See Wohl 2015: 35 on the tension between form and content.

The all-seeing sun, often called as a witness to oaths, is here omitted, perhaps because of the connection between Helios and Apollo.[64] Instead Creusa calls first upon the "star-studded seat" of Zeus, who as the guarantor of justice and as Apollo's father has power over his son. In second place she invokes Athena, specifically in her role as protectress of the Acropolis and of "my cliffs," where both the rape and the abandonment took place. Apollo's assault upon Creusa represents a violation against Athena herself; a virgin has been raped under the cliffs that are sacred to the virgin goddess.[65] The invocation of Athena also looks forward to the goddesses' epiphany in the *exodos*. There Athena, whose clear pronouncements dispel the ambiguity about Ion's past and future, emerges as an alternative model of divine guidance. At the end of the play, Creusa and Ion will leave Apollo and his riddling oracles to live in the city of Pallas. Apollo thus is in some ways replaced by Athena, as Delphi is replaced by Athens; the god of private contemplation and private grievance gives way to the goddess of communal civic engagement.

Creusa's oath ends with a parenthetical plea for sympathy. If the unstated metaphor of the three witnesses is a legalistic *agōn*, the more overt metaphor for Creusa's motivation is medical. Consequently, she steps back from explicit combat in order to invoke pity, also a potent weapon. She resolves to tell the story of her rape so that when she has thrust the burden from her heart, she will be "easier" (ῥᾴων, 875). The metaphor is taken from the realm of medicine and I have translated it as "healed": Apollo is not only the god of music but of sickness and recovery as well.[66] The monody will be a purgation of the pain and anger that Creusa has carried for so many years; her "sick" or "suffering" spirit will pass through a crisis and begin to mend.

In the first episode Creusa seeks to conceal her weeping when she sees the temple of Apollo (245–248); now she calls attention to the tears that stream from her eyes:

> στάζουσαι κόραι δακρύοισιν ἐμαί,
> ψυχὴ δ' ἀλγεῖ κακοβουλευθεῖσ'
> ἔκ τ' ἀνθρώπων ἔκ τ' ἀθανάτων,
> οὓς ἀποδείξω
> λέκτρων προδότας ἀχαρίστους. (876–880)

---

[64] For oaths to the sun, compare *Medea* 752 and *Choephoroi* 985. On the unusual addressees of this oath, see Delcourt 1938.
[65] Thorburn 2000: 42. [66] Lee 1997: ad 875. Compare LSJ s.v., *Heracles* 1407.

My eyes drop tears,
and my soul is sick, schemed against
by men and by gods,
whom I will reveal as
graceless betrayers of beds.

Creusa moves into full lyrics once again for her condemnation of Apollo. This second section of the monody itself falls into two parts: Creusa accuses Apollo of misconduct in the past (881–906) and in the present (907–922). In the first section of the monody Creusa fought with her own soul and her sense of shame, a performed ψυχομαχία where she wavered between song and recitative; in the second section each accusation begins with a musical cry that makes explicit her engagement with Apollo (ὦ, 881; ὠή, 907). In this way Creusa's internal conflict is externalized as an attack against the god. The second section of the monody takes the form of the speech for the prosecution in a trial; to approach her adversary more forcefully, the condemnation is delivered not in speech but in song.[67]

The return to lyric is strongly marked in that it coincides with the first description of Apollo in his role as god of music. Creusa's song sets itself against the invoked song of Apollo in a contest of performance; she will undermine his paean with her lyrical accusation:

ὦ τᾶς ἑπταφθόγγου μέλπων
κιθάρας ἐνοπάν, ἅτ' ἀγραύλοις
κεράσιν ἐν ἀψύχοις ἀχεῖ
μουσᾶν ὕμνους εὐαχήτους,
σοὶ μομφάν, ὦ Λατοῦς παῖ,
πρὸς τάνδ' αὐγὰν αὐδάσω.   (881–886)

O you who make the seven strings of the kithara
sing out, a sound that rings in the rustic soulless horn,
with the Muses' harmonious hymns,
against you I will speak out, O child of Leto,
toward the rays of this sun.

Creusa declares that she will speak out (αὐδάσω) toward the rays of the sun (πρὸς τάνδ' αὐγάν). By speaking "toward" the sun she is also speaking against Apollo in his role as the god of light. The language recalls Ion's hymn to the glories of the rising sun (ὦ Λατοῦς παῖ, 127 = 143); the

---

[67] Compare Rynearson 2014, who sees Creusa's monody as a self-conscious echo of Clytemnestra's defense in the trial-like scene at the end of *Agamemnon*, where she blames Agamemnon for the loss of the child they shared (*Agamemnon* 1523–1530).

repeated imagery of light emphasizes the difference between Ion's conception of Apollo and Creusa's: where Ion apostrophizes the bright god of morning, Creusa calls to the full and blinding light of midday, which will reveal the truth of the god's misconduct.

The first lines of lyric draw attention to sound and music; the next passage concentrates instead on visual imagery:

> ἦλθές μοι χρυσῷ χαίταν
> μαρμαίρων, εὖτ' ἐς κόλπους
> κρόκεα πέταλα φάρεσιν ἔδρεπον
> ἀνθίζειν χρυανταυγῆ· (887–890)

> You came to me with hair that
> sparkled gold, while I was harvesting
> saffron-yellow petals in the folds of my cloak,
> the blooms reflecting a golden light.

The interpretation of these lines has been the subject of much debate. How is Creusa's adversary Apollo portrayed? Certainly, the language emphasizes the visual glory of Apollo's epiphany; the detail of the golden flowers ablaze with the golden radiance of the god is an arresting image of overwhelming sensuality.[68] After the spondaic rhythm of the opening lines, the run of short syllables in line 889 creates a sense of excitement like a sudden quickening of breath. For Anne Burnett, the beauty of Apollo in this passage hints that Creusa was in fact attracted to the god; she gave in to his seduction more willingly than she would like to think.[69] Naomi Weiss comments that this passage suggests an "unacknowledged wish fulfillment."[70] At the other end of the spectrum, Adele Scafuro writes that the absence of explicit and unambiguous language of violence is in accord with the modesty of Creusa's character, but there is no doubt of sexual assault.[71] Douglas Kearns goes so far as to call Apollo a "brutal rapist."[72] John E. Thorburn takes a middle position, drawing attention to the tension between beauty and violence in the scene.[73]

These interpretations all seek to find within Creusa's narrative a factual account of the rape. But, of course, the actual original experience is beyond

---

[68] LaRue 1963: 132 and Swift 2010: 96 emphasize that these references to beauty and light ironically recall the traditional language of hymns.
[69] Burnett 1962. Compare Barlow 1986: 16 and Rabinowitz 1993: 189–222.
[70] Weiss 2008: 43. [71] Scafuro 1990. See Sommerstein 2006 on rape and consent in tragedy.
[72] Kearns 2013: 63. For a discussion of sexual misconduct in Euripidean tragedy with references to Attic law, see Mirto 2009: 63–74.
[73] Thorburn 2000.

recovery. Creusa's description of the rape is reconstructed as a rhetorical device, not an objective history, and the power of the monody as a form for her accusation lies in its subjectivity. As her behavior in the early parts of the play suggests, Creusa has long brooded in solitude upon the rape, her pregnancy, the birth of her son, and his supposed death. In the lonely, rageful years that have passed, the memory has been reworked; in the process, as Adele Scafuro writes, "some of its features may have been altered, some softened, some emphasized, in an attempt, over the years, to create a memory that is acceptable, inhabitable or even publicly presentable."[74] Her account in the monody is a persuasive strategy deployed against the god. Creusa's attack in this *agōn* depends on eliciting sympathy, and here the lyrical beauty of the lines makes the violence of the god more striking.

The actual consummation of the rape is related only in oblique and impressionistic terms:

> λευκοῖς δ' ἐμφὺς καρποῖς
> χειρῶν εἰς ἄντρου κοίτας
> κραυγὰν Ὦ μᾶτέρ μ' αὐδῶσαν
> θεὸς ὁμευνέτας
> ἆγες ἀναιδείᾳ
> Κύπριδι χάριν πράσσων.   (891–896)

> Entwining my pale wrists, while I shrieked
> – "O Mother!" – you, a god, my lover,
> led me in shamelessness to bed in a cave,
> to do the grace of the Cyprian.

In this section, sympathy is created through the inversion of language describing maidens and marriage. The detail of Creusa's "pale wrists" (λευκοῖς καρποῖς) recalls the traditional formula of the Athenian wedding ritual, specifically the moment at which the groom takes possession of the bride.[75] The cry to her mother, introduced as a sudden vocative, emphasizes her fear and unwillingness.[76] The intrusion of dochmiacs in lines 894–896, after three entirely spondaic lines, accentuates the panic Creusa felt in the moment. The change in rhythm substitutes for explicit language: the phrases "bed in a cave" (ἄντρου κοίτας) and "lover" or "bedfellow"

---

[74] Scafuro 1990: 145.
[75] On this gesture and its role in maiden choral songs and in marriage, see Chiu 2005 and Olsen 2021: 94–98.
[76] *Contra* Burnett 1962: 91, who argues that Creusa's reluctance is only a conventional gesture to show that she was not a loose woman; in fact, she was receptive to Apollo's advances.

(ὁμευνέτας), and the mention of Aphrodite (Κύπριδι), are the only references to the actual act of intercourse.[77]

The rape is only the first of Creusa's complaints against the god. Equally painful is the memory of the birth and abandonment of her child. The double use of "wretched" frames the description of Creusa's own sufferings; over the course of the passage Creusa moves from agent (δύστανος in the nominative) to passive victim (δύστανον in the accusative):

> τίκτω δ' ἁ δύστανος σοι
> κοῦρον, τὸν φρίκᾳ ματρὸς
> εἰς εὐνὰν βάλλω τὰν σάν,
> ἵνα με λέχεσι μελέαν μελέοις
> ἐζεύξω τὰν δύστανον. (897–901)

> And I, wretched, bore you a boy,
> whom I cast with a mother's shudder
> into your bed, the one where you yoked me to you,
> miserable, a bed of miseries, in my wretchedness.

Creusa then mourns her infant son's probable fate as food for scavenging birds:

> οἴμοι μοι· καὶ νῦν ἔρρει
> πτανοῖς ἁπρασθεὶς θοίνα
> παῖς μοι καὶ σός, τλᾶμον. (902–904)

> Alas! And now he is gone,
> mauled as a meal for the birds:
> my son, reckless one, and yours.

The "winged creatures" (πτανοῖς) that Creusa fears recall the birds of Ion's monody. Throughout the play birds are a symbol for liminality, for the space between outside and inside, profane and sacred, nature and civilization. Here the birds define the boundary between known and unknown, and between life and death. By exposing her child to the birds, Creusa has given him over from the human world to the wild nature and the gods. But the symbolism of birds in the play is twofold: they are, on the one hand, rapacious scavengers who will feast on an infant; on the other, they are the messengers of the gods whom Ion ultimately scruples to shoot.[78] In Ion's monody, as we have seen, the birds are connected to the divine realm, and

---

[77] See Scafuro 1990 on the non specificity of language in descriptions of sexual union.
[78] In a clever turn, Ion, whom Creusa feared would be threatened by birds as an infant, as an adolescent still perceives them as a threat.

their appearance prefigures that of Xuthus and Creusa. Here too the birds are the agents of the gods. Creusa believes that they are like Apollo, singers who feel no pity for her child; but her fear, like Ion's threat, is founded on a misunderstanding. The birds force mortals, with their moralism and their tidy dichotomies of justice and injustice, to come to terms with mystery and myth.[79]

A second charge against Apollo in his role as the god of music frames this section of the monody. The ring composition emphasizes again the contrast between Apollo's paean and Creusa's. The word Creusa uses, κλάζεις, is closer to "shriek" than to "sing" – in Homer it is used of the cry of the eagle and the barking of dogs as well as of the rattling of Apollo's own arrows.[80] The alliteration of kappa adds to this sense of musical dissonance:

> σὺ δὲ κιθάρι κλάζεις
> παιᾶνας μέλπων.   (905–906)

> But you shriek with your lyre,
> singing your paeans.

The final section of the monody begins with another direct address to attract attention, showing Creusa's mounting courage and aggression.[81] The passage repeats many of the same words used in earlier sections of the monody: αὐδῶσαν (893) and αὐδῶ (907); χρυσῷ (887) and χρυσέους (909); τάνδ᾽αὐγάν (886) and αὐδάν (911); ἀχαρίστους (880), χάριν (896), and χάριν (914). Creusa is concerned with speaking and being heard; with the falsity of Apollo's golden exterior; with the beams of the sun, both witnesses to Apollo's transgression and stand-ins for the god; and with the demands of faith and reciprocity. As in Ion's monody, where the insistent accumulation of words indicates the young man's deepest preoccupations, Creusa's fixations are made increasingly clear through diction and vocabulary.

In mock-hymnal form, Creusa lists the usual attributes of Apollo in his role as patron of Delphi. Where the first extended lyric section focused on Apollo's wrongs in the past, this section concentrates on his wrongs in the present. The change from past to present is intensified by a change in the epithets by which Creusa calls upon the god. He is no longer simply the god of music but the god of oracular prophecy, whose temple is immediately visible on the stage. Creusa has been forbidden from entering the temple

---
[79] See Zeitlin 1996: 285–286.
[80] LSJ s.v. Of the eagle, *Il.* 12.207; of dogs, *Od.* 14.30; of arrows, *Il.* 1.46.
[81] See Lee 1997: ad 907.

and will not enter it in the course of the play.[82] The mention of the Apollo in his oracular role is a summoning. Creusa imagines Apollo inside the temple, just out of her reach; his proximity makes his refusal to appear and answer her charge all the more worthy of censure:

> ὠή, τὸν Λατοῦς αὐδῶ,
> ὅς ὀμφὰν κληροῖς,
> πρὸς χρυσέους θάκους
> καὶ γαίας μεσσήρεις ἕδρας. (907–910)

> You, you, I call on you, Leto's son,
> who deliver your voice
> by the golden chair, your holy seat in the earth's deep core.

Since Apollo himself will not come forth, Creusa again turns to the daylight as a substitute for the god. Her final charge is that Apollo favors Xuthus, whose supposed son is contrasted with the wretched child of Creusa (μέν, 913; δ', 916):

> ὁ δ' ἐμὸς γενέτας καὶ σός, ἀμαθής,
> οἰωνοῖς ἔρρει συλαθείς,
> σπάργανα ματέρος ἐξαλλάξας. (916–918)

> And that son, born of me and of you,
> unfeeling one, he is gone, preyed on by birds,
> leaving behind the swaddling bands of his mother.[83]

The monody ends with an image of Apollo's own birth and infancy. The effect of the allusion is to connect Leto with Creusa and Apollo both with his own abandoned son and his father Zeus. The fullest version of the myth is told in the *Homeric Hymn to Apollo*: Leto, pregnant with Apollo, was turned away from countless lands as she sought to bear her son; at last, she found refuge on the floating island of Delos. For nine days and nine nights she struggled in painful labor, until the goddess Eilethyia arrived to ease her birth-pangs.[84] Thus far the myth provides a parallel for Creusa, who

---

[82] Compare lines 369–380. Mastronarde 2010: 253–254 comments on the spatial inversion of the play; Creusa, a woman, operates in the open, while interior spaces, such as the temple and the tent where Ion holds his feast, are heavily identified with the male. Weiss 2008 describes the Delphic shrine as a womb, where all of Ion's needs are met; his process of "rebirth" takes him beyond infancy into the real adult world.

[83] The vocative ἀμαθής is difficult to translate. It may have a negative connotation, "ignorant, stupid, without moral feeling," or a more neutral one, "without knowledge, untaught." Here the closest parallel seems to be the use in *Hercules Furens* 347, where Amphitryon accuses Zeus of cruelty and injustice. Compare LSJ s.v.

[84] *Homeric Hymn to Apollo* 14–125.

conceived, bore, and exposed her child in pain and isolation.⁸⁵ Here the similarities end, for once Apollo was born, Leto rejoiced, and the other goddesses helped to wash and dress him and to feed him with ambrosia.⁸⁶ Creusa adds the detail that Leto gave birth in the gardens of Zeus, thereby emphasizing his presence in Leto's ordeal; Zeus watches over the mother in her labor and accepts Apollo as his rightful son. The persuasive strategy is indirect, but powerful: Apollo should have taken pity on Creusa, who suffered as his own mother did; and he should, like Zeus, have acknowledged and protected his own son:

> μισεῖ σ' ἁ Δᾶλος καὶ δάφνας
> ἔρνεα φοίνικα παρ' ἁβροκόμαν,
> ἔνθα λοχεύματα σέμν' ἐλοχεύσατο
> Λατὼ Δίοισί σε κάποις.   (919–922)

> Delos hates you, and the shoots of laurel
> beside the palm with its delicate leaves,
> where Leto gave birth to you,
> a holy birth, in the gardens of Zeus.⁸⁷

As we have seen, Creusa in her monody uses a number of rhetorical strategies to present her agonistic case against Apollo: she ironically undercuts the conventions of the paean, calls for witnesses, addresses the god directly, elicits sympathy by describing her own sufferings, and adduces mythical parallels in support of her argument.⁸⁸ Her song creates tremendous sympathy, but at the same time the factual error at the center of her argument detracts from her case. She cannot "win the contest" against Apollo in any meaningful sense.

The monody is also agonistic in the larger context of the play, in counterpoint to the much lighter portrayal of Apollo in Ion's monody. Apollo is the most important figure in both songs but he is addressed very differently by the two singers. Ion thinks of the god in terms of brilliance and refers to him by his title Φοῖβος; his personal reverence is emphasized

---

⁸⁵ Athena later declares that Apollo caused Creusa to give birth "without illness" (ἄνοσον, 1595) but, as Creusa's account makes clear, the birth was not without emotional suffering.
⁸⁶ *Homeric Hymn to Apollo* 120–124.
⁸⁷ The reading of κάποις, "gardens," as the final word in the monody is not certain. The manuscripts have καρποῖς, "fruits." De Poli 2011, Martin 2018, and Gibert 2019 prefer κάποις, and I am persuaded by Kearns 2013: 64–65, who discusses three other passages in which these "gardens of Zeus" appear as a fitting place for a divine marriage and resultant birth. The evocation of an idealized mythical pattern would thus be brought into contrast with the force used by Apollo against the unwilling mortal woman.
⁸⁸ For rhetorical strategies in Euripides, see Mastronarde 2010: 207–222.

by the number of times he calls upon the god with this epithet. Creusa, by contrast, only addresses Apollo in the vocative twice, and never by his proper name (885, 907). She too emphasizes the brightness and golden gleam of the god, especially in the description of the rape, but here the imagery is of light as blinding and a source of fear.

Creusa's monody echoes Ion's in her concern with parentage: this is the driving mystery of the play, and the need to resolve it is the force linking mother and son. The theme is signaled in the opening recitative section as Creusa laments that she is deprived of children (στέρομαι παίδων, 865) and recalls the birth of her lost son (τόκους πολυκλαύτους, 869). She twice thinks of her own mother, from whom she withheld the truth of her rape, pregnancy, and labor (ὦ μᾶτερ, 893; φρίκα ματρός, 898). Even Apollo is referred to by his matronymic in preparation for the lines associating Creusa with Leto (ὦ Λατοῦς παῖ, 885; τὸν Λατοῦς, 907).

The theme of song, delivered in song, is also common to both monodies. Ion describes the melodious chanting of the Pythia on her sacred tripod, communicating the prophecies of Apollo to mortals (91–93), and compares the singing of the swan to the music of the lyre (164–168). Creusa twice depicts Apollo singing (881–884, 905–906). There is an ironic disparity between the imagined song of Apollo and the performed song of Creusa: his song is initially fair sounding (ὕμνους εὐαχήτους, 884) but later he is described as "shrieking" (κλάζεις, 905).

These shared themes are in tension with the very different diction and syntax of the two monodies. Ion does not speak of himself for a full twenty lines and then uses the universalizing first-person plural (ἡμεῖς, 102). He describes his tasks and narrates their execution rather than directly revealing his own inner state; still, his feelings do emerge obliquely, in the repetition of certain words and ideas. By contrast, Creusa's song focuses obsessively on herself and her sufferings. The first-person verbs of hesitation in the opening of the monody – σιγάσω (859), ἀναφήνω (860), ἀπολειφθῶ (861), and κρύψω (874) – give way to more determined vocabulary: ἀποδείξω (879), αὐδάσω (886), τίκτω (897), βάλλω (899), αὐδῶ (907), and καρύξω (911). The emphasis on her own experience is central to Creusa's argument: after she takes possession of her own past through narrative, she can move into the realm of action in the present.

The monody of Creusa is thus agonistic on several levels. On the level of explicit legalistic argument, Creusa battles first with her own soul and sense of shame in the recitative section; then, in the lyric section, she accuses Apollo directly for crimes both past and present. Performatively, through the very act of singing, Creusa throws down a challenge at the feet of the gnomically silent god of music, as her harsh anti hymn contradicts the exalted hymns of praise sung to or by Apollo. The more abstract *agōn* that pits Creusa against Ion as singers exists only in the minds of the audience. The questions, "Who is my father?" on the one hand and "Where is my child?" on the other are complementary. The yearning for a reconciliation of purity and pollution implicit in Ion's song and in his work is made explicit as a personal demand by Creusa. The combative relationship, this metatheatrical *agōn*, between diametrically antithetical, apparently irreconcilable points of view forces the action forward. In the final scene of the play, this indirect *agōn* of song will become a performed *agōn* of violence.

1.4 *Exodos* (1250–1622): Beyond the *Agōn*

The *exodos* first enacts and then resolves the conflict prefigured by the monodies. As Victoria Wohl has described, in this play Euripides uses all of his structural and poetic resources to make the audience yearn for the *anagnorisis* of mother and son and to present the final recognition, when it eventually comes, as emotionally satisfying.[89] On the level of form, this sense of satisfaction is brought about through the reintroduction of the programmatic language of the *agōn* and the return of solo song as a mode in the *exodos*.

At this point in the play, Creusa's plot to kill Ion has been discovered; she takes refuge at the altar of Apollo to claim protection as a suppliant. When Ion and his retinue enter in pursuit, Creusa identifies these men as her "adversaries," bringing back the metaphor of the *agōn* (ἀγωνισταί, 1257). This desperate *agōn* will be Creusa's last stand against the god, even as she calls upon him. In the ensuing iambic argument between Ion and Creusa, two competing concepts of morality – human justice and divine holiness – are brought into direct opposition. Ion declares that Creusa crouches at the altar of the god to avoid "paying the penalty" for her deeds (δίκην δώσουσα, 1280). Creusa opposes him with a religious defense, calling her body "sacred" (ἱερόν, 1285). Ion too claims a special relationship to Apollo, declaring that he is "of the god" (τὸν τοῦ θεοῦ, 1286), referring to his service in the temple, his longstanding relationship with the god, and his righteous revenge against Creusa.[90] Creusa argues that the balance has shifted: now, as a suppliant, she is the one who belongs to the god (νῦν δ' ἐγώ, σὺ δ' οὐκέτι, 1291). Ion criticizes the

---

[89] Wohl 2015: 29–31. For Wohl, this sense of closure serves an ideological end, manipulating Euripides' spectators into cheering at the restored good fortune of an elite ruling family; she points out that *Ion* was produced in a period of intensifying class conflict in Athens.

[90] For the audience, the genitive may be understood as a patronymic, an instance of dramatic irony.

laws that protect suppliants as unjust (τοὺς νόμους, 1312; ἐνδίκοις, 1316). The terms of justice and injustice, piety and impiety, alternate in this dialogue: Ion speaks of δίκη and νόμος, while Creusa defends herself as ἱερά. Yet Ion, in claiming to have both human and divine justice on this side, is in the wrong, as the intervention of the Pythia will show. Creusa has taken refuge at the altar of the god and put herself under his protection, however unwillingly; and the god, making good his earlier negligence, will save her.

The rest of the scene dramatizes the victory of divine justice over human justice, marked in this play by weakness, fear, and the desire for revenge. The Pythia enters and forestalls Ion's attempt to drag Creusa from the altar and in so doing the priestess' account of Ion's adoption convinces Creusa that this is the son she once abandoned. Two of Creusa's central accusations against Apollo – that he left his child to die and that he granted a son to Xuthus rather than to her – are proven false. The case built up by Creusa in her monody has been dismantled.

And yet, wonderfully, Creusa is not defeated by this revealed truth, but by virtue of it emerges victorious. She has stood silent for eighty lines. The musical arrangement of the *exodos* reverses the pattern of Creusa's monody: where she once broke her silence to reveal her secret pain, here she breaks her silence to accept a greater truth beyond her previous comprehension. The recognition scene that follows takes the form of an *epirrhema*, where Creusa sings in astrophic lyrics and Ion responds in iambic trimeter (1439–1509).[91] The resolution of the conflict is underscored by the return of solo song as a mode, and more specifically by an inversion of the language that appeared in Creusa's monody, or rather of its valence: the same words and images now appear in a positive context.[92] As she and Ion embrace, Creusa rejoices at finding her child. Images of light displace the vocabulary of secrecy and concealment that began Creusa's monody (e.g., σιγάσω, 859; σκοτίας, 860). Because her son lives, she revises her earlier view:

ὦ τέκνον, ὦ φῶς μητρὶ κρεῖσσον ἡλίου
(συγγνώσεται γὰρ ὁ θεός), ἐν χεροῖν σ' ἔχω,
ἄελπτον εὕρημ', ὃν κατὰ γᾶς ἐνέρων
χθονίων μέτα Περσεφόνας τ' ἐδόκουν ναίειν. (1439–1442)

---

[91] On the duet, compare Cyrino 1998, who comments that the arrangement of the scene highlights Creusa's greater emotional intensity in contrast to the calmer reflections of Ion. Creusa does, however, accept comfort from Ion, unlike the singing heroines described by Chong-Gossard 2003. On the staging of the scene, see also Mueller 2010.

[92] Swift 2010: 100. Compare Mueller 2016: 80–84, who traces a similar pattern of reversal in the preceding recognition scene as the various tokens that confirm Ion's identity are brought to light from the darkness of the basket where they have been kept in secret for so many years.

> My child, light stronger for your mother than the sun
> (the god will forgive me), I hold you in my arms,
> a discovery beyond hope, who dwelt, as I thought,
> under the earth with Persephone and those below.

In Creusa's monody, speech was associated with distress, as when she called to her absent mother to save her from Apollo (αὐδῶσαν, 893), or with accusation (αὐδῶ, 907). In this final song, her cry instead expresses wonder and joy:

> ἰὼ ἰὼ λαμπρᾶς αἰθέρος ἀμπτυχαί,
> τίν' αὐδὰν ἀύσω βοάσω; πόθεν μοι
> συνέκυσ' ἀδόκητος ἡδονά;
> πόθεν ἐλάβομεν χαράν; (1445–1448)

> O O enfoldings of bright ether,
> what voice shall I call, shall I shout aloud?
> From where has this unexpected joy come to me?
> From where did I receive this delight?

Ion's miraculous appearance has brought back sunshine and sight to the royal house of Athens:

> ἄπαιδες οὐκέτ' ἐσμὲν οὐδ' ἄτεκοι·
> δῶμ' ἑστιοῦται, γᾶ δ' ἔχει τυράννους,
> ἀνηβᾷ δ' Ἐρεχθεύς·
> ὅ τε γηγενέτας δόμος οὐκέτι νύκτα δέρκεται,
> ἀελίου δ' ἀναβλέπει λαμπάσιν. (1463–1467)

> No longer am I childless, without an heir.
> The heart of the house is secure, the land has a ruler,
> Erectheus is young again.
> The house of the earth-born no longer looks upon the night,
> but its sight is restored by the rays of the sun.

The epiphany of Athena puts an end to all questioning of the god. Ion recognizes that he is the son of Apollo, while Creusa expresses an even more radical change of perspective:

> τἀμὰ νῦν ἄκουσον· αἰνῶ Φοῖβον οὐκ αἰνοῦσα πρίν,
> οὕνεχ' οὗ ποτ' ἠμέλησε παιδὸς ἀποδίδωσί μοι.
> αἵδε δ' εὐωποὶ πύλαι μοι καὶ θεοῦ χρηστήρια,
> δυσμενῆ πάροιθεν ὄντα. νῦν δὲ καὶ ῥόπτρων χέρας
> ἡδέως ἐκκρημνάμεσθα καὶ προσεννέπω πύλας. (1609–1613)

> Hear me now. I praise Phoebus, though before I did not,
> Because he returns the child that he once neglected.
> These temple doors and the shrines of the god, once my enemies,
> are lovely to me. Now it is sweet for me to grasp the door handle
> with my hands and to address the gates.

1.5 Conclusion

We have seen that Ion and Creusa engage in an indirect *agōn* of song about the nature of Apollo. We must now ask whether the two monodies give us an objective frame of reference for interpreting the behavior of the god and the events of the play. Do they have transcendental validity, or are they merely the subjective beliefs of two flawed human characters, partially valid at best? The points of view expressed by the two songs are marked as highly personal, not least by the use of monody as a form. In each case, the character has only a limited understanding as a basis for argument. Ion sings of his relationship to Delphi and to Apollo and also expresses anxiety about his identity and his place in the larger world. Creusa's monody is not only an emotional recounting of past trauma but also a rhetorically sophisticated invective delivered against the silent god. Yet her argument is based on a false premise, and she claims to abandon her anger when she is reunited with her lost child at the end of the play. As several scholars have discussed, the happy *exodos* does not in all respect resolve the darker aspects of the tragedy; Creusa's final words of praise do not erase her previous sufferings, depicted with such detail in her monody.[93] As often in Euripides' late work, in *Ion* questions about the morality of the gods, the limits of human knowledge, and the potential for mortal growth and flourishing are raised in a provocative way that ultimately transcends any simple understanding, perhaps indeed any understanding at all.

Yet it is because of their very subjectivity that the monodies are dramatically effective. Song allows access to the inner state of the characters more directly and forcefully than is possible in iambic dialogue. And, because the preoccupations of the characters are put forth so vividly, the monodies elicit tremendous identification and sympathy. Ion's monody invites the

---

[93] Compare Martin 2018: 7, who writes, "A sour aftertaste may linger; the very abruptness of Creusa's change of judgment and the surprising degree of general happiness should make us wary of this unequivocal ending." The openness of the ending is also discussed by Rabinowitz 1993: 219–220; Pedrick 2007: 186–192; Swift 2008: 86–100; Wohl 2015: 19–38; Radding 2017; and Olsen 2021: 98–99.

audience to join with the young man in his pure love and devotion to the god. In displaying her all-too-real suffering, Creusa does win a partial victory in the *agōn*, even though she loses on the facts of the case, for she engages the emotions and arouses pity and outrage through the imagistic register of song. Here Euripides shows his empathetic *bona fides* with and for women, as a formal innovator expanding the registry of roles granted a full and public voice.

Apollo, though offstage, is no vaporous and idealized being from outside the human world; like all the Greek gods, he is an embodiment of terrible forces and contradictions. From the standpoint of human morality, therefore, he must be an ambiguous figure. He is sickness and healing, cruelty and benevolence, justice meted out and immeasurable fate. At the end of the play, the pain of past experience is not wiped clear; instead, through the mysterious action of the god, the characters pass through disillusion to a more mature piety. This resolution, uneasy though it may be, is brought about on a formal level through Euripides' use of solo song. In the monodies of Ion and Creusa, Euripides moves away from the traditional connection of solo song and lamentation; rather, the poet uses monody to explore the shifting perspectives of the two central figures in the play and to set them against one another. After this musical *agōn*, Euripides again turns to solo song as a coda in the *exodos*, when Creusa reverses her earlier view of the god and embraces her son, miraculously restored to her. In these three musical scenes that mark the high points of the play, the poet brings together agonistic argument and the emotional expression inherent in solo song, collapsing separate forms into a new and dramatically powerful hybrid structure.

2 | Iphigenia among the Taurians

Memory and Movement

Iphigenia among the Taurians, first produced around 414–412 BCE, shows Euripides harnessing the potential of monody to express the psychological state of a single, central female figure as it changes over the course of the tragedy.[1] The play dramatizes Iphigenia's passage from stasis to decisive action. In her role as priestess in the cult of Artemis, Iphigenia is constrained to repeat upon others the sacrifice that was once performed on her, never healing, trapped in an endless process of remembrance and reenactment.[2] It is only when she rediscovers her family and repositions herself within it that she can move forward, ultimately escaping the harsh land of Tauris and returning to Greece. This repositioning involves several stages, traversed through questioning and through song.

In the play, Iphigenia sings two monodies, which constitute definitive statements of the beginning and end stages of the heroine's emotional journey. In her first monody – which comprises two extended lyric sections, connected by interaction with the chorus – Iphigenia mourns the unfulfilled potential of her young life, where each status was canceled, each promised doing undone. She mirrors her own situation by singing in a language of paradox, where every charged term is promptly undermined by its negation: her father who was no father, her wedding that was no wedding, her homeland that is no homeland. This first monody establishes her paralyzed state, drawing on the traditional association of monody and lamentation. Iphigenia's second monody, delivered after the reunion scene with Orestes, marks a shift in her mind and a crisis in the plot. Here we see Euripides taking the traditional form and turning it to new and innovative purpose, as monody becomes a vehicle for both deliberative thought and decisive action. The playwright builds on the convention of the "deliberation speech," a specialized type of tragic *rhesis*, to create a unique "deliberative monody"

---

[1] For dating, see Kyriakou 2006: 39–41 and Parker 2016: lxxvi–lxxx. Wright 2005 argues that *Iphigenia among the Taurians* formed part of a thematically connected trilogy of "escape tragedies" along with *Helen* and *Andromeda*, produced in 412 BCE. Marshall 2009 proposes a wider range of possible dates from 419 to 413 BCE.

[2] Chiu 2005 and Mueller 2018 offer psychological interpretations of Iphigenia's inability to move forward.

that not only dramatizes the process of thought but also highlights it through song.³ Iphigenia's words are urgent and immediate, yet at the same time they are rational and lead to a solution. It is by serving this complex purpose that Iphigenia's second monody can be said to instantiate a "collapse" or "liberation" of form: single, separate functions and their corresponding aspects of form are here brought together into close alignment and focus.

When the play begins, Iphigenia is literally isolated on an island in time as well as in space: just as she cannot escape from the barbarian land where she presides over gruesome rites of slaughter, she cannot leave behind the pain of her own past.⁴ Iphigenia had been on the point of being slaughtered in Aulis, but when the fatal act was stopped, time for her stopped with it. Condemned forever to dwell within that instant, suspended between life and death, she is folded in a secret dimension that opened up when the knife touched her throat. The life course that was apparently her destiny, the royal family she was born into, the glorious marriage she expected: these things had proved to be fragile or false, betrayed by fate and by her father's misdeed, impious and unnatural. Change seems impossible: only an unforeseen, unforeseeable event can shock her into motion. At the same time, her prison lies also within her own mind. To escape from the iron grip of the past, she must envision and desire an alternate future. The arrival of Orestes and Pylades propels her to purposeful movement; yet it is Iphigenia alone who can come up with a plan to save the last descendants of the line of Atreus.

As Edith Hall has suggested, Iphigenia in this play possesses a unique status among the female protagonists of Greek tragedy. She stars in a plot not teleologically directed at romance, sex, marriage, or motherhood; she travels across large spaces, even crossing the hostile sea between Greece and Tauris; she has a special relationship with the goddess Artemis; she possesses both religious authority and moral stature; and she exhibits tremendous resourcefulness, cunning, loyalty, and intelligence.⁵ Indeed, Iphigenia is an exemplar for her sex, a quest heroine. She is also a figure connected with song in many of her appearances in dramatic poetry.⁶ In Aeschylus' *Agamemnon*, for example, the chorus of Argive elders picture the young Iphigenia singing

---

³ On the deliberation speech in tragedy, compare Mannsperger 1971 and Fowler 1987. Within the play, Orestes' address to Pylades in the prologue exemplifies the "deliberation speech" (93–103).
⁴ Much scholarship on the play focuses on issues of sacrifice and ritual or has used the play to reconstruct actual cultic practice: see Burkert 1966; Sansone 1975; Parker 1983; O'Connor-Visser 1987; Dowden 1989; Hughes 1991; Wolff 1992; Mirto 1995; Goff 1999; Tzanetou 1999–2000; O'Bryhim 2000; Zeitlin 2011; and Bremmer 2013.
⁵ Hall 2013: 27–46.
⁶ Compare Hall 1999: 116, who writes, "Certain female characters seem almost pre-programmed to sing (Electra, Hecuba, Iphigenia, Cassandra)."

a paean in her father's banqueting halls, a memory of ritual festivity that pathetically contrasts with the silence enforced on the girl at the moment of her slaughter.[7] And Euripides himself would return to the story of Iphigenia at the end of his life, in his posthumously produced tragedy *Iphigenia in Aulis*.[8] Perhaps recalling the famous image of Iphigenia singing the paean from Aeschylus' *Agamemnon*, in *Iphigenia in Aulis* Euripides presents her actually singing a paean onstage to Artemis at the climax of the play, while the chorus respond in admiring solidarity.[9] As the tragedy moves toward its close, Euripides uses the relationship of choral and solo song to show the heroine's increasing status and confidence as her willing acquiescence in her own sacrifice becomes vital to the success of the Greek expedition to Troy.

In *Iphigenia among the Taurians*, Euripides develops both the heroine's status as exemplar and her connection with song. Iphigenia's two monodies in the play, by marrying passion and logic, demonstrate that she contains within herself a diversity of attitudes and potential.[10] Her first monody vividly portrays her static grief at the opening of the play. Despite the heroine's enduring *aporia*, her second monody is a forceful articulation of her reawakened sense of purpose.[11] Once Iphigenia is able to share with her brother the story of her sacrifice, she can situate her own experience within the larger context of her family's fate. Orestes' present troubles, more pressing than her own past suffering, compel Iphigenia to think of the future: she picks up the dropped thread of her life as she joins her fate with his. Through this second monody, Euripides sounds new notes in the delineation of character as specifically responsive to time and circumstance.

This chapter falls into two sections. In the first, I discuss Iphigenia's memory of Aulis as presented in the early scenes of the play, especially in her first monody. In this scene, both Iphigenia and the chorus utilize a vocabulary of musical terms to emphasize the rituals and rhythms of an idealized past life in Greece. In verses rife with oxymoron and internal contradiction, the women lament the loss of their families, friends, and homeland and their participation in the ceremonies of civilized society.

---

[7] *Agamemnon* 240–247. On musical imagery in this scene of *Agamemnon*, see Weiss 2018a: 39–40; on evocations of the *Oresteia* in *Iphigenia among the Taurians*, see Goff 1999 and Zeitlin 2006.

[8] The play was probably first performed posthumously along with *Bacchae* in 405 BCE, produced by Euripides' son or nephew.

[9] See Weiss 2018a: 191–231.

[10] See Mastronarde 2010: 223, writing of Phaedra: "While the juxtaposition of ... different modes is sanctioned by the formal conventions of the genre, Euripides seems to go farther than others in asking his audience to accept that these modes are capacities within a single person and that the search for any single unity of *ēthos* is futile." Compare also di Benedetto 1971: 5–24.

[11] *Contra* Chong-Gossard 2008: 104.

This loss is articulated as the heroine and the chorus call up again their old songs, now gone; the absence of these happy songs is emphasized as they are invoked through onstage performance. Euripidean choruses often lament the loss of their role in cult in the hope of future reintegration; here the *topos* is given particular force by the participation of Iphigenia, whose life was stalled at the precise moment of ritual transition from virgin to wife.[12] The heroine's song shows her imprisoned by the memory of Aulis, which separated her forever from the life she should have led as a woman.[13] Euripides here draw on the traditional connection of monody and lament, but with a striking effect of dramatic irony: this lament is performed for a man whom the audience knows to be still living, by a woman who considers herself dead. This irony foreshadows the dramatic development that is to follow, where Orestes moves toward greater passivity and Iphigenia toward greater action. Meanwhile, the following scenes lead both Iphigenia and Orestes through despair to knowledge: each thinks the other is dead, and both are wrong.

The second section of the chapter examines Iphigenia's remarkable deliberative monody, which prepares her to move from passive victim to the agent of her own rescue and that of her family. The unique nature of this second monody may be appreciated more clearly in contrast with Iphigenia's first song as well as with instances of deliberation in iambic trimeter elsewhere in the play. Iphigenia's second monody revisits and reverses patterns of imagery that have been developed in earlier scenes: travel and escape, fortune and misfortune, and the role of chance or luck (τύχη). In marked contrast to Orestes' inconclusive deliberative speech in the prologue, Iphigenia's song casts into sharper relief her growing authority and determination.

2.1 Iphigenia's First Monody: Memory (Lines 143–235)

Iphigenia's first monody takes the form of two lyric passages in alternation with the chorus in the *parodos*. I categorize Iphigenia's two sections of solo lyric as a single monody because they are part of a unified musical composition; each section is of substantial length, approximately thirty lines, and metrically independent from the contribution of the chorus. That is,

---

[12] For example, *Heraclidae* 777–783, 892–895; *Hecuba* 466–474; *Heracles* 672–700; *Phoenician Women* 220–225, 232–237, 784–791; *Bacchae* 862–865.

[13] Mueller 2018 traces a mirroring between "inner and outer landscapes" in the play, with the desolate, uncanny land of Tauris as a parallel to Iphigenia's perturbed inner state in the opening scenes.

Iphigenia and the chorus do not sing in strophic responsion to one another; this stands in contrast to other *parodoi* in Euripidean tragedy that are shared between a soloist and a sympathetic chorus.[14] Thus, even as Iphigenia is joined to the chorus by their common identity as Greek women, the heroine's relative musical independence emphasizes her isolation from the communal group and prefigures the separation of her fate from theirs as the play develops.

The significance of Iphigenia's first monody becomes evident through comparison to the other versions of the Aulis story in this same play. In the opening scenes, Iphigenia is obsessed and imprisoned by the memory of the central moment of her life, her sacrifice at the hands of her father. As Froma Zeitlin has written, Iphigenia is the haunted child of a past she has inherited, a past that is textually based in earlier versions of the myth of the house of Atreus, chief among them Aeschylus' *Oresteia*.[15] Action in the first half of *Iphigenia among the Taurians* is ruled by the forces of memory and desire, repetition, and reenactment. Euripides in this play will signify dramatic progression through a series of recognizable forms – iambic *rhesis*, lyric song, and iambic dialogue – that retell the same story but vary in the emotion they express. Over the course of the play, six times Iphigenia remembers and six times she retells her experience at Aulis: in the prologue (24–29); in her first monody (214–217); after she has resolved to kill the two young Greeks who have been captured on the shores of Tauris (361–371); when questioning Orestes, his identity still unknown, about the fate of the house of Atreus (563–566); in her letter (783–786); and finally in her lyric duet with her brother (852–867).[16] The story is sometimes embellished, sometimes told in brief; but the past remains always before the heroine's eyes.[17]

Iphigenia's first monody is the second version of the Aulis story, and it is both the longest and set apart from the five other retellings through its use of lyric song. The conventions of actor's song as a medium allow for a particularly immediate, open expression of Iphigenia's grief. The emotional

---

[14] For example, *Electra* 112–212, *Trojan Women* 153–229, and *Helen* 164–251.
[15] Zeitlin 2006.
[16] All versions of the Aulis story reflect previous accounts of the myth; see Caldwell 1974–5; Sansone 1975; O'Brien 1988; Lübeck 1993; Aretz 1999; Wright 2005: 56–157; Zeitlin 2006; and Bremmer 2013.
[17] We may compare Creusa in *Ion*, who tells the story of the rape and the abandonment of her child various times and before various audiences, and who is imprisoned by this memory; in both plays Euripides makes the monody of the heroine the most unrestrained and emotional retelling of the event, a necessary step before she can move forward and build a new relationship with the male relative she thought was lost.

force established in the monody extends backward to the prologue and forward to subsequent scenes. Each telling of the story is different, determined by its particular motivation, onstage audience, and mode of delivery. In the prologue, the focus is on exposition: Iphigenia relates the bare facts of her history without commenting on her own feelings. In her first monody, by contrast, she is more open: she pities herself and explicitly calls for the pity of others. Here she has a sympathetic audience, the women of the chorus. Faced in the first episode with the prospect of preparing the two Greek strangers for sacrifice, Iphigenia steels herself by recounting again the horrors she suffered at the hands of her own people. In her questions to Orestes and in her letter, the fourth and fifth retellings of the story, she is brief and restrained – she is, after all, facing a supposed stranger. At last reunited with her brother, she relates the misery of her false marriage with great pathos in the sixth retelling, drawing a parallel between her father's murder of his daughter and her own preparations to slaughter her brother. Under the dictatorship of the past, Iphigenia has come to the brink of repeating Agamemnon's crime, but at the last possible moment disaster is averted. In saving Orestes, Iphigenia breaks the cycle of kin-killing that has for generations plagued the house of Atreus. This sixth and final retelling lays to rest the obsessive remembering of her own past and prepares her for change.

Her father's murderous and public betrayal was the core event, the traumatic and generative moment, that established time zero for her existence. These six very different retellings underscore the particular dramatic significance of the first monody, where for the first time Iphigenia describes her sacrifice in terms that expose her own feelings about that event. The monody is related to the other versions of the Aulis story through complex patterns of similarity and contrast both formal and thematic. In addition, the outpouring of emotion in the monody seems to effect a change in Iphigenia's ability to express her own feelings. In the third telling, after the monody, she reveals new details of her experience at Aulis and even reexperiences the event through first-person speech. The fourth and fifth versions of the story move from a private expression to a public one. Finally, in the sixth retelling the dramatic irony that has marked the play until this point is collapsed in the long-awaited reunion between brother and sister. Each retelling, as we shall see, engages in different ways with the themes of paralysis, of actual death as mirrored by suspended or frustrated life, and of understanding versus error; each version provides an essential step in Iphigenia's journey from stasis to decisive action.

The first presentation of the Aulis story brings into sharper focus the special intensity achieved later through the use of monody, where Iphigenia's obsessive focus on her own suffering is expressed through the language of lyric. The brief, unadorned, chronological version of Iphigenia's history in the prologue provides a template against which all future versions of the story are measured. Here Iphigenia's exposition is clear and matter-of-fact. The narrative proceeds in linear fashion from the past to the present:

> καί μ' Ὀδυσσέως τέχναις
> μητρὸς παρείλοντ' ἐπὶ γάμοις Ἀχιλλέως.
> ἐλθοῦσα δ' Αὐλίδ' ἡ τάλαιν' ὑπὲρ πυρᾶς
> μεταρσία ληφθεῖσ' ἐκαινόμην ξίφει·
> ἀλλ' ἐξέκλεψέ μ' ἔλαφον ἀντιδοῦσά μου
> Ἄρτεμις Ἀχαιοῖς· (24–29)

> And by the arts of Odysseus
> I was taken from my mother on the pretext
> of marriage to Achilles. I came to Aulis, wretched,
> and lifted high above the pyre I was about to be slaughtered
> with a sword; but Artemis stole me away, and gave
> to the Achaeans a deer in my place.

In the short clause describing the actual moment of the sacrifice, only one adjective, "wretched" (τάλαιν'), and the passive participle "lifted" (ληφθεῖσ') show Iphigenia in the position of a victim. Her emotions remain unexpressed and unexplored. The event seems to be fully in the past, buried and no longer affecting the present. Iphigenia does not speak of her own fear or of her anger at her father and the other Greek captains. She does not attribute responsibility to Artemis, who both demanded Iphigenia's sacrifice and saved her from death. She shows neither resentment nor gratitude toward the goddess.[18]

In the *parodos*, by contrast, Iphigenia expresses the emotions of sadness and anger that were only hinted at in her monologue. The song takes the form of a *kommos*, or shared lament, in which Iphigenia's part is substantially longer than that of the chorus. The assignation of lines in this passage is somewhat vexed; here I follow the arrangement favored by most recent editors of the play.[19] In this arrangement, the *parodos* progresses through four lyric sections. The chorus enter, announcing their identity as free-born Greek maidens who now serve as slaves at the temple of Artemis and asking Iphigenia for news (123–142). In her first passage of lyric, Iphigenia laments

---

[18] For the range of mythological accounts describing the reason for the sacrifice, see Kyriakou 2006: ad 15–16. For Iphigenia's relationship to Artemis in the play, see Hartigan 1991: 89–106.

[19] See Cropp 2000; Kyriakou 2006: ad 123–142; de Poli 2011: 157–173; and Parker 2016: ad 123–235. In brief, the manuscript L gives 123–136 to Iphigenia and 137–142 to the chorus, but 126–136 must belong to the chorus because the women identify themselves as slaves of the priestess.

for Orestes, whom she presumes dead on the evidence of her dream (143–177).[20] The chorus respond by offering dirges for the dead man (178–202). Finally, in the longest and most metrically varied passage, Iphigenia grieves for her own misfortune (203–235). In the remote land of the Taurians, shared lamentation serves to solidify the bond between these helpless and beleaguered Greek women. Yet the chorus do not so much answer Iphigenia as second her words; it is mainly her song and her feelings that are explored.

The formal arrangement of this *parodos* draws on a long tradition of laments shared between a female soloist and a group. This literary form has its roots in actual funereal practice; as the foundational work of Margaret Alexiou demonstrates, continuities in the performance of female lament can be traced from archaic epic and Classical poetry all the way through to modern Greek communities, a tradition spanning perhaps 3,500 years, if not more.[21] In Greek literature, the *locus classicus* for shared female mourning is Book 24 of the *Iliad*, where Hecuba, Andromache, and Helen each lead a lament for the dead Hector as a soloist among a wider group of women and bards.[22] As we saw in the Introduction, lamentation plays a substantial role in the works of all of the Greek tragedians that have come down to us and provides numerous opportunities for arresting song on the tragic stage. More than Aeschylus and Sophocles, Euripides seems to have been especially fond of structuring his opening *parodoi* as sorrowful duets between heroine and chorus. He experimented with this technique in several plays produced within a few years of *Iphigenia among the Taurians*: *Electra* (lines 168–212), *Trojan Women* (lines 153–229), *Helen* (lines 164–251), and the fragmentary *Andromeda*.[23] In all of these cases, the heroine's passage or passages of solo song, placed early in the play, reveal with particular intensity the emotional state and preoccupations of the enthralled central figure and establish a close relationship between her and the chorus.

Compared to the shared opening laments in these other plays, however, the monody of Iphigenia is rendered more complex because it is heard as one of a series of recounted versions of the heroine's central calamity. Musically, too,

---

[20] On the dream and its interpretation, compare Zeitlin 2006: 208–212 and Trieschnigg 2008.

[21] Alexiou 1974.

[22] On lamentation in Greek culture, see the Introduction, pp. 21–36, as well as discussion in Alexiou 1974; Loraux 1987: 45–49 and 2002 [1999]; Hall 1989: 83–84, 121–133; Foley 1993 and 2001: 21–29; Segal 1993; Sultan 1993; McClure 1999; Murnaghan 1999; Suter 2003 and 2008; Dué 2006: 30–56; Swift 2010: 298–367; Nooter 2011; Weiss 2017; and Curtis and Weiss 2021: 261–310.

[23] These passages are discussed by Weiss 2018a: 61–75. In each play, Weiss argues, Euripides draws on the dynamics of traditional female chorality to present the relationship as one between a (potential) chorus leader and her chorus. Compare Mossman 2005 on the emotional authenticity of women's voices in tragedy.

Iphigenia is more independent from the chorus than other Euripidean heroines, as evidenced by the lack of strophic responsion and the runs of short syllables that only occur in her verses and further set her apart from the group (e.g., lines 213, 220, 231, 232). The example of *Helen*, produced in 412 BCE, shows how much more closely Euripides could link heroine and chorus.[24] Indeed, the figure of Helen is closely associated with chorality throughout Greek literature as well as in myth and cult more broadly.[25] As Naomi Weiss has argued, Euripides' *Helen* is dramatically centered on Helen's position as the chorus leader *par excellence*; Helen begins the tragedy as a leader of lamentation for her exiled fellow Greek women in Egypt and will later become a leader of choral dance in Sparta, following her escape back to Greece with Menelaus.[26] Helen's role as future chorus leader is emphasized in the *parodos* through musical responsion: Helen sings an opening strophe (167–178) and the chorus of enslaved Greek women respond with a matching antistrophe (179–190); after a second strophe and antistrophe pair shared in this way (191–228), Helen concludes the *parodos* with an independent epode (229–251).[27] Although Helen's three sections of lyric in the *parodos* can be seen as constituting a single monody, the responsive role of the chorus in this scene frames her as closely bonded to them.

By contrast with Helen, Iphigenia is granted a second monody at the midpoint of the play that, through contrast with the first, shows the very process of change in how she sees and situates herself, including an evolution in the relation of chorus to heroine. As we saw in the previous chapter, Euripides uses a similar technique of multiple retellings to explore the emotions of Creusa in *Ion*. In that play, Creusa's monody is the climactic version of her story, and all previous versions look forward to it and create suspense for its final outpouring; in addition, the monody stands in opposition to Ion's monody in the opening scene. Iphigenia, by contrast with Creusa, is granted a lyric voice almost immediately. She is the only figure in the play who expresses herself through lyric song; there is no one with whom she can be brought into a lyric conflict except her own later self.

The *parodos* creates an intimate connection between the women of the chorus and Iphigenia: they share a background as displaced Greeks, and in Tauris they are in a similar position of bondage and vulnerability.[28] The

---

[24] For the dating of *Helen*, see Allan 2008: 1–4.
[25] Calame 1997: 191–202; Martin 2008: 119–126; Murnaghan 2013. [26] Weiss 2018a: 144–156.
[27] For scansion, see de Poli 2011: 197–215; for discussion of the musical arrangement, see Allan 2008: 165–166 and Marshall 2014: 27.
[28] Chong-Gossard 2008: 168–171 discusses the solidarity between the chorus and Iphigenia. The women of the chorus benefit from keeping Iphigenia's plans secret and from deliberately misdirecting Thoas and are rewarded for their "positive" deceit by return to Greece.

unity of thought and feeling is expressed through related – though never entirely matched – meters: the *parodos* consists almost entirely of "mourning" anapests, with the substitution of some dactyls and many spondees to create a slow, measured tone appropriate for lamentation.[29] On the level of diction and vocabulary, the chorus and Iphigenia share a common language of contradiction. As several scholars have explored, such language of negation is a typical feature of ancient Greek laments; this is especially true of tragedy, where lament itself is conceptualized as paradoxical, at once a highly articulate lyrical performance and an inarticulate noise of grief.[30] In Charles Segal's felicitous phrase, lament in tragedy is "negated song."[31] In this play, the paradoxical nature of lament – its status as at once music and its opposite, unruly noise – is further heightened by setting and context: in the shadowland of Tauris, nothing is as it should be.

In the first lines of her song, Iphigenia addresses the chorus directly:

> ὦ δμωαί,
> δυσθρηνήτοις ὡς θρήνοις
> ἔγκειμαι, τᾶς οὐκ εὐμούσου
> μολπᾶς βοὰν ἀλύροις ἐλέγοις, αἰαῖ,
> ἐν κηδείοις οἴκτοισιν,
> αἵ μοι συμβαίνουσ' ἆται
> σύγγονον ἁμὸν κατακλαιομένα
> ζωᾶς. οἵαν ἰδοίμαν
> ὄψιν ὀνείρων
> νυκτὸς τᾶς ἐξῆλθ' ὄρφνα.   (143–152)

> O attendant women,
> how I lie wrapped in ill-chanted chants,
> the cry of unmusical song with lyre-less laments, alas,
> in piteous wailing for my loved ones,
> weeping for the disasters that have fallen upon me,
> for the life of my brother.
> Such was the dream vision I saw
> coming in the dark of the night now ended.

This passage emphasizes Iphigenia's arrested state through a series of phrases in which one term negates or contradicts the other: "ill-chanted chants" (δυσθρηνήτοις θρήνοις), "unmusical song" (οὐκ εὐμούσου μολπᾶς), "lyre-less

---

[29] On meter, see Sansone 1981: 56–58; Cropp 2000: ad 123–235; and Kyriakou 2006: ad 123–235.
[30] Alexiou 1974; Segal 1993; McClure 1999: 40–47; Wilson 1999–2000; Murnaghan 2011; Weiss 2017.
[31] Segal 1989: 343.

laments" (ἀλύροις ἐλέγοις). As Naomi Weiss has remarked, the language of negation in these lines draws our attention to Iphigenia's own musical skill (and to that of the actor in this role).[32] Several times Iphigenia asserts the musicality of her lament, but each time she immediately undermines it. The usual acts of mourning that a sister should perform for a brother are impossible in this context: there is no corpse, and Iphigenia's own misinterpretation of her dream is the only evidence of Orestes' death. In the perverted lineage of Atreus, not even death takes place as it should.

Iphigenia then describes the rituals of burial – pouring libations of milk, wine, and honey (157–169).[33] She performs these rites alone, without the other members of her family, far from her homeland. She addresses Orestes directly, a bitter irony given his recent onstage appearance:

> ὦ κατὰ γαίας Ἀγαμεμνόνιον
> θάλος, ὡς φθιμένῳ τάδε σοι πέμπω.
> δέξαι δ'· οὐ γὰρ πρὸς τύμβον σοι
> ξανθὰν χαίταν, οὐ δάκρυ' οἴσω.
> τηλόσε γὰρ δὴ σᾶς ἀπενάσθην
> πατρίδος καὶ ἐμᾶς, ἔνθα δοκήμασι
> κεῖμαι σφαχθεῖσα, τλάμων.   (170–177)

> O child of Agamemnon below the earth,
> as to one dead I send you these offerings.
> Accept them: for to your tomb I shall not bring
> a golden lock of hair, I shall not bring tears.
> For I have been sent far away from your homeland,
> and from mine, where they suppose that
> I lie slaughtered, poor sufferer.

Iphigenia's actions commemorate her own death in addition to that of Orestes: the mourner as well as the mourned man is thought of as dead, "lying slaughtered" on a foreign shore (κεῖμαι σφαχθεῖσα). Iphigenia's first passage of song thus becomes her own performed funeral lament. For many years, as the prologue reveals, she has remained in a liminal space between life and death. To be far from her homeland is for her a kind of death. The supposed loss of Orestes removes all hope that she will ever escape this state of suspension: she will never leave Tauris, never return to life in Greece. The

---

[32] Weiss 2017: 247. In tragedy lament is often described as a distortion of normal song; for example, Aeschylus, *Suppliants* 681, *Agamemnon* 990–992, *Eumenides* 331–333; Sophocles, *Oedipus at Colonus* 1221–1222; and Euripides, *Phoenician Women* 784–791.

[33] For the physical and ritual actions associated with lament in tragedy, see Dillon 2002 and Dué 2006: 8–21.

monody expresses her complete despair through the language of paradox, in which every potential movement is annihilated by its anti-movement. These contradictions suggest an untenable dramatic condition: Iphigenia will have to move from stasis to action, whether in death or through rebellion against her condition. As we shall see, this transformation occurs in the second monody and takes effect immediately after it.

Iphigenia sings of a death, a funeral, and a house that have all been perverted; the chorus respond with language that explicitly echoes hers:

> ἀντιψάλμους ᾠδὰς ὕμνων τ'
> Ἀσιητᾶν σοι βάρβαρον ἀχὰν
> δεσποίνᾳ γ' ἐξαυδάσω,
> τὰν ἐν θρήνοισιν μοῦσαν
> νέκυσι μελομέναν, τὰν ἐν μολπαῖς
> Ἅιδας ὑμνεῖ δίχα παιάνων.   (179–185)

> Antiphonal songs, the barbarian cry
> of Asiatic hymns I shall cry forth
> in response to you, my mistress,
> music in laments proper for the dead,
> music that Hades chants in songs, without paeans.

The chorus situate themselves in musical alternation with Iphigenia, a "twanging" (ψαλμός) set against (ἀντί) her lament. Their lyrics are "Asiatic" and "barbarian" (Ἀσιητᾶν, βάρβαρον): in inhospitable Tauris, there is no place for the proper Hellenic songs of mourning.[34] Their cries of despair and death are contrasted with hymns (ὑμνεῖ) and specifically with the paean (δίχα παιάνων), which, as we explored in the previous chapter, is usually a communal performance of joy, gratitude, or prayer.[35] Since these contradictory references to song take place within the context of an onstage musical performance, the effect is to heighten the contrast between absent and enacted music, music here standing for all the activities of life that it rightly accompanies: prayer, festivity, celebration, transition, mourning. In the next section of the monody Iphigenia's self-referential song will further develop this dichotomy.

---

[34] On the relationship between mourning and barbarian songs, see Hall 1989; Loraux 2002 [1999]: 54–65; and Weiss 2017.
[35] On the paean as a genre, see Käppel 1992: 32–86; Rutherford 1994–5 and 2001: 3–136; and Swift 2010: 61–103.

The chorus conclude their second lyric passage with a final oxymoron describing Iphigenia's situation: some divine force presses upon her things that should not be pressed (σπεύδει δ' ἀσπούδαστ' ἐπὶ σοὶ δαίμων, 201–202). The δαίμων to which they attribute Iphigenia's misfortunes carries several shades of meaning: it is at once an unspecified divine power and Iphigenia's personal and personified fate.[36] The exchange between heroine and chorus thus establishes the misery and hopelessness of Iphigenia's current situation now that Orestes has died. In her second, longer passage of lyric, Iphigenia imagines Orestes' death as the culmination of the series of misfortunes that began with the sacrifice at Aulis. The confines of her world have shrunk to the size of her own obsessively remembered past: here she fully leaves behind shared lament and approaches the self-absorption of a monodist, fully intent on her own experience.

Taking up the language of the chorus, Iphigenia speculates that this most recent evil is only the latest chapter in the disastrous legacy of the house of Tantalus. She narrates her own part in this familial misfortune from the very beginning:

> ἐξ ἀρχᾶς μοι δυσδαίμων
> δαίμων τᾶς ματρὸς ζώνας
> καὶ νυκτὸς κείνας· ἐξ ἀρχᾶς
> λόχιαι στερρὰν παιδείαν
> Μοῖραι συντείνουσιν θεαί·
> ἃ μναστευθεῖσ' ἐξ Ἑλλάνων,
> ἃν πρωτόγονον θάλος ἐν θαλάμοις
> Λήδας ἁ τλάμων κούρα
> σφάγιον πατρῴᾳ λώβᾳ
> καὶ θῦμ' οὐκ εὐγάθητον
> ἔτεκεν ἔτρεφεν εὐκταίαν·
> ἱππείοις δ' ἐν δίφροισι
> ψαμάθων Αὐλίδος ἐπέβασαν
> νύμφαιον, οἴμοι, δύσνυμφον
> τῷ τᾶς Νηρέως κούρας, αἰαῖ. (203–217)

> From the start my fate has been ill-fated,
> since the night I came from my mother's womb;
> from the start the goddesses of Fate,
> attendants at my birth,
> have drawn tight for me a harsh upbringing.
> I was wooed by the Greeks,
> the firstborn shoot in the chambers

---

[36] Compare Mikalson 1991: 22–28.

of Leda's daughter, a wretched girl,
sacrificial offering for a father's atrocity
and joyless victim of his vow –
for this I was born and nurtured.
In horse-drawn carriages
they set me on the sands of Aulis,
a bride who was no bride – ah, me! –
for the son of the daughter of Nereus, alas.

In contrast to the earlier description of the sacrifice in the *parodos*, here Iphigenia uses elaborate rhetorical devices, including anaphora (ἐξ ἀρχᾶς, ἐξ ἀρχᾶς), alliteration (θάλος ἐν θαλάμοις), and asyndeton (ἔτεκεν ἔτρεφεν εὐκταίαν). She invites pity through her description of herself as unfortunate (ἁ τλάμων κούρα) and through interjected cries (οἴμοι, αἰαῖ). Where previously she placed no guilt on Agamemnon or the Greek captains, here she speaks of Agamemnon's action as her "father's outrage" (πατρῴᾳ λώβᾳ) and her sham marriage as a disastrous contradiction in terms, a "marriage that was no marriage" (νύμφαιον δύσνυμφον).

Now Iphigenia has no share in the life of a Greek woman: she is marriageless, childless, city-less, friendless, a total negation emphasized by a striking line entirely composed of short syllables (ἄγαμος ἄτεκνος ἄπολις ἄφιλος, 220).[37] The perversion of her current existence is further expressed through the terms and imagery of music:

νῦν δ' ἀξείνου πόντου ξείνα
δυσχόρτους οἴκους ναίω,
ἄγαμος ἄτεκνος ἄπολις ἄφιλος,
οὐ τὰν Ἄργει μέλπουσ' Ἥραν
οὐδ' ἱστοῖς ἐν καλλιφθόγγοις
κερκίδι Παλλάδος Ἀτθίδος εἰκὼ
<καὶ> Τιτάνων ποικίλλουσ', ἀλλ'
αἱμορράντων δυσφόρμιγγα
ξείνων αἱμάσσουσ' ἄταν βωμοὺς
οἰκτρόν τ' αἰαζόντων αὐδὰν
οἰκτρόν τ' ἐκβαλλόντων δάκρυον. (218–228)

[37] Compare Fleming 1977 and Finkelstein 2010, who traces Aeschylus' novel use of alpha privatives and negated language in the *Oresteia* in order to show that the proliferation of these words emphasizes the destruction of social and sexual relations. At 113–123 Finkelstein discusses the afterlife of this vocabulary in *Iphigenia among the Taurians*. Euripides, she argues, deliberately echoes the language of the *Oresteia* to create a connection between the Taurian land, the chthonic Erinyes, and the Underworld: alpha privatives thus characterize the land of the Taurians as a kind of underworld from which Iphigenia and Orestes must escape.

> And now as a stranger I dwell in a house
> that borders on a Hostile Sea,
> marriage-less, childless, city-less, friendless.
> I do not sing for Hera at Argos,
> nor on the sweet-voiced loom
> do I portray Attic Pallas and the Titans,
> embroidering them with my shuttle,
> but I bloody the altars
> with the streaming blood of strangers,
> a fate unfit for the lyre,
> while they wail with piteous cries
> and shed piteous tears.

Iphigenia sets up a contrast between joyful music, associated with longed-for life in Greece, and the mournful, dissonant music of her present life among the Taurians. Her singing (μέλπουσ') for Hera at the loom, itself a sweet-voiced instrument (καλλιφθόγγοις), has been replaced by the piteous wailing of sacrificial victims (αἰαζόντων) and sounds that do not suit the lyre (δυσφόρμιγγα). Her only activity – polluting the altar with the blood of strangers – is compelled, forced upon her. Her monody ends with a renewed lament for the dead Orestes:

> καὶ νῦν κείνων μέν μοι λάθα,
> τὸν δ' Ἄργει δμαθέντα κλαίω
> σύγγονον, ὃν ἔλιπον ἐπιμαστίδιον   231–232
> ἔτι βρέφος, ἔτι νέον, ἔτι θάλος
> ἐν χερσὶν ματρὸς πρὸς στέρνοις τ'
> Ἄργει σκηπτοῦχον Ὀρέσταν.   (229–235)

> And now I have forgotten these things:
> it is the one dead in Argos that I weep for,
> my brother, whom I left behind a nursling at the breast,
> still a newborn, still a youth, still a tender shoot,
> in the arms and embrace of his mother,
> the scepter-bearing king of Argos, Orestes.

Another run of short syllables indicates the culmination of Iphigenia's distress as she recalls her brother as she last saw him, an innocent infant at their mother's breast in Argos (231–233).[38] His proper name, postponed for the entire song, climactically concludes the lament.

---

[38] On the line division and meter, see Kyriakou 2006: ad 123–235 and de Poli 2011: 164.

2.1 Iphigenia's First Monody

Iphigenia's first monody thus demonstrates the full extent of the heroine's grief and loss, as well as the dramatic conditions with which the play opens, signified by her internal conflict. Language of paradox, especially the negation of musical terms, emphasizes her complete deracination. This fuller exposition of Iphigenia's inner state creates tension for the scenes that follow and establishes the vital role that monody plays in the dramatic development of the play. Orestes' death has killed her as well: for her, his loss is a second Aulis, a second death of hope and the family. She has now been turned into a ruthless killer of others, so much so that she will narrowly avoid sacrificing her own brother.

Coming after the account of the sacrifice in the prologue, the first monody precedes two further tellings in iambic trimeter of that same sacrifice. These two accounts, the third and fourth versions of the Aulis story, explore the conflict between the emotionality of the first monody and the "hardening of heart" that Iphigenia experiences after she concludes that Orestes is dead. Immediately after the *parodos*, a herdsman arrives from the shore, bringing news that two young Greeks have been captured and must now be prepared for death. Iphigenia's subsequent iambic speech is essentially a soliloquy in the presence of the chorus as signaled by the opening address to her heart (ὦ καρδία τάλαινα, 344). She asserts that the death of her brother has hardened her heart toward all strangers (334–350). The pity she once felt for helpless Greeks has become anger and a desire for revenge, especially against those she blames for her current state: Helen and Menelaus. Their hated names remind her of Aulis:

> οἴμοι – κακῶν γὰρ τῶν τότ' οὐκ ἀμνημονῶ –
> ὅσας γενείου χεῖρας ἐξηκόντισα
> γονάτων τε τοῦ τεκόντος, ἐξαρτωμένη,
> λέγουσα τοιάδ'· ὦ πάτερ, νυμφεύομαι
> νυμφεύματ' αἰσχρὰ πρὸς σέθεν· μήτηρ δ' ἐμὲ
> σέθεν κατακτείνοντος Ἀργεῖαί τε νῦν
> ὑμνοῦσιν ὑμεναίοισιν, αὐλεῖται δὲ πᾶν
> μέλαθρον· ἡμεῖς δ' ὀλλύμεσθα πρὸς σέθεν.
> Ἅιδης Ἀχιλλεὺς ἦν ἄρ', οὐχ ὁ Πηλέως,
> ὅν μοι προσείσας πόσιν, ἐν ἁρμάτων ὄχοις
> ἐς αἱματηρὸν γάμον ἐπόρθμευσας δόλῳ.   (361–371)

> Alas – for I cannot un-remember the evils of that day –
> how many times I darted forth my hands at the cheek
> and at the knees of my father, clinging to them,

saying: "Father, I am led into a shameful marriage
by you. Now, as you kill me, my mother and the Argive women
sing wedding hymns, and all the house is filled with pipe-music –
but I am destroyed at your hands. Achilles was Hades, then,
not the son of Peleus, whom you offered to me
as a husband, then brought me in the shelter of a carriage
to a bloody wedding, by deceit."

In this passage the narrative precision of the prologue and the emotional force of the monody are carried forward to create an account of striking intensity. The memory begins in the past tense (ἐξηκόντισα) but is made more vivid through the switch to the present tense in Iphigenia's direct address to Agamemnon (νυμφεύομαι, ὑμνοῦσιν, αὐλεῖται). As in the *parodos*, musical imagery emphasizes the terrible perversion of the civic, sacred, and familial rite.[39] While Iphigenia pleads for her life, Clytemnestra, ignorant of the truth, raises the joyful wedding hymn at home with the women of Argos (ὑμνοῦσιν ὑμεναίοισιν), and the whole house is filled with the music of the aulos (αὐλεῖται). The juxtaposition of the names of Achilles and Hades (Ἅιδης Ἀχιλλεύς) conflates the intended bridegroom with death. Just as Iphigenia is caught between life and death, so she is caught between girl and woman, trapped forever in her virgin status. This third retelling continues the emotional memory of the *parodos* and contrasts the pain Iphigenia felt at Aulis with her self-proclaimed pitilessness in the present. As Iphigenia herself says, she "cannot un-remember" what happened at Aulis (οὐκ ἀμνημονῶ, 361). Her straightforward speech in the prologue, her emotional lamentation in her first monody, and her passionate monologue in the first episode establish her state of paralysis. She cannot escape from the grip of the terrible memory.

The next two recountings of the Aulis story, although brief, mark a crucial turning point in her effort to come to terms with the past. For the first time, Iphigenia tells her story to strangers. Where previously she has had only herself and the enslaved women of the chorus as an audience, now the two young Greeks present her with an opportunity to share her story and to gain new information in return.

Throughout their long iambic dialogue in the second episode, Orestes and Iphigenia conceal their true identities. The effect is one of dramatic irony and increasing tension, as time and again the recognition is

---

[39] For perverted wedding imagery in tragedy, see Seaford 1987.

2.1 Iphigenia's First Monody

tantalizingly approached and then deferred. In her series of questions about the fate of the ruling family of Argos, Iphigenia asks first about Electra and then about herself:

Ιφ.   τί δέ; σφαγείσης θυγατρὸς ἔστι τις λόγος;
Ορ.   οὐδείς γε, πλὴν θανοῦσαν οὐχ ὁρᾶν φάος.
Ιφ.   τάλαιν' ἐκείνη χὠ κτανὼν αὐτὴν πατήρ.
Ορ.   κακῆς γυναικὸς χάριν ἄχαριν ἀπώλετο.   (563–566)

Iph.   And is there any report of the daughter who was slaughtered?
Or.   None, except that she died and no longer looks upon the light.
Iph.   Wretched girl, and wretched too the father who killed her.
Or.   She perished as thankless thanks for an evil woman.

At this point Iphigenia makes no move to correct Orestes. She hopes to hear, perhaps, that she still lives in some sense, in the memories and intentions of her family, but Orestes' reply tells her that to them she no longer exists. She is no longer mourned and sought. Therefore what he has said is essentially true – although she does "look upon the light," she is dead, trapped in the land of the Taurians with no hope of rescue.

Iphigenia's next line, that Agamemnon is also unfortunate, reverses her earlier expressions of anger against her father. She has heard that he is dead, slaughtered by his wife; that his wife is dead; that Electra lives, but – she imagines at this point – that two of his three children are dead. The family of Atreus has all but disappeared. Her grief and pity now extend beyond herself; she mourns her sufferings within the larger context of her destroyed family. Here Iphigenia moves beyond the description of her own misfortune as displayed in the first monody; the seeds of change exist in the outward extension of her sympathy.

These two abbreviated versions of her own sacrificial slaughter, in her stichomythia with Orestes and in her letter, constitute the fourth and fifth retellings of the Aulis story. Together they create suspense through dramatic irony for the outpouring of her second monody, as we shall see in the next section, and for the rest of the play. In the first monody Iphigenia has displayed the full agony of her betrayal, and in the second she bids farewell at last to the paralyzing memory of Aulis and prepares herself for change.

2.2 Iphigenia's Second Monody: Movement (Lines 868–899)

In the first monody, as we have seen, Euripides presents Iphigenia's inner state at the beginning of the play. This state is complicated by the overwhelming dramatic irony of her situation: her grief is based on a misapprehension. Like Creusa's monody in *Ion*, the first monody of Iphigenia creates a distancing effect, as the compelling tone of the song stands in tension with the factual error of its content. Thus the first monody contains an emotional and dramatic potential energy, soon converted into action. The innovative second monody occurs once Iphigenia sees more clearly. The change from a more conventional monody of mourning to a unique monody of deliberation parallels the change in the play from stasis to action.

Of course, in a more evident way, the alternation between plainer speech and unrestrained song – that is, between the iambic scenes and the two monodies taken together – moves in tandem with the action of the play. Euripides uses the pattern of song and speech to explore the two extremes of Iphigenia's emotional state: desperation and the rebirth of hope. The two monodies assume places of special importance in the drama. When she is convinced that Orestes is dead and her last hope of rescue is lost, Iphigenia gives vent to her grief in her first monody. This new depth of misery hardens her heart for the killing of the unknown Greeks. Her second monody acknowledges the connection between the two intended murders and finally quells the drive toward further incestuous violence.[40]

The change in mood embodied by the second monody is ushered in by the fifth and sixth versions of the Aulis story: Iphigenia's letter and her reunion duet with Orestes. Iphigenia finally asks the Greek strangers about her central concern, the fate of Orestes (567–569). When she learns that her brother has not died and that her interpretation of her dream was false, her behavior shifts. She quickly offers a plan, which, as she says, will benefit both the strangers and herself (578–580). The stratagem of the letter is presented as something long prepared and pondered, kept in readiness for just such an opportunity (584–590).[41] Despite her stated helplessness, Iphigenia has never fully abandoned the hope that a Greek sailor might land on the shores of the Taurian land and carry her message back to Greece.

---

[40] For the relationship between the two sacrifices, compare O'Brien 1988.
[41] See Mueller 2016: 178–184 on the role of the *deltos* as a significant prop in the play.

In the stichomythia with Orestes in the previous scene, Iphigenia learns that she is considered dead and chooses not to dispute it by revealing herself. But now in her letter she announces that she is simultaneously alive and dead: the report of Orestes' survival has brought back the possibility of change, of reintegration into the Hellenic world. She is both "slaughtered" (σφαγεῖσ') and "living" (ζῶσ'):

Ιφ.	ἄγγελλ' Ὀρέστῃ παιδὶ τἀγαμέμνονος· Ἡ 'ν Αὐλίδι σφαγεῖσ' ἐπιστέλλει τάδε ζῶσ' Ἰφιγένεια, τοῖς ἐκεῖ δ' οὐ ζῶσ' ἔτι.	
Ορ.	ποῦ δ' ἔστ' ἐκείνη; κατθανοῦσ' ἥκει πάλιν;	
Ιφ.	ἥδ' ἣν ὁρᾷς σύ· μὴ λόγων ἔκπλησσέ με. Κόμισαί μ' ἐς Ἄργος, ὦ σύναιμε, πρὶν θανεῖν ἐκ βαρβάρου γῆς, καὶ μετάστησον θεᾶς σφαγίων ἐφ' οἷσι ξενοφόνους τιμὰς ἔχω.	
Ορ.	Πυλάδη, τί λέξω; ποῦ ποτ' ὄνθ' ηὑρήμεθα;	(769–777)

Iph.	Announce these things to Orestes, son of Agamemnon: She who was slaughtered at Aulis sends you these words, Iphigenia, who lives, although to those there she lives no longer.
Or.	Where is she? Has she come back from the dead?
Iph.	She is the one whom you see! Don't interrupt my words. Take me to Argos before I die, brother, away from this barbarian land, and release me from the sacrifices of the goddess where I officiate over the slaughter of strangers.
Or.	Pylades, what shall I say? Where do we find ourselves?

The recounting of the contents of the letter thus shows an intermediate stage in Iphigenia's journey from stasis to movement: no longer fully without hope, she is now entering into the passage from death to life.[42] The part that death still has of her derives not only from the physical entrapment from which she calls to be released and the sacrificial rites she presides over but also from her family's belief. Although the letter reiterates information already familiar to the theater audience from the prologue, the presence of Orestes onstage crucially changes its import. The letter, which speaks with Iphigenia's voice, brings about the longed-for reunion.

Once the recognition between the two siblings has been achieved, Iphigenia tells the story of Aulis for the sixth and final time. She is no longer

---

[42] Mueller 2016: 178–184 offers a complementary interpretation of the letter as a metatheatrical "script" that has been rendered obsolete and must be laid aside before a new story pattern can emerge.

dead or even trapped between death and life, but has fully come back to life. In sharing the memory with her brother, and in receiving his sympathy, she is finally able to let go of the past that has held her captive for so long. This climactic action is further heightened by the use of song. The two siblings lament the fate of their family in a composition of mixed modes, where Iphigenia sings and Orestes responds in spoken iambic trimeter:

Op.	γένει μὲν εὐτυχοῦμεν, ἐς δὲ συμφοράς,	
	ὦ σύγγον', ἡμῶν δυστυχὴς ἔφυ βίος.	
Ιφ.	ἐγῷδ' ἁ μέλεος, οἶδ, ὅτε φάσγανον	
	δέρᾳ 'φῆκέ μοι μελεόφρων πατήρ.	
Op.	οἴμοι. δοκῶ γὰρ οὐ παρών σ' ὁρᾶν ἐκεῖ.	
Ιφ.	ἀνυμέναιος, ὦ σύγγον', Ἀχιλλέως	
	ἐς κλισίαν λέκτρων δόλιον ἀγόμαν·	
	παρὰ δὲ βωμὸν ἦν δάκρυα καὶ γόοι.	
	φεῦ φεῦ χερνίβων ἐκείνων· οἴμοι.	
Op.	ᾤμωξα κἀγὼ τόλμαν ἥν ἔτλη πατήρ.	(850–859)

Or.   In our birth we are fortunate, but in our circumstances,
      sister, our life has been one of ill fortune.
Iph.   I know it, miserable as I am, I know that my
      miserable-minded father thrust the knife at my throat.
Or.   Alas! For I seem to see you there, though I was not present.
Iph.   Without wedding songs, brother,
      I was brought to the deceitful tent for the bed of Achilles.
      By the altar were tears and cries of lamentation.
      Ah, ah, the lustral vessels there! Ah me!
Or.   I too cry in sorrow at the bold deed that our father dared.

Such "recognition duets" between a male and female character appear to have been a popular feature of late Greek tragedy. In most cases, as here, the female character sings, while the male character responds in iambic trimeter.[43] K. O. Chong-Gossard has explored these duets as a specialized kind of female language, which unlocks or reveals the fictional inner life of the singer, a self "connected to a traumatic past that is dictated by myth."[44] Chong-Gossard proposes further that female lyric in these recognition duets includes a component of persuasion: "the

---

[43] Other recognition duets appear in Sophocles, *Electra* 1232–1287; Euripides, *Ion* 1439–1509, *Helen* 625–697, and the fragmentary *Hypsipyle* TrGF 5.2, fr. 759a, 1579–1632. Only the Sophoclean example is in strophic response. Menelaus in Euripides' *Helen* does sing a few brief snatches of lyric, but it is unclear how it was delivered.

[44] Chong-Gossard 2008: 28.

female singer ... must prove a truth about her past to her male kin before the drama can go forward or be resolved."[45] This element of persuasion is essential to Iphigenia's song. Through the recollection of her experience, Iphigenia makes Orestes a virtual witness to Agamemnon's violation and thereby persuades him of its veracity. Her brother empathically enters into her memory – he imagines his sister at the moment of her sacrifice and exclaims with sorrow. The two siblings focus their grief also on their father, whose miserable state of mind (μελεόφρων) led to an act of terrible daring (τόλμαν). Orestes' participation in this final telling of the Aulis story is crucial, for his presence makes possible Iphigenia's release from the land of the Taurians.

In an article on sex, status, and song, Monica Cyrino suggests that Iphigenia's greater emotional intensity in this scene is highlighted by her use of lyric, in contrast to Orestes' more "rational" trimeter, and that the song ultimately places her in a subordinate position to Orestes.[46] I agree with Cyrino that the duet creates a "lyric space" that showcases Iphigenia's vulnerability in the immediate dramatic situation. Yet I would argue against the idea that Iphigenia is therefore shown to be subordinate; rather, by focusing on Iphigenia's experience, the song reveals her growing power and agency. Certainly, in the subsequent scene Iphigenia takes the lead in devising the escape plot; but even in the lyrical exchange just quoted it is Iphigenia who introduces a theme and Orestes who reacts to it. Iphigenia first brings up Agamemnon and then the sacrifice at Aulis; Orestes responds to her, imaginatively entering into the scene she describes as a spectator (δοκῶ σ' ὁρᾶν, 854). He aligns his response to hers (ᾤμωξα κἀγώ, 859) and does not try to silence his sister, restrain her in any way, or take control of her narrative. Put simply, he listens. Orestes' lack of lyrical expressivity is not indicative of his greater emotional control or "rationality" but rather of his lesser knowledge; as he himself says, he was not present when these events took place (οὐ παρών, 854) and therefore must learn about them. Iphigenia's song provides a connection to what is absent, invisible, intangible, and existing only in her mind, as she remembers the abuse of her body and her betrayal at the hands of her nearest kin. The reunion duet thus reinforces what Iphigenia has suffered and survived, and the validation of her experience is its primary focus. By acknowledging her past vulnerability and sharing it with her brother and Pylades, she paradoxically establishes her authority in the present.

---

[45] Chong-Gossard 2008: 57. [46] Cyrino 1998.

It is also the newly authoritative Iphigenia who brings the lyric exchange to an end. In her last lines in the duet, she turns away from what has come before and looks instead to the future:

> ἀπάτορ' ἀπάτορα πότμον ἔλαχον.
> ἄλλα δ' ἐξ ἄλλων κυρεῖ
> δαίμονος τύχᾳ τινός. (864–866)

> My portion was an unfatherly, unfatherly fate.
> But different things are emerging,
> by the fortune of some divinity.

These alpha privatives – ἀπάτορ' ἀπάτορα – are the last that Iphigenia uses to describe her own situation in the play. As we have seen, self-canceling alpha privatives have been associated in the language of Iphigenia and of the chorus with the state of limbo in which they find themselves. Their disappearance signals a shift toward activity and toward a full experience of living.

With Orestes and Pylades standing silently onstage, Iphigenia turns from the recognition duet to an independent monody. Here I take a position distinct from that of some other scholars, who consider this passage an extended coda to Iphigenia's lyric duet with Orestes.[47] I would argue that both metrically and in content the thirty-two lines of the monody (869–899) stand apart from what has come before. In the preceding lyric duet (827–868), Iphigenia sings short snatches: her longest passage is eight lines (842–849), while the majority of her parts are only three or two lines, always punctuated by a response from Orestes. The syntax of the lyric duet underscores the growing sympathy between the siblings; brother and sister repeat thematically important words from one another's lines (e.g., πατήρ, 862; ἀπάτορα, 863), as in stichomythic exchange, and Orestes' verses make use of particles to emphasize logical connections to what his sister has just said (e.g., κἀγώ, 831). The meter of Iphigenia's lines in the duet is predominantly iambo-dochmiac. Dochmiac verse is a form virtually unique to Attic tragedy and is the meter most clearly expressive of a consistent ethos, that of extreme agitation or excitement; it is appropriate to convey Iphigenia's wonder and delight at being reunited with her brother, while the iambic element ensures that her lines of song fit together with Orestes' spoken responses

---

[47] De Poli 2012 classifies lines 869–899 as an independent monody; for the contrary position, compare Chong-Gossard 2008: 41, who terms these lines "a large portion at the song's end," and Parker 2016: ad 827–899, who considers them an ending section to the recognition duet.

in iambic trimeter.[48] In several ways, therefore, the lyric duet emphasizes the closeness and connection between the two siblings.

Yet after Orestes' last line of trimeter at 868, the mood changes. Iphigenia begins to deliberate in an intensely introspective fashion about alternative courses of action. It is as though she has temporarily stepped apart from the other figures onstage, looking away from them or perhaps up to the sky, and now takes counsel with herself. Although the dochmiac rhythm continues from her lines in the lyric duet, in the monody a new meter, the enoplian, is introduced.[49] Thus the musical rhythms of the scene evolve in a way that underscores Iphigenia's developing process of thought. I therefore agree with Mattia de Poli and Edith Hall, who emphasizes that these lines are not simply a section of a standard reunion duet, "with formulaic musings on the vicissitudes of fortune and worry about the future."[50] Rather, this is a fully fledged monody, embodying the shift in Iphigenia's attention from the past to the future.

All that has been revealed to this point has set the stage for Iphigenia's meandering meditation, akin to a sung soliloquy, which includes a purposeful yet open-ended consideration of the facts as they are, a setting of goals, and a weighing of possibilities. The monody falls into two sections: in the first part of the song, Iphigenia reflects on her narrow escape from repeating her father's crime and slaying her brother (869–872); in the second and longer section, she considers the various paths by which the Greek exiles might escape (873–899). The shift from past to future is thus contained and condensed within the monody itself.

Iphigenia first pauses to take stock of herself, calling upon her own "wretched soul" (ὦ μελέα ψυχά, 881).[51] "Wretched," she says, using the same word for her soul trapped in this *aporia* that she has just used to describe her father's mind at the moment of her sacrifice – a remarkable reach of empathy. This capacity to empathize is a further sign that Iphigenia is no longer imprisoned in the past. Her hard-heartedness has dissipated as she expands her pity to include the other members of her family. She has realized that some telling shift of fortune has taken place. Now she wonders what this new fortune will be and how her own choices will affect the outcome. The insistent series of

---

[48] Mastronarde 2002: 107.
[49] See Sansone 1981: 59–60 and Kyriakou 2006: ad 827–299 for detailed metrical commentary.
[50] Hall 2012: 37.
[51] As we saw in the previous chapter, Creusa's monody in *Ion* also begins with an address to her own soul (*Ion* 859).

questions – τίς, τίς, τίνα – indicate irresolution, but her use of a strong first-person indicative verb in the future tense shows her growing agency (πέμψω):

> ἃ δ' ἐπ' αὐτοῖσι τίς τελευτά;
> τίς τύχα μοι συγχωρήσει;
> τίνα σοι πόρον εὑρυμένα
> πάλιν ἀπὸ πόλεως, ἀπὸ φόνου πέμψω
> πατρίδ' ἐς Ἀργείαν,
> πρὶν ἐπὶ ξίφος αἵματι σῷ πελάσαι;
> τόδε τόδε σόν, ὦ μελέα ψυχά,
> χρέος ἀνευρίσκειν. (874–882)

> What ending will there be for these things?
> What fortune will come to me?
> What path will I find for you,
> to bring you from slaughter in a foreign land
> back to our Argive homeland,
> before the sword draws near to your blood?
> This, this, my wretched soul, you must find out.

In these lines, Iphigenia takes responsibility for the escape from the land of the Taurians. This is her task, as she emphasizes by using a second-person adjective to address herself, a feature of deliberation speeches in tragedy (σόν). She next considers the various plans she might undertake:

> πότερον κατὰ χέρσον; οὐχὶ ναί,
> ἀλλὰ ποδῶν ῥιπᾷ.
> θανάτῳ πελάσεις ἄρα βάρβαρα φῦλα
> καὶ δι' ὁδοὺς ἀνόδους στείχων· διὰ κυανέας μὰν
> στενοπόρου πέτρας μακρὰ κέλευθα να-
> ΐοισιν δρασμοῖς. (883–892)

> Should it be on land? Not by ship,
> but by the rushing of feet.
> Then you will come close to death
> from barbarous tribes, traveling
> also along pathless paths.
> But the route for ship-borne flight
> through the narrow passage
> of the dark rocks is long.

The alternatives she proposes – by land or by ship – are both uncertain and dangerous. The alpha privatives in this passage are applied not to Iphigenia but to the journey that is to come (ὁδοὺς ἀνόδους, πόρον ἄπορον). Her relentless focus on herself has been replaced by a focus on the means of escape, and the introduction of dual forms (δυοῖν τοῖν μόνοιν Ἀτρείδαιν) emphasizes the shift in her thinking. Iphigenia's command of geographical knowledge shows her intelligence and resourcefulness. Yet she soon lapses into a seeming hopelessness:

> τάλαινα τάλαινα.
> τίς ἂν οὖν τάδ' ἂν ἢ θεὸς ἢ βροτὸς ἢ
> τί τῶν ἀδοκήτων
> πόρον ἄπορον ἐξανύσας δυοῖν
> τοῖν μόνοιν Ἀτρείδαιν φανεῖ
> κακῶν ἔκλυσιν; (893–899)

> Miserable, miserable!
> What, whether god or mortal
> or something unexpected,
> will appear as a release from evils,
> accomplishing the unpassable passage
> for the only two descendants of Atreus?

Iphigenia's song ends in *aporia*; it is only with the assistance of her friends in the next scene that she will overcome questioning in favor of decisive action. This monody thus takes the form of a "deliberation speech," which resembles but can also be distinguished from a "desperation speech," as described by R. L. Fowler.[52] A typical "desperation speech," in Fowler's definition, consists of a series of questions that are rhetorically posed and rejected, one after the other. Famous examples from Greek tragedy include Ajax's speech of anguish in Sophocles' *Ajax* (430–480) and Medea's speech about whether or not to kill her children in Euripides' *Medea* (1019–1080). Fowler posits that the desperation speech was a structure with the status of convention, almost a *Bauform*, in Greek tragedy, and that Euripides innovates against the background of this convention.[53] And yet, unlike in a desperation speech, Iphigenia does not deliberate about *whether* she should take action but about *how* that action should be taken. By ending her song with an open question – "What will appear to us as a release from these evils?" – rather than with a statement of hopelessness, Iphigenia leaves open the possibility of a solution.

Of all the monodies in the extant corpus of Euripides, this is the only one that has the act of deliberation as its central theme and a successful action as

---

[52] Fowler 1987; Hall 2012. [53] Fowler 1987.

its outcome. Euripidean monodies often contain rhetorical questions, which in most cases contribute to a sense of hopelessness: so, for example, Phaedra in *Hippolytus* wonders how she can turn aside her misfortune, but finds no solution (668–679); Polymestor in *Hecuba* searches here and there to lay hold of his enemies, but is foiled in his blindness (1056–1082); the Phrygian in *Orestes* wishes to fly either to the sky or to the encircling sea, both clearly impossible (1368–1379). In other cases, the options proposed in the monody are immediately criticized or forestalled, as when Hermione in *Andromache* considers various ways of committing suicide after she has been detected in her plot to murder Andromache (846–850), but is rebuked by the Nurse for her excessive and unnecessary fear (866–878). The closest parallel to Iphigenia's monody may be the opening section of Creusa's song in *Ion*, discussed in the previous chapter, where Creusa struggles with her own soul, addressed in a vocative, about whether she should speak or keep silent (859–864). In that play, Creusa's hesitation creates suspense for the scathing indictment of Apollo that follows; here, Iphigenia's deliberation itself becomes the sole matter of the monody.

Thus Iphigenia is unique among figures in other Euripidean plays who pose questions in song. Within the play, she is distinguished from Orestes, who also deliberates, but in iambic trimeter, and without making a decision that leads to action and a successful outcome. In the second scene of the prologue, Orestes considers how he and Pylades might enter the temple precinct and steal the statue of Artemis. He proposes several options but soon gives up hope of ever succeeding in this difficult venture, preferring flight instead:

> ἥκω δὲ πεισθεὶς σοῖς λόγοισιν ἐνθάδε
> ἄγνωστον ἐς γῆν, ἄξενον. σὲ δ' ἱστορῶ,
> Πυλάδη – σὺ γάρ μοι τοῦδε συλλήπτωρ πόνου –
> τί δρῶμεν; ἀμφίβληστρα γὰρ τοίχων ὁρᾷς
> ὑψηλά· πότερα δωμάτων προσαμβάσεις
> ἐκβησόμεσθα; πῶς ἂν οὖν λάθοιμεν ἄν;
> ἢ χαλκότευκτα κλῇθρα λύσαντες μοχλοῖς –
> ὧν οὐδὲν ἴσμεν; ἢν δ' ἀνοίγοντες πύλας
> ληφθῶμεν ἐσβάσεις τε μηχανώμενοι,
> θανούμεθ'. ἀλλὰ πρὶν θανεῖν, νεὼς ἔπι
> φεύγωμεν, ᾗπερ δεῦρ' ἐναυστολήσαμεν.   (93–103)

> So I have come, trusting in your words,
> here to an unknown, inhospitable land. But I ask you,
> Pylades – for you are my partner in this labor –

what shall we do? For you see the high fortifications
of the walls. Shall we ascend on scaling ladders?
How then could we avoid detection?
Or should we loosen the bronze-made bolts
with crowbars, of which we know nothing?
But if we are caught in the act of opening the gates
and devising a means of entry, we will die.
No, before we die let us flee on the ship
by which we sailed here.

Orestes' speech of deliberation in iambic trimeter does not lead to decisive action. Only when Pylades reproaches him for his cowardice does Orestes agree to hide in a nearby cave until nightfall (104–105); even then, no definite plan is advanced, and the onset of Orestes' madness drives the pair out of hiding and into the hands of the Taurians. Orestes in the prologue thus establishes a model for ineffective deliberation that will be reversed and corrected by Iphigenia's second monody. She, not her brother, will devise a means of stealing the statue and escaping to Greece. Thus the monody signals in dramatic terms the contrast between Iphigenia and Orestes and constitutes the critical moment in which she realizes her potential for action.

Returning to the second monody: at the close of Iphigenia's song, Pylades urges the siblings to cease from sorrowing and face the problem at hand: how can they escape? Pylades has not fully recognized the change in Iphigenia's will; the iambic exchange that follows convinces him utterly. Iphigenia does not reply directly, but instead asks about her sister Electra. Orestes answers that she is married to Pylades (915); in response to further questions, he declares that Pylades is a cousin of the house (919). These facts allow Iphigenia to accept Pylades as a member of her family (922). She later refers to him as one of her "dearest" (φιλτάτους, 1065); his fortune is now tied to hers, and he must be saved as well. Now that her task is clear, Iphigenia thinks of a stratagem that will use elements of truth to deceive the king. Orestes' eager questions bring out the details of her plan: to bring both statue and victims down to the sea for fictitious rites of purification and then escape on board ship. In her monody she asks her own soul for a "discovery" that will save the last descendants of Atreus (εὑρυμένα, 876); now she has hit upon just such a "novel discovery" (καινὸν ἐξεύρημά τι, 1029), a verbal repetition that emphasizes the connection between the *aporia* of her song and the solution she has now found.

This scene is Iphigenia's last exchange with the women of the chorus. Her second monody marks a shift in her allegiance: she is no longer only one of many captive women but a sister and a sister-in-law whose first responsibility is to her family. She is awake, alive, newly embracing of her identity. She asks the chorus to conceal her plan, appealing to them on the basis of their shared femininity: "we are all women, a group concerned for one another, most firm in looking after our common welfare" (1061–1062). She further promises that if she survives, she will bring them to Greece (1067–1068). Although Iphigenia has no further interaction with them, their loyalty to her is rewarded: Athena in her epiphany guarantees their safe return.

2.3 Conclusion

I have argued that *Iphigenia among the Taurians* contains two monodies that Euripides uses to emphasize Iphigenia's drastic shift in thought and in action over the first half of the play. Both monodies resemble other established musical forms – a *parodos* in alternation between the heroine and the chorus in the first case, and a reunion duet where a female character sings and a male character responds in iambic trimeter in the second – and fall along a continuum of flexible musical scenes in tragedy; the distinction between monody and lyric exchange is not always absolute. Nevertheless, in Iphigenia's songs we encounter something singular that goes beyond formal innovation: an increased focus upon the individual figure and her shifting emotions.

Iphigenia's first monody, placed early in the play, shows her to be intelligent and sensitive as well as closely connected with the chorus; at the same time, she is trapped in the moment when her promised life was stolen from her. This song draws on the traditional connection between monody and lament but expands the heroine's part and musically emphasizes her independence from the chorus through a lack of strophic responsion. The monody expresses Iphigenia's inner turmoil by contrast with her self-possession in the prologue. It is both her strength and her depth of feeling that have been established. In the scenes that follow, Iphigenia masters her emotions so successfully that she narrowly avoids sacrificing her own brother. The second monody, positioned at the play's midpoint, marks the moment when Iphigenia moves from thinking obsessively and exclusively about herself and her own past to thinking of others and of the future. The use of monody to highlight the act of deliberation is, I suggest, unique to this play and to this heroine; by expressing the process of Iphigenia's thought in song, Euripides emphasizes her status as a woman called to action.

2.3 Conclusion

Both monodies invite the audience to see through Iphigenia's eyes. Music rouses the emotions; it not only permits but even induces a degree of resonant empathy. The direct presentation of grief in Iphigenia's first monody expresses the truth of her experience at that particular moment. Insofar as her song allows her to be known, the first monody has built up a credit that is paid forward into the second monody. At other points, as in her dealings with Thoas, Iphigenia is capable of sophisticated rhetoric and intentional deceit.[54] By contrast, in her two songs she does not lie or attempt to conceal her feelings. It is her unadulterated experience that emerges and the direct connection between her thought and her deed. In the next chapter, we shall see Euripides expanding the role of monody still further, showcasing in *Phoenician Women* three distinct singing characters whose individual perspectives take on a position of central thematic interest and importance in dramatizing the fall of the royal house of Thebes.

---

[54] See Hartigan 1986 on the connection between salvation and deceit in the play.

3 | Phoenician Women

The Lyric Voice of a Shattered House

Phoenician Women, produced c. 410 BCE, is a richly allusive play, self-consciously positioned against a backdrop of earlier literary and dramatic treatments of the fall of Thebes.[1] Euripides' innovative use of monody thus stands out with particular clarity in this tragedy. Musically and dramatically, Euripides here displaces the communal perspective of the chorus from its position as a center of gravity in order to draw greater attention to the individual perspectives of the singing actors. Remarkably, the actors in this play sing more than the chorus does: indeed, *Phoenician Women* is framed by monody, positioned at the beginning and end of the play.[2] The prominence of solo song is a formal means of highlighting a central zone of thematic interest. *Phoenician Women* stages a horrifyingly modern world in which communal, civic, and religious structures have lost their meaning, their legitimacy, and their hold. Instead, the mere selfish desires of individuals tyrannize a fragmented public life. The singing actors in the play – Antigone, Jocasta, and Oedipus – stand at the very center of the city, yet are powerless to save it. The four scenes of solo actor's song in the play dramatize individual emotional reactions to the disaster of Thebes.

The action of *Phoenician Women* is complex and diffuse. The plot involves a large ensemble of figures drawn from the myth of the house of Labdacus: Jocasta and Oedipus and their sons Eteocles and Polyneices, but also their daughter Antigone, Jocasta's brother Creon, the prophet Tiresias, and his son Menoeceus. The sheer number of speaking roles necessitates a reduction in any one individual's influence on the course of events; indeed, many of the characters seem helplessly caught up in a catastrophe beyond their control. Yet this apparent chaos is part of a deliberate strategy by Euripides, consciously playing against expectations of unity and simple order.[3] Within this flexible structure, the formal element of monody,

---

[1] For dating, see Craik 1988: 40–41 and Mastronarde 1994: 11–14.
[2] Csapo 1999–2000 gives the percentages for choral song and actors' song as follows: choral song makes up 13.6 percent of the play and choral song plus recitative 14.2 percent, while actor's song makes up 14.4 percent and actor's song plus recitative 17.6 percent. The total percentage of the play delivered to musical accompaniment is 31.8 percent.
[3] On unity, see Ferrante 1996: 11–13.

concentrated at crucial points in the development and assigned to crucial figures, shapes, and organizes the action of the play.

In total, solo actor's song makes up more than a quarter of the play, concentrated into four scenes: the *epirrhema* between Antigone and the Old Servant in the *teichoskopia* (103–192); Jocasta's monody celebrating the return of Polyneices (301–354); the monody of Antigone (1485–1538), which leads into her first *amoibaion*, or lyric duet, with Oedipus (1539–1581); and the second *amoibaion* of Antigone and Oedipus, which concludes the *exodos* (1710–1757). The roles may be divided in several ways, but it is likely that all three actors would be called upon to sing in the course of the drama, which presupposes highly trained professional performers with great vocal ability.[4] The four scenes of solo actor's lyric are placed in two pairs quite near the beginning and end of the play, distant yet in a number of evident ways counterposed to each other. The contrasts thus set up constitute an arc that spans the entire work.

In an ostensibly episodic plot, the placement of solo actor's song reveals a consistent strategy. The four scenes of solo actor's song by their positioning serve to underscore the analogies between disparate events; the scenes are distributed in a chiastic pattern, situated at the beginning and end of the play. The two scenes of lyric dialogue are counterposed in form and content, as are the two extended monodies.[5] The middle portion of the drama, by contrast, develops through iambic argument rather than music: here the focus is on the intense ideational *agōn* between Eteocles and Polyneices, on the prophecy of Tiresias and the suicide of Menoeceus, and on the reports of the battle and the deaths of Eteocles and Polyneices. The songs of the chorus are woven through this central section but their contributions have a different focus from those of the singing actors, reflecting on the history and implications of the house's disorder. At the end of the play, the solo song with which the drama begins then returns but, as it were, in a minor key; the analogies between the opening and closing scenes of lyric thus lead the audience toward a recognition of latent connections of similarity and contrast.

The audience of the play is thrust into the experience of the solo singers from the outset; the choral perspective is allowed to develop more gradually and with a tranquility of observation entirely absent from the songs of the actors. The women who make up the dramatic chorus are, as the title of the play indicates, *Phoenician* women, on

---

[4] For role division, see Craik 1988: 46 and Mastronarde 1994: 16.
[5] Compare Ludwig 1954: 130–135 on the symmetrical positioning of the lyric scenes in the play.

their way from Phoenicia to Delphi. These transients stand outside the troubles of the royal family of Thebes; and yet the siege prevents them from continuing their journey to Delphi and temporarily traps them within the city.[6] In ritual terms, they are not yet a chorus: only at Delphi will they take up their cult post as a real chorus, singing and dancing in honor of the god (234–238; cf. χορὸς γενοίμαν, 236).[7] Although they feel sorrow for the descendants of Oedipus, who are distant kin through their shared descent from Cadmus, they remain largely uninvolved in the action. Their songs are linked by a continuity of thought and theme; taken together, they sound a note of deep pessimism. The odes explore the connection between the present ills of Thebes and Cadmus' original crime at its founding – that is, between the present and the distant past.[8] As Helene Foley has described, a "contrapuntal relation" develops between the unfolding onstage action of the play and the choral odes, which describe the history of Thebes in mythical terms.[9]

If the chorus are outsiders to Thebes, the actors who sing stand at the very heart of the city, its inmost, incestuous natives. They must make sense of the house's calamity not as mythology but as autobiography. In a play of 1,776 lines, the five songs of the chorus amount to only 224 lines. This relative scarcity emphasizes by contrast the lyric of the actors, particularly that of Antigone. In fact, Antigone's first two lyric scenes usurp places that would ordinarily be occupied by choral song: the position immediately following the prologue – that is, the *parodos* – and the position after the speech of the messenger who relates the disastrous news of the three deaths of Eteocles, Polyneices, and Jocasta. The playwright gives to Antigone, rather than to the chorus, the principal lyric voice of the play. She alone sings almost as much as the chorus does, and her dominant mode is song: of her 223 lines, 178 of them – that is, 80 percent – are in lyric meters. The effect is highly personal, in content as well as form. Antigone's three scenes of lyric trace an emotional arc from youth and inexperience to knowledge and sorrow.

The singers in this play – Antigone, Jocasta, and Oedipus – are a young woman, just beyond childhood; a mother; and an old, blind man. Their

---

[6] Compare Rawson 1970 on the importance of the chorus' identity as "exiles" from their native land and Murnaghan 2005 on the more typical role of female choruses as supportive to young women like Antigone.
[7] On the cultic role of the chorus in this play, see Prodi 2018.
[8] On the odes in this play, see especially Kranz 1933: 228; Arthur 1977; Parry 1978: 166–173; Medda 2005; and Tsolakidou 2012: 48–97.
[9] Foley 1985: 111.

songs share an emphasis on the values of community, family, and religion. The common concerns of the singers are symptomatic of the larger political and social situation in Thebes, where adult men are manifestly unable to provide stable and enduring leadership. It falls to the characters on the fringes of civic life – women, children, old men, and the foreign women of the chorus – to try to keep the fabric of the family and of society from disintegrating entirely. Jocasta and Antigone can provide continuity only through the customary duties of Greek womanhood: marriage, motherhood, and lamentation. Traditional female roles, however, are confounded by the incestuous history of the royal house: Jocasta is the mother not only of Polyneices, Eteocles, and Antigone but of Oedipus as well. Antigone, too, cannot fulfill her expected role in religious, social, or familial life, and at the end of the play she relinquishes her prospective future as a wife and mother to become the lifelong virginal companion of her aged, debilitated father. Male attempts at leadership, the focus of the iambic scenes in the middle of play, all fail disastrously. Oedipus in the *exodos*, ghostly and weak, is proof of this failure.

Because *Phoenician Women* is an especially intricate and allusive play, this chapter is structured as a series of short sections following the chronology of the action. I begin by discussing the relationship between *Phoenician Women* and Aeschylus' *Seven against Thebes*, a canonical treatment of the myth of Thebes that profoundly influenced Euripides' own version of the story. I then treat each of the four scenes of solo actor's song in some detail. These musical scenes give the tragedy its contours both by their structural relationship within the play and by their continuity of theme. The *teichoskopia* and the monodies of Jocasta and Antigone emphasize the isolation of the individual members of the house; the final duet of Antigone and Oedipus reunites what remains of the family through the shared experience of grief. The three scenes of lyric featuring Antigone – the *teichoskopia*, her monody of lament over the corpses of her mother and brothers, and her duet with Oedipus – trace her progression from a sheltered maiden to a distraught mourner and finally to a mature, albeit unmarried, woman who takes charge of her own and her family's fate. As in the case of Iphigenia in *Iphigenia among the Taurians*, the songs of this virginal heroine show a progression from a position of powerlessness to the assumption of greater agency. Euripides here experiments with monody not only as a structural device to shape plot and create meaning but also as a vehicle for the development of a complex female figure whose varied and varying state of mind constitutes a center of interest in the play.

3.1 *Phoenician Women* and *Seven against Thebes*

Euripides highlights the prominent role of solo actor's lyric in *Phoenician Women* through elaborate intertextual – and inter-musical – engagement with Aeschylus' *Seven against Thebes*. Aeschylus' play, produced in 467 BCE, deals with the same portion of the Theban myth as Euripides' *Phoenician Women*. Euripides himself may have seen the original production in his youth.[10] But is it plausible that Euripides' audience, more than fifty years after the original performance, could be counted on to appreciate sophisticated relationships of similarity and contrast? Here we are in a remarkably fortunate position, as Marcel Lech has made a strong case that *Seven against Thebes* was reperformed in Athens between 411 and 405 BCE.[11] The date of *Phoenician Women* is uncertain but likely between 411 and 409 BCE.[12] This would mean that not only could Euripides have created his own version of the myth with the older drama freshly in mind but also that his audience might have recently seen a staging of Aeschylus' play with which to compare it.

The possibility of a reperformance of *Seven against Thebes* is tempting to imagine, but ultimately beyond proof. Even if we do not assume a recent reperformance, scholars have traced numerous allusions in Euripides' work to Aeschylus' earlier treatment. For instance, Helene Foley offers a sequential comparison of scenes in *Phoenician Women* with their predecessors in *Seven against Thebes* and concludes that the later play acquires its meaning in large part by calling attention to its differences from the earlier poetic text.[13] Froma Zeitlin and Barbara Goff have described the emphatic and self-aware intertextuality of the shields of the Argive attackers in Euripides' play; here the shields lack any observer capable of reading and deciphering their emblems, an instance of the breakdown between signifier and signified in the world of the drama.[14] Other scholars have discussed the roles of men and women in the two plays, the different depictions of the city of Thebes, and the ways in which Euripides responds to Aeschylus in describing – and not describing – the attackers and their shields.[15]

---

[10] The *agōn* between Euripides and Aeschylus in Aristophanes' *Frogs* (405 BCE) takes for granted that Euripides was intimately familiar with the work of his great predecessor; as the character of Euripides himself says, "I know him [Aeschylus] well and have long examined him" (ἐγᾦδα τοῦτον καὶ διέσκεμμαι πάλαι, 836); compare Dover 1993: 7–21.

[11] Lech 2008. For a more cautious approach to the evidence, compare Marshall 1996 and Hanink and Uhlig 2016.

[12] Mastronarde 1994: 12.   [13] Foley 1985.   [14] Goff 1988; Zeitlin 1990, 1994, and 2009 [1982].

[15] Goldhill 2007; Lamari 2007 and 2010; Burian 2009; Torrance 2013.

Building on the work of these scholars, I would suggest that Euripides has adapted the meters and thematic concerns of the choral songs of *Seven against Thebes* and set them into scenes of solo actor's lyric in his own play. The singing chorus of Theban women of Aeschylus' play become the individual singing Theban women – that is, Jocasta and Antigone – of Euripides' play. This change has the effect of redefining the emotional center of the work. Instead of a focus on the impact that the war has on the community at large, the main interest of *Phoenician Women* derives from the experiences of the characters most affected by the brothers' quarrel but pathetically unable to influence its outcome: Jocasta, Oedipus, and above all Antigone. The impulse toward death and disorder that has destroyed Thebes is given form in the progression of the four scenes of solo actor's lyric.

3.2 *Teichoskopia* (88–201)

The *teichoskopia*, the view from the wall by Antigone and an aged servant, introduces solo actor's song as a mode of central importance in the play. The epirrhematic dialogue in this scene takes the place of the choral song the audience might usually expect at this point. Toward the end of the scene, Antigone sings three extended lyric passages (161–169, 175–180, 183–192), which in their length and relative independence from the brief responses of the old man in iambic trimeter approach independent monody. By situating the lyrics of Antigone immediately after Jocasta's prologue and before the *parodos*, the playwright ensures that the voice of the singing actor is the first point of entry into understanding the danger that besets Thebes.

Scholars both ancient and modern have called the authenticity of the *teichoskopia* into question, but it is now generally accepted that the scene belongs to the original play.[16] For the purposes of this study I treat the *teichoskopia* as genuine, basing my decision on considerations of both formal and thematic integrity. The scene serves several important dramatic functions. It presents the initial emotional state of Antigone, whose youthful exuberance will subsequently be undone by her family's fate. Her words illustrate the strength and ferocity of Polyneices and his army and emphasize the justice of their cause. As we shall see, the lyric dialogue also looks

---

[16] Using formal arguments that take into account vocabulary, meter, and lyric structure, Mastronarde 1994: ad 88–201 concludes that the *teichoskopia* is of a piece with the rest of the play. For a summary of thematic arguments and a persuasive defense of the scene, see in particular Burgess 1988.

forward to the shared lament of Oedipus and Antigone in the *exodos*, whose connection to the earlier scene is signaled by the repeated gesture of an old man and a young woman joining hands.[17] In addition, by its very setting, the *teichoskopia* establishes the paramount importance of the theme of boundaries. There is a sense in which the entire play is staged at the wall.[18]

Close literary precedents for the *teichoskopia* are few and unmistakable. The two that would almost certainly have been present and relevant to the viewing audience, as well as in the mind of the poet, are the *teichoskopia* in Book 3 of the *Iliad*, where Helen identifies various Greek heroes in response to Priam's questions, and the *parodos* of Aeschylus' *Seven against Thebes*, where the chorus describe the sights and sounds of the Argive army attacking the walls of the city. A more distant *comparandum* may be found in Sophocles' *Antigone*, produced c. 440 BCE, because of the shared central figure. Euripides' allusions to these scenes in earlier literature at times reinforce and at times reframe the apparent meaning of the action in *Phoenician Women*. Given the high canonical status of the prior poetry, everything that Euripides does in constructing his *teichoskopia* stands out against the backdrop of Homer, Aeschylus, and Sophocles. Euripides' scene is noteworthy as much for what it omits as for what it includes.

The *teichoskopia* of *Phoenician Women* resembles the scene in the *Iliad* in its basic situation: two characters, a young woman and an old man, stand on the high walls of a city and observe enemy soldiers on the battlefield below.[19] Euripides reverses the structure of the Homeric scene, as here it is the young woman who asks questions and the old man who answers them. Antigone inquires about everything she sees, while the old man twice justifies his knowledge, which comes from first-hand experience as a negotiator in the Argive camp (95–98, 142–144). The disparity in experience and point of view between the characters is signaled on a formal level through the juxtaposition of the old man's lines of trimeter and Antigone's flights of lyric.[20] Antigone's first utterance, a series of breathless short

---

[17] For an analysis of this joining of hands as a "significant action," compare Altena 1999–2000.

[18] On walls in Greek literature, see Wiles 1993; Scodel 1997; Ieranò 2002; and Goldhill 2007. Zeitlin 1993: 171–182 explores the possibility that *Phoenician Women* was part of a trilogy with the fragmentary plays *Hypsipyle*, which also has a *teichoskopia*, and *Antiope*, which is much concerned with the walls of Thebes.

[19] On the female observer and her lack of agency in Euripides, see Scodel 1997.

[20] Cyrino 1998 discusses scenes in which Euripides uses lyric dialogue to establish the singing character as more vulnerable, subordinate, and feminized in contrast to the responding speaker. She notes that the one example of a male/female duet on terms of equality is the lyric dialogue between Antigone and Oedipus at the end of *Phoenician Women*; as we shall see, the shared

syllables, defines the contrast between the old man and herself. She is young and he is old, yet she requires his help to climb onto the palace roof:

> ὄρεγέ νυν ὄρεγε γεραιὰν νέᾳ
> χεῖρ᾽ ἀπὸ κλιμάκων
> ποδὸς ἴχνος ἐπαντέλλων. (103–105)
>
> Stretch out, stretch out your hand
> from the ladder, aged to young,
> helping me to place the track of my foot.

The servant reassures Antigone, telling her to "have courage" (θάρσει, 117) and encouraging her to ask about what she sees (118). The pointed change from the literary precedent of the *Iliad* presents Antigone from the first lines of the scene as a sort of anti-Helen: chaste, innocent, inexperienced, and unknowing.[21] Euripides' use of this Old Servant for the Priam-figure also underscores the absence of Oedipus. It ought to be the king of the city standing on the wall and taking stock of the attacking army. Polluted, broken in spirit, and unable to see the army ranged below, Oedipus cannot fulfill his proper role, and his son Eteocles is nowhere in evidence.

Even as it recalls the scene in the *Iliad*, the *teichoskopia* of Euripides' play calls into question the function of walls. In the *Iliad*, the walls of Troy are crossed by Trojan warriors and by Priam, but never by the Greeks; yet the original audience knew very well that the walls must at last be breached, Helen extracted, and the city destroyed. The division between inside and outside of Troy is dichotomous and absolute. This is not the case in the incestuous, unrighteous city of Thebes, at war with itself, where the proper boundary between inside and outside – like that between native and foreign, or between ally and enemy – is repeatedly undermined.[22] Over the course of the play, the walls of Thebes, unlike those of Troy in the *Iliad*, are revealed to be permeable. In the *teichoskopia* Antigone looks over the walls and wishes to be transported beyond their confines to embrace her brother on the battlefield; Polyneices, a declared adversary, enters the city alone under the truce brokered by Jocasta; Menoeceus leaps from the walls onto the battlefield in his attempt to save the city by self-sacrifice; Jocasta and Antigone leave the

---

song in this passage looks back to the exchange between Antigone and the Old Servant, where the balance of knowledge and of lyric is decidedly unequal.

[21] Antigone is also, as we shall see, implicitly in contrast with the women of the chorus of *Seven against Thebes*, whom Eteocles rebukes for their clamor and effrontery (181–202). On Eteocles, see Caldwell 1973; Byrne 1997; and von Fritz 2007.

[22] Zeitlin 1986 and 1993 has written on the way in which myths set at Thebes move between the extremes of rigid inclusions and exclusions, on the one hand, and radical confusions, on the other.

city and enter the fray of battle to intervene between the two brothers; in the *exodos* the corpses of Jocasta and her sons traverse the walls; and in the play's final moments expulsion from the city is decreed for the body of Polyneices, while Antigone and Oedipus are driven out into permanent exile. By recalling the *teichoskopia* of the *Iliad* in this early scene, Euripides sets into high relief the contrasting characteristics of this city and these walls.

We have already seen how, in consequence of the unusually strong shadow presence of Homer as one antecedent model text, the *teichoskopia* of *Phoenician Women* operates with a paired rhetoric of what it is and what it is not. A similar allusive game can be posited with Aeschylus' *Seven against Thebes*: that is, the *teichoskopia* of the later work can be usefully examined in contrast to the *parodos* of the earlier. Clearly, the imagined presence of Aeschylus' pattern behind that of Euripides is not nearly as straightforward as in the case of Homer, and it is by the richness of the plausible ideas it generates that any analysis in those terms stands or falls.

There is, as I have suggested, some evidence that *Seven against Thebes* may have been reperformed shortly before the premiere of *Phoenician Women*, and that therefore a reworking of defining scenes and situations can be viewed partially as a response. In contrast to *Seven against Thebes*, the central actions of *Phoenician Women* are undertaken by women and the young. Of course, the chorus in *Seven against Thebes* do try to intervene in the war and dominate the end of the play with their lamentation. The identity of the singing figures, virginal and native to Thebes, remains constant across the two plays: Euripides' innovation consists in giving the initial musical scene of the play to a single woman rather than to a group.

In both plays, the scenes by the wall serve primarily to delineate the initial emotional state of a principal figure or figures, whether the chorus of Theban women or Antigone. Euripides challenges the expectations built up by Aeschylus by introducing solo actor's lyric to his version of the scene. He presents the coming siege through the eyes of the excited, impressionable, and inexperienced Antigone. By this formal innovation, Euripides adds a layer of dramatic irony to the scene of the sort that calls for additional pity. Antigone, as a virgin and a member of the royal family, should exist in an enclosed, peaceful realm, apart from war and suffering.[23]

Antigone's first perspective on the action is characterized by both literal and figurative distance: she stands far above the army, does not know the names of the warriors or what the devices on their shields represent, and is

---

[23] See Blok 2001 for a historical approach to proper behavior for an unmarried Greek woman, as well as Foley 1985: 117, who compares the Servant's concern for the propriety of Antigone to Eteocles' emphasis in *Seven against Thebes* on the proper place of women.

unable to understand the consequences that would follow if the city fell. Despite her agitation, she finds order and brightness in the scene on the battlefield.[24] Yet her youthful vision of order is based on formulaic and naïve expectations and on an implicit sense of safety that cannot withstand experience.[25] The wall she stands upon proposes a set of isomorphic boundaries that prove, in essence, illusory; for there is at this juncture in Thebes no proper dichotomy between in and out, us and them, native and foreign, right and wrong.

In Aeschylus' *Seven against Thebes*, the *parodos* portrays the panic of the chorus at the sounds of the approaching Argive army (78–181).[26] Nowhere in *Seven against Thebes* is there solo actor's lyric, whereas the chorus have a leading role.[27] Indeed, choral lyric accounts for nearly 50 percent of the total lines of *Seven against Thebes*. As Theban maidens – not visitors from a distant city – the chorus of *Seven against Thebes* are directly affected by the action taking place onstage. They represent the whole life of the city: its relations with the land and with the gods.[28] If the city is saved, these maidens will marry, bear children, and create a society free from the polluting influence of the Labdacids. At the moment when the play begins, however, their lives have been entirely disrupted by the war. In Euripides' *Phoenician Women*, by contrast, the chorus of Phoenician women have no such vested interest in the outcome of the dynastic struggle of the house of Oedipus. Rather, it is Antigone who represents the future life of Thebes and the possibility of marriage, childbirth, and social order. Accordingly, her lyric scene – which echoes the corresponding scene in *Seven against Thebes* in meter, placement, and content – conveys what the siege means for the women of the city. Yet here Euripides creates an atmosphere not of uncontrolled panic but of mingled anxiety and admiration.

The *parodos* of *Seven against Thebes* falls into two parts, with some overlap of content: first the Theban women express panic at the imminent attack of the Argives, and then beseech the gods to come to the aid of the city. Instead of a stately progression onto the stage, the maidens rush in

---

[24] On spectacle in this scene, see Hawley 1998 and Lamari 2007.
[25] On the rhetoric of fear in this scene, see Papadodima 2016.
[26] On the chorus in *Seven against Thebes*, see Brown 1977; Bruit-Zaidman 1991; Valakas 1993; Goff 1995; Edmunds 2002; Murnaghan 2005; Stehle 2005; Giordano-Zecharya 2006; and Trieschnigg 2016.
[27] In the ending of *Seven against Thebes* as it stands, it is possible that Antigone and Ismene appear in the last scene and may have joined with the chorus in their final lines, but I do not accept this passage as original, as I discuss further in Section 3.7. On the ending of *Seven against Thebes*, see Dawe 1967; Orwin 1980; Flintoff 1980; and Torrance 2007: 19–20, 108–120.
[28] Thalmann 1978: 7.

from all quarters, singing in astrophic dochmiacs.[29] The meter is marked: although sporadic dochmiac cola appear in Pindar, their systematic use is peculiar to drama and characteristic of tragedy. Aeschylus' *Seven against Thebes* is the first extant tragedy in which this meter is used extensively, but dochmiacs appear in every extant tragedy, and their tone is always urgent or emotional. Here, the chorus cannot see over the wall and instead describe the sounds they hear, making the offstage world vividly present in the space of the theater.[30] They sing of the clang of shields, the tramping of horses, the rattling of armor, the whirring of spears, the clatter of chariots, and the crash of stones against the walls of the city:

> ἒ ἒ ἒ ἔ, 150
> ὄτοβον ἁρμάτων ἀμφὶ πόλιν κλύω·
> ὦ πότνι' Ἥρα.
> ἔλακον ἀξόνων βριθομένων χνόαι.
> Ἄρτεμι φίλα, ἒ ἒ ἒ ἔ,
> δοριτίνακτος αἰθὴρ δ' ἐπιμαίνεται. 155
> τί πόλις ἄμμι πάσχει, τί γενήσεται;
> ποῖ δ' ἔτι τέλος ἐπάγει θεός; (150–157)[31]

e e e e!
I hear the rattle of chariots encircling the town.
O lady Hera!
The hubs are creaking beneath the axles' load.
Beloved Artemis! *e e e e!*
The air rages at the shaking of spears!
What is happening to our city? What will the future bring?
To what final end does the god lead us?

The initial impact of the song is to create a mood of fear, disorder, and impending disaster. The women's agitation is conveyed verbally by the repeated cry ἒ ἒ ἒ ἔ, by the invocations to Hera and Artemis, and by an escalating series of rhetorical questions (τί, τί, ποῖ, 156–157). After this frenzied opening, the maidens appeal in a strophe-antistrophe pair to the Olympian gods, who may have been present onstage in the form of statues

---

[29] Hutchinson 1985: ad 78–108 comments that the dochmiac meter here contrasts with the spoken anapests often used to mark the entrance of the chorus in Aeschylus. On the dochmiac meter in tragedy, see Conomis 1964; Dale 1968: 104–119; and West 1982: 108–115.

[30] On meter, music, and sound in this passage, see Haldane 1965; Calame 1994–5; Edmunds 2002; Trieschnigg 2016; Gurd 2016: 74–78; Griffith 2017: 125–127; Nooter 2017: 65–69, 94–96; and Weiss 2018b: 171–176. In particular, the synesthetic phrase κτύπον δέδορκα ("I have seen the crashing," 103) brings what is outside the walls into the space of the theater – the chorus can both see and hear the attacking army, while the audience can do neither.

[31] Text of Page 1972. West 1990 differs slightly, but I prefer the punctuation used by Page.

(128–180).³² Eva Stehle argues that the metrical progression of the *parodos*, which moves from astrophic dochmiacs to strophic dochmiacs and ultimately to strophic cretics and iambics, represents a struggle "to mold terror into religiously pleasing appeal to the gods."³³ The success of this struggle, poetic as much as psychological, is an omen of the city's survival.

If the musical shape of the *parodos* of *Seven against Thebes* progresses from astrophic chaos to greater strophic order, the *teichoskopia* of *Phoenician Women* moves in the opposite direction. Over the course of the scene, the lyric patterns become increasingly complex. The Old Servant speaks in iambic trimeter throughout, while Antigone, after a few spoken verses in trimeter, sings twelve astrophic systems, culminating in a final outpouring of lyric that some scholars have classified as an independent monody.³⁴ Antigone's lyrics feature dochmiacs – an echo of Aeschylus – with an admixture of syncopated iambic, anapestic, dactylic, and enoplian elements. Here, as in *Seven against Thebes*, the effect of the meter is to create a sense of agitation, but in this case the heightened emotion is individual rather than collective. As the scene progresses, this individuality, even isolation, becomes even more pronounced: Antigone's lyric sections become both longer and more divorced from her interlocutor, directed increasingly not to the Old Servant but to herself and the natural environment.

Where the focus of the *parodos* of *Seven against Thebes* was on the sounds of the approaching army, from her very first lyric section Antigone draws attention to sight and spectacle.³⁵ As soon as she appears on the roof, she sees the whole plain "flashing with bronze" (κατάχαλκον ἅπαν / πεδίον ἀστράπτει, 110–111). She asks about the different warriors and points out details of their armor. Hippomedon, for instance, is conspicuous for his white plume and bronze shield

---

[32] Wiles 1993. [33] Stehle 2005: 108.
[34] See Mastronarde 1994: ad 88–201 and de Poli 2011: 225–232.
[35] The *teichoskopia* may also be compared to the long central episode of *Seven against Thebes*, where Eteocles hears and responds to descriptions of the seven shields of the seven attackers. In *Phoenician Women* the warriors and their shields are not riddles to be deciphered but objects of spectacle. The focus of the scene is Antigone's point of view. Attempts to interpret Euripides' description of warriors, gates, and shields as symbolic have been unsuccessful and, as Foley 1985: 128 writes, "the lack of significant pattern becomes a statement in itself." The attacking army does not suggest the construction of a cosmology, like the shield of Achilles in the *Iliad*, or the workings of a familial curse, as in Aeschylus. On the shield of Achilles, see Taplin 1980; Alden 2000: 48–73; Purves 2010: 45–55; and Minchin 2021. On the polysemy of the *teichoskopia* in this play, see Goff 1988: 138 and Zeitlin 1994.

(119–121). His glorious appearance excites not only terror but wonder as well:

> ἒ ἒ, ὡς γαῦρος, ὡς φοβερὸς εἰσιδεῖν,
> γίγαντι γηγενέτᾳ προσόμοιος
> ἀστερωπὸς ὡς ἐν γραφαῖσιν, οὐχὶ πρόσ-
> φορος ἁμερίῳ γέννᾳ. (127–130)

> Ah, ah! How proud, how fearful to see,
> like an earthborn giant
> in a painting, dazzling-faced,
> not resembling the mortal race.

Here again *Seven against Thebes* lurks behind the Euripidean text. There the shield of Hippomedon is described as "not made by a lowly craftsman" (ὁ σηματουργὸς δ' οὔ τις εὐτελής, 491), bearing as its ensign the monster Typhon breathing dark smoke, surrounded by coiling snakes (493–496). The image of the giant appears as well in *Seven against Thebes*, applied to Capaneus (γίγας, 424). There the warriors are terrible, boastful, violent; here, although the passage is textually difficult, the sense seems to be that Antigone cannot compare Hippomedon's appearance to anything she has seen in real life but only to something seen in art.[36] It is the warrior himself, not his shield, that is ekphrastic. Euripides includes the images and language of *Seven against Thebes* only to place them at one remove: Antigone sees the entire plain as a painting.

Euripides' engagement with Aeschylus' *Seven against Thebes* in the *teichoskopia* is pointed and omnipresent; a subtler contrast may be drawn in the way he depicts the central figure – that is, between the Antigone of *Phoenician Women* and the one of Sophocles' earlier play.[37] In the prologue of Sophocles' *Antigone*, Antigone appears outside the walls of the city alone, without a male chaperone, determined to defy Creon's edict and bury her brother Polyneices. Her sister Ismene begs her to remember that she is a woman and must be ruled by those in power (49–68), but Antigone is adamant. From the very first lines of the play, Sophocles' Antigone stands forth as a strong-willed woman, committed to performing the rites that she

---

[36] The intricacies are discussed by Mastronarde 1994: ad 128–129. Characters in tragedy may use comparisons to art to convey the striking strangeness or monstrosity of a sight; for example, Aeschylus, *Suppliants* 282–283, *Eumenides* 49–51; Euripides, *Hippolytus* 1005, *Trojan Women* 687, *Ion* 271. Barlow 1971: 59 suggests that Antigone's words evoke contemporary highlighting and painting techniques so that the audience imagine what is not present for them to see. See further Stieber 2011.

[37] See Saxonhouse 2005 for a comparison of political action in the two plays.

believes are dictated by family, duty, and religion. In her confrontation with Creon, she appeals with confidence to the universal, unwritten laws of the gods (450–470). After she has been sentenced to death, however, Antigone mourns her own fate in an antiphonal lament with the chorus (806–802). By contrast, Euripides' Antigone in *Phoenician Women* begins the play as a well-behaved, well-guarded maiden. Unlike Sophocles' Antigone, who moves into the register of lyric song only before her own death, Euripides' Antigone sings from her first entrance but about the seemingly superficial topics of brightness and appearance. Looking forward, Euripides' Antigone will sing two more passages of lyric in the *exodos*. In these final scenes she will surpass her prototype in Sophocles' play both in musical ingenuity and in the depth of the grief she must convey.

To return to the *Phoenician Women*, the *teichoskopia* culminates in two extended passages of lyric. Although addressed to the Old Servant, these passages are long, self-contained, and thematically coherent; that is, Antigone has moved, over the course of the scene, from *epirrhematic* dialogue toward monody.[38] Antigone feels a connection to the warriors on the field and even wishes to be among them. When Antigone finally catches sight of Polyneices, she sings of her desire to escape from the walls and embrace her brother on the battlefield:

> ὁρῶ δῆτ' οὐ σαφῶς, ὁρῶ δέ πως
> μορφῆς τύπωμα στέρνα τ' ἐξῃκασμένα.
> ἀνεμώκεος εἴθε δρόμον νεφέλας
> ποσὶν ἐξανύσαιμι δι' αἰθέρος
> πρὸς ἐμὸν ὁμογενέτορα – περὶ δ' ὠλένας   165
> δέρᾳ φιλτάτᾳ βάλοιμι χρόνῳ –
> φύγαδα μέλεον. ὡς
> ὅπλοισι χρυσέοισιν ἐκπρεπής, γέρον,
> ἑῴοις ὅμοια φλεγέθων βολαῖς ἀελίου.   (161–169)

I see him, yes, but not clearly, I see somehow
the outline of his form and the likeness of his chest.
If only I could speed through the air on my feet,
like a cloud before the wind,
to my own dear brother – throw my arms
around his beloved neck at last –
a wretched exile. How marvelous he is
with his golden armor, old man,
flashing like the rays of the burning sun!

---

[38] See de Poli 2011: 225–232.

Antigone cannot see her brother clearly, and the "outline of his form" and "likeness of his chest" are insufficient to satisfy her longing for him. Antigone's language foreshadows events to come: her wish to be among the warriors prepares for the later scene in which she and Jocasta will physically enter the battlefield, and her desire to touch Polyneices will be grimly fulfilled in the *exodos*, where she embraces the corpse of her brother.[39] But in this first scene, ignorant of what is to come, she is dazzled by the beauty of his golden armor. Her lyrics emphasize the visual, rather than the moral, implications of his panoply.

Antigone in the *teichoskopia* has been agitated, even at times afraid, but has never voiced any specific dread about what will happen to her if the city falls.[40] This is in strong contrast to the chorus of Aeschylus' *Seven against Thebes*, who imagine in horrifying detail the plunder and rape awaiting them if the besieging army is successful. They foresee the women taken captive and led away, "young and old together, dragged by their hair like horses, their clothes being torn off" (327–329); and, after the sack, "slave-girls new to suffering will endure captive coupling with a fortunate man ... the outcome of their wretched afflictions" (363–368). In her final outburst of lyric in the *teichoskopia* of *Phoenician Women*, Antigone too envisages what may happen if the attacking army succeeds in conquering the city:

> ἰώ,
> Νέμεσι καὶ Διὸς βαρύβρομοι βρονταὶ
> κεραύνιόν τε φῶς αἰθαλόεν, σύ τοι
> μεγαληγορίαν ὑπεράνορα κοιμίζεις·
> ὅδ' ἐστίν, αἰχμαλωτίδας   185
> ὃς δορὶ Θηβαίας Μυκηνηίσιν
> 〈   〉
> Λερναίᾳ τε δώσειν τρίαιναν,
> Ποσειδανίοις Ἀμυμωνίοις
> ὕδασι δουλείαν περιβαλών.
> μήποτε μήποτε τάνδ', ὦ πότνια,   190
> χρυσεοβόστρυχον ὦ Διὸς ἔρνος,
> Ἄρτεμι, δουλοσύναν τλαίην.   (182–192)

> O Nemesis, and deep-resounding thunder of Zeus,
> and blazing lightning fire, lull to sleep
> this presumptuous boasting;
> this is the man who says he will give

---
[39] See Lamari 2007: 17 on female agency in the play.
[40] See Chong-Gossard 2008: 101, who comments that Antigone is "disturbingly unafraid" in this scene.

> the women of Thebes as spear-captives
> to the women of Mycenae, to the Lernaean trident,
> and to the waters of Amymone, dear to Poseidon,
> casting them into slavery.
> Never, never, o lady Artemis,
> golden-haired offshoot of Zeus,
> may I endure that slavery.

Antigone invokes Nemesis, the personified goddess of retribution, as well as the fire of Zeus in his role of guarantor of justice. Her address to Artemis recalls the words of Aeschylus' chorus, who call upon the goddess to protect the city (154). Antigone seems finally to have entered the expected emotional state of a virgin in a city under siege.

Yet even here Antigone's fear of becoming a spear-captive (αἰχμαλωτίδας, 185) and being sold into slavery (δουλείαν, 189) is held at a distance. The fate that she foresees for herself and the other women of Thebes is service to Mycenean women beside the springs of Lerna and Amymone; that is, domestic tasks such as washing and water-carrying, not sexual subjugation, humiliation, or mistreatment. Antigone's expectation is thus very different from the vivid evocations of future rape and slavery voiced, for instance, by Andromache in the *Iliad*, Tecmessa in Sophocles' *Ajax*, or the choruses in Aeschylus' *Seven against Thebes* and Euripides' *Trojan Women*. Antigone is made to seem so naïve that she cannot even imagine the sexual dimension of the horrors that await the women of a captured city. These are Antigone's last lines in the scene; perhaps in response to her words about future captivity, the Old Servant urges her to go back to her maiden chamber inside the house (κατὰ στέγας/ἐν παρθενῶσι, 193–194). He worries that other women will speak ill of Antigone if she is found outside of the confines of the palace (196–201). This concern for propriety echoes the opening lines of the *teichoskopia*, where the Old Servant explains that only her mother's permission allows Antigone to leave her maiden quarters (παρθενῶνας, 89).[41] The temporary license granted to Antigone has now run its course, and she will not appear again until her mother's urgent summons to leave behind "choral dances and girlish pursuits" and accompany her to the battlefield (χορείαις ... παρθενεύμασιν, 1265).[42]

We have seen that through sophisticated engagement with Homer, Aeschylus, and Sophocles, Euripides has shaped the *teichoskopia* of *Phoenician Women* to accentuate his unique portrayal of Antigone. The

---

[41] On the traditional limits for female behavior, see Foley 2001: 272–300.
[42] Foley 1985: 139–141.

scene emphasizes by contrast Antigone's inexperience at the beginning of the action; the extent of her change over the course of the play is thereby thrown into relief.[43] Antigone's final lyric section in the *teichoskopia*, a quasi-monody, gives way to the *parodos*. The effect of the *parodos* is to present an entirely new understanding of the current situation, one that takes into account the mythological past, the rhythms of divine worship, and the geographical extent of the Hellenic world, from the Tyrian Sea to Sicily. The songs are contrasted both formally and in their content: the solo voice yields to a collective chorus; variable dochmiacs give way to uniform glyconic cola; and the perspective of a young girl hopelessly caught up in her family's conflict broadens to include the detached observations of outsiders.

3.3 *Parodos* (202–260)

The three lyric scenes that open the play – the *teichoskopia*, the *parodos*, and Jocasta's monody – set up a difference in perspective between actors and chorus. This stark defining of distance is accomplished through differences of meter, vocabulary, syntax, and imagery. Antigone's lyrics in the *teichoskopia*, as we have seen, establish her as young, inexperienced, hopeful, and naïve through allusive contrast with figures from Homer, Aeschylus, and Sophocles. Jocasta's monody similarly plays on audience expectation, using the familiar tropes of the "recognition duet" to enhance the audience's perception of her isolation. Situated between these two scenes of actor's lyric, the *parodos* introduces a new mode, choral lyric, and a new understanding of the house's calamity. Although monody, not choral lyric, is the subject of our study, we will briefly consider the *parodos* here because of its key location and function in the play: it is like the sea between two islands.

The *parodos* defines the emotional distance of the chorus from Antigone and from Jocasta. The Old Servant's last words in the *teichoskopia* suggest that the women of the chorus are gathering because of the confusion that reigns in the city; but the women who enter are nothing like the agitated women in the *parodos* of *Seven against Thebes*. This chorus introduce themselves as Phoenician maidens sent by the Agenoridae of Tyre to serve as "first-fruits" in the temple at Delphi (ἀκροθίνια Λοξίᾳ, 203). There they will attend upon the god, a holy service entirely different from

---

[43] Chong-Gossard 2008: 109–110 proposes that the *teichoskopia* may be compared to Ion's opening monody in *Ion* in its emphasis on the innocence of a central character.

the slavery awaiting the captured women of Thebes, which Antigone cannot fathom. Their journey to Apollo's city has been interrupted by the war and they have taken refuge at Thebes. After the agitation and anxiety of Antigone's lyrics, their tone in the first strophe-antistrophe pair is calm, even tranquil: they recall that the wind on the sea as they sailed made "the loveliest sound" (κάλιστον κελάδημα, 213), and they themselves are offered as "loveliest gifts" to the god (καλλιστεύματα, 215). In the second strophe-antistrophe pair their thoughts turn to the war that has come to the city.[44] They sing of their sympathy for the people of Thebes because of their shared kinship as descendants of Io for "sorrows are common among friends" (κοινὰ γὰρ φίλων ἄχη, 243). Although they feel fear at the might of Argos and at what the gods may bring (256–258), they recognize the justice of Polyneices' cause and do not blame his actions (258–260).

The chorus' objectivity as outsiders and their consequent state of emotional distance is unusual and has a direct consequence in defining by contrast Jocasta's anxious isolation. After the serene, expository *parodos*, Jocasta's monody once again creates a heightening of excitement and emotionality. Jocasta's monody is the third consecutive musical scene in the play. For nearly 250 lines, with only a short iambic interlude marking Polyneices' entrance, the play has been delivered entirely in song. However, the two modes, choral song and solo actor's song, remain entirely separate. Antigone makes her exit before the chorus enters; and, although the chorus call Jocasta out from the house, they do not interact with her: they share neither her joy at seeing Polyneices nor her sorrow at his long absence. In other plays of this period – *Ion*, *Iphigenia among the Taurians*, and *Orestes* – Euripides creates a strong bond of sympathy between the female protagonist and the female chorus. Jocasta, by contrast, is isolated from the foreign women of Phoenicia, who have no part in the life of Thebes or of its royal family. She rejoices and grieves alone.

Jocasta's segregation from the women of the chorus is of crucial importance to Euripides' portrayal of the myth. The central role played by Jocasta in the Battle at the Seven Gates may have been Euripides' own innovation.[45] In contrast to Aeschylus' *Seven against Thebes* and Sophocles' *Oedipus Tyrannus*, in Euripides' play Jocasta has not committed suicide after

---

[44] See Podlecki 1962 on the transition between the two halves of the ode.
[45] The story was told at greater length in the lost epic *Thebaid*, but we do not know Jocasta's fate in this poem. In the Lille fragment of Stesichorus, the name of the mother does not survive; she is only referred to as δῖα γυνά, "noble lady" (232). Most scholars assume that this refers to Jocasta, but for the argument that Stesichorus presented Euryganeia, the second, non-incestuous wife of Oedipus, compare March 1987: 127–131; Tsitstibakou-Vasalos 1989; and MacInnes 2007.

Oedipus' true identity is revealed. She has raised her children, cared for her blind husband, and shared the burden of rule with her brother Creon. As we shall see, Jocasta's alienation is also conveyed through costuming and staging. Her monody is remarkable for its wealth of "internal stage directions," details of movement and gesture that would be performed alongside the words to echo and enhance their impact.[46] In the monody, Jocasta's position, at once solitary and authoritative, is conveyed visually and aurally by her distance from the women of the chorus.

3.4 Jocasta's Monody (301–354)

The monody reveals, by both its form and content, the isolated position that Jocasta occupies in all spheres of her life. The song progresses through a sequence of topics: Jocasta emerges from the palace (301–303); embraces and dances around Polyneices (304–316); describes the effect of the separation on herself and on Oedipus (317–336); laments her son's foreign marriage and the ceremonies in which she had no share (337–349); and finally curses the cause of the current conflict and reiterates her own woes (350–354). In its overarching movement from reunion to lamentation, the monody touches upon several themes, which recur and undergo various poetic transformations over the course of the drama. These themes are couched as antitheses: youth versus age, male versus female, light versus darkness, native-born versus foreign, and joyful dance versus the sorrowful gestures of mourning. The interplay of these opposing forces provides structure and unifies the disparate portions of the song. Each of these antitheses underscores many successive domains of Jocasta's life where she occupies an inverted or perverted position.

The progression of the monody is adapted to the shifting emotions that it contains. In its metrical shape, the monody presents an alternation of dochmiac and iambic rhythms.[47] Dochmiacs are predominantly associated

---

[46] For the "grammar" of dramatic technique and gesture in ancient acting, see Taplin 1977; Halleran 1985; Csapo 2002; and Green 2002.

[47] Jocasta's halting entrance is accompanied by dochmiacs, an unusually excited meter to express the ills of old age; when she sees her son at 304, the rhythm shifts to pure iambic, and in 312–317 her dance of joy is marked by syncopation. The lamentations that focus on Jocasta herself (318–326) are almost entirely dochmiac, while the description of Oedipus' despair (327–336) is more varied. The pure iambic rhythm returns for the lament over the foreign marriage (337–343), but as Jocasta sings of her own absence from the wedding ceremony, she once again shifts to dochmiacs. The concluding lines initiate a new dactylic rhythm, which adds solemnity to Jocasta's final curse.

3.4 Jocasta's Monody (301–354)

with Jocasta's personal suffering, while iambic and other meters underscore the wider effect of the separation on the family and on the city. This division of meters in the song accompanies the oscillation between personal and public sorrow. The monody's exploration of the contradictions and inversions that permeate Jocasta's role in the city and in her family situates her further and further beyond the pale of ordinary life.

Let us now move through the substance of the monody, noting in particular how Jocasta's emotions are presented. The opening of the song sets up the expectation of a joyful reunion between mother and son, only to frustrate that expectation. As in the *teichoskopia*, the first lines of Jocasta's monody introduce a contrast between youth and age and the theme of generational passage:

> Φοίνισσαν βοὰν κλύουσα
> ὦ νεάνιδες, γηραιῷ ποδὶ
> τρομερὰν ἕλκω ποδὸς βάσιν.   (301–303)

> Hearing your Phoenician cry,
> young women, I drag the trembling step
> of my foot with aged tread.

Jocasta's greeting is marked by motifs typical of scenes of reunion: she dwells on her son's face (σὸν ὄμμα, 304–305); urges him to embrace her (ἀμφίβαλλε ... ὠλέναισι, 306–307); and emphasizes her long yearning for their meeting (μόλις, ἄελπτα κἀδόκητα, 310–311).[48] But Euripides raises the hope of a recognition scene only to leave it tantalizingly unfulfilled. Unlike in *Ion* or *Iphigenia among the Taurians*, where long-separated relatives are reunited at the climax of the play, this early scene does not lead to a reintegration of the family. Indeed, Jocasta's wishful words emphasize how far the house of Thebes stands from any joyful reconstitution:

> ἰὼ τέκνον, χρόνῳ σὸν ὄμ-
> μα μυρίαις τ' ἐν ἁμέραις   305
> προσεῖδον· ἀμφίβαλλε μα-   306a
> στὸν ὠλέναισι ματέρος,   306b
> παρηίδων [τ'] ὄρεγμα βοσ-   307
> τρύχων τε κυανόχρωτα χαί-
> τας πλόκαμον, σκιάζων δέραν ἁμάν.

---

[48] Compare Shisler 1942 on the portrayal of joy in tragedy and Rawson 1970 on the "emotionally and psychologically realistic style" of Jocasta's lyrics. Scharffenberger 1995 comments on Euripides' use of comic precedents to heighten the *pathos* of this scene.

> ἰὼ ἰώ, μόλις φανεὶς 310
> ἄελπτα κἀδόκητα ματρὸς ὠλέναις. (304–311)

> Oh, my child, after all this time,
> after many days, I see your face.
> Throw your arms around your mother's breast,
> and bring close to my face your outstretched cheek
> and the dark curly locks of your hair, shading my neck.
> Oh, oh, you have only just appeared in your mother's arms,
> unlooked-for, beyond hope.

Jocasta next enacts her feelings of joy and pleasure. Her wish is to capture her son in words (λόγοισι, 313) just as she caresses him with her hands (χερσί, 313). The transference of epithet in the phrase "much-whirling pleasure" (πολυέλικτον ἁδονάν, 314) emphasizes the excitement of Jocasta's movements as she dances around her son (περιχορεύουσα, 316).[49] The language may also allude to the musical daring of these lines, in the "whirling" imagery often associated with the New Music.[50] As Sarah Olsen has demonstrated in her work on solo dance, idiosyncratic patterns of movement on the tragic stage may underscore that characters are acting in transgressive or disruptive ways.[51] Here we can imagine that the choreography of Jocasta's dance would show her agitation and vulnerability, at the same time emphasizing the paradoxical combination of delight and trepidation expressed in her song. Movement and words come together to create meaning:

> τί φῶ σε; πῶς ἅπαντα
> καὶ χερσὶ καὶ λόγοισι
> πολυέλικτον ἁδονὰν
> ἐκεῖσε καὶ τὸ δεῦρο
> περιχορεύουσα τέρψιν παλαιᾶν λάβω
> χαρμονᾶν; (312–317)

> What shall I say of you? How in every way,
> both with hands and with words,
> dancing about you, to that side and this side,
> a much-whirling pleasure,
> shall I take the delight of joys long missed?

As Jocasta begins to sing of the effects of Polyneices' absence on the royal house, the tone shifts from joy to bereavement. She for the first time

---

[49] Compare Podlecki 1962: 370, who writes, "She must here be supposed to go through some choral steps with appropriate gestures as she sings."
[50] See Csapo and Slater 1994: 333 and Weiss 2018a: 9. [51] Olsen 2021: 1–22.

condemns Eteocles' behavior, stating that Polyneices has been driven into exile by his brother's "outrage" (λώβᾳ, 319). She does not reproach Polyneices for bringing an army to the gates of his native city or for threatening his family and the populace with destruction. Indeed, she imagines that even now, in his role as general, Polyneices is desired by all of Thebes:

> ἰὼ τέκος,
> ἔρημον πατρῷον ἔλιπες δόμον
> φυγὰς ἀποσταλεὶς ὁμαίμου λώβᾳ,
> ἦ ποθεινὸς φίλοις,
> ἦ ποθεινὸς Θήβαις. (317–321)
>
> Alas, my child,
> you left your paternal house desolate,
> driven into exile by your brother's outrage,
> much desired by your dear ones,
> much desired by Thebes!

Jocasta goes on to describe her own miserable appearance. Her white hair, and the regal white robes she once wore as queen, contrast with the black rags in which she now appears:

> ὅθεν ἐμάν τε λευκόχροα κείρομαι
> δακρυόεσσαν ἱεῖσα πενθήρη κόμαν,
> ἄπεπλος φαρέων λευκῶν, τέκνον,
> δυσόρφναια δ' ἀμφὶ τρύχη τάδε
> σκότι' ἀμείβομαι· (322–326)
>
> For this I have cut short my white hair
> and unbound my locks, weeping in grief;
> no longer dressed in white garments, my child,
> I have changed my robes, putting around my body
> these rags, dusky and dark.

This reference to her shorn, unbound hair contrasts with the very different description of Polyneices' luxurious dark locks (κυανόχρωτα χαίτας πλόκαμον, 308–309). The words make clear the visual differences between mother and son, whose opposite costuming would set them against one another as types on the stage. Jocasta's pointed references to her own appearance and costume also suggest a degree of metatheatrical self-awareness: in this scene she takes on a particular role, that of a mother in a "reunion scene," one she will later cast off in favor of an arbitrating role, as the situation requires.

Jocasta's words, movements, and gestures are carefully calculated to draw sympathy from her estranged son. By commenting on her attire, Jocasta also draws attention to the perversion of ritual that marks and mars the house of Oedipus. The queen wears the traditional garb of mourning, dark robes with close-cropped hair, even though no one in the family has died. Jocasta's words ring strangely in their immediate context because both of her sons are still alive; not until the end of the play will her costume and tonsure of grief fit the current situation.[52] Her actions, whirling and dancing, are also jarringly out of place for a woman dressed in mourning. The monody of mourning thus foreshadows the deaths not only of Eteocles and Polyneices but also of Jocasta herself, who will stab herself with the weapons of her slain sons. These antitheses between youth and age, between son and mother-grandmother, are especially striking in light of the imploded, incestuous generational structure of the house of Laius.

In the following section, where Jocasta speaks of her son's foreign marriage, the theme of proper behavior for men and women is brought together with issues of foreign and native birth:

> σὲ δ', ὦ τέκνον, καὶ γάμοισιν δὴ
> κλύω ζυγέντα παιδοποιὸν ἁδονὰν
> ξένοισιν ἐν δόμοις ἔχειν,
> ξένον τε κῆδος ἀμφέπειν,
> ἄλαστα ματρὶ τᾷδε Λα-
> ΐῳ τε τῷ παλαιγενεῖ,
> γάμον ἐπακτόν, ἄταν. (337–343)

> But you, my son, I hear
> that you are yoked in marriage
> and have the pleasure of siring children
> in foreign halls,
> that you seek a foreign alliance,
> a disaster for your mother here
> and for your ancient ancestor Laius,
> an alien marriage, ruin.

For the royal house of Thebes, with its history of incest, a foreign bride threatens to bring an end to the concentrated power of the family. This concern with exogamy is overweighted, given the pathologic endogamy of the

---

[52] As we observed in the previous chapter on *Iphigenia among the Taurians*, Iphigenia in the *parodos* draws on the language of mourning with a strongly ironic effect; she mourns for herself, still alive in the land of the Taurians, and for her brother, who, the audience knows, is not yet dead.

house; Jocasta's song draws attention to the way that the family of Oedipus closes in upon itself and foreshadows the brothers' mutual slaughter.

Polyneices' marriage is ruinous not only because the bride is of foreign birth but also because the ceremony took place in a foreign land. Jocasta laments her own absence from the wedding, which is figured as the absence of the usual sacraments: the light of torches, the cleansing water of the ritual bath, and the song that accompanies the bridal procession. Instead, Polyneices' marriage took place in darkness, without purification, and in silence:

> ἐγὼ δ' οὔτε σοι πυρὸς ἀνῆψα φῶς
> νόμιμον ἐν γάμοις, ὡς πρέπει
> ματρὶ μακαρίᾳ·
> ἀνυμέναια δ' Ἰσμηνὸς ἐκηδεύθη
> λουτροφόρου χλιδᾶς, ἀνὰ δὲ Θηβαίων
> πόλιν ἐσιγάθη σᾶς ἔσοδοι νύμφας.   (344–349)

> I did not kindle for you the blazing torch
> that is customary in weddings,
> as befits a mother blessed;
> The river Ismenus contracted this marriage
> without hymns, without the luxury of a ritual bath,
> and in the city of Thebes
> the procession bringing your bride was silent.

To summarize the discussion thus far, Jocasta's reunion with Polyneices in the first portion of the monody introduces contrasts between youth and age, between joy and sorrow, and between *polis* and individual, while also raising uncomfortable implications about the nature of Jocasta's affection for her son. In the second half of the song, categories that should remain separate blend, shift, and exchange places. In Jocasta's description of Oedipus, even male and female roles are inverted. Jocasta, by arranging the truce and presiding over the meeting of the two brothers, has taken upon herself a role of political and familial leadership that would ordinarily be performed by the father. By contrast, Oedipus lives like a woman, secluded within the house, weeping and mourning:

> ὁ δ' ἐν δόμοισι πρέσβυς ὀμματοστερής   327
> ἀπήνας ὁμοπτέρου τᾶς ἀποζυγείσας δόμων   328/329
> πόθον ἀμφιδάκρυτον ἀεὶ κατέχων   330
> ἀνῆξε μὲν ξίφους
> ἐπ' αὐτόχειρά τε σφαγὰν
> ὑπὲρ τέραμνά τ' ἀγχόνας,
> στενάζων ἀρὰς τέκνοις·

σὺν ἀλαλαῖσι δ' αἰὲν αἰαγμάτων
σκότια κρύπτεται. (327–336)

> He in the halls, the old man deprived of sight,
> in never-ending, tearful longing
> for the pair of brothers
> now unyoked from the house,
> first took up the sword
> to inflict slaughter by his own hand,
> then hung nooses from the rafters,
> groaning for the curses on his children.
> With continual cries of woe and sorrow
> he hides himself in the dark.

Oedipus' attempts to end his own life, by hanging and with a self-inflicted sword wound, are typically associated with female suicide.[53] The familial relationships of the line of Laius are perverted both in generation and in gender.[54]

In the final section of the monody, Jocasta compares the unknown agent that has caused these evils to a reveling band (κῶμος; cf. κατεκώμασε, 352). Throughout the play, the calm, all-seeing god of Delphi is contrasted with the war-maddened Ares and anarchic Dionysus.[55] Here, the abstract concept of "the divine" (τὸ δαιμόνιον) stands in for the proper name of any one god; but the image of a wild, unstoppable, irrational force bursting in upon the house combines the fury of Ares and the riot of Dionysus.[56] The curse closes the monody:

ὄλοιτο τάδ' εἴτε σίδαρος
εἴτ' Ἔρις εἴτε πατὴρ ὁ σὸς αἴτιος,
εἴτε τὸ δαιμόνιον κατεκώμασε
δώμασιν Οἰδιπόδα·
πρὸς ἐμὲ γὰρ κακῶν ἔμολε τῶνδ' ἄχη. (350–354)

> May it be damned, whether it was the sword
> or Strife or your father who caused these things,
> or if the divine realm has burst furiously in
> upon the halls of Oedipus;
> for upon me has come the pain of these evils.

---

[53] Loraux 1987: 7–30.
[54] See Swift 2009 on the distortion of sexual relationships within the play.
[55] Arthur 1977.
[56] Compare Aeschylus, *Agamemnon* 1189, κῶμος Ἐρινύων.

In its movement through a sequence of disparate topics, Jocasta's song resembles the second, "deliberative" monody of Iphigenia in *Iphigenia among the Taurians*: here the queen uses the musical form to think through her situation in an immediate and emotional manner. Unlike Iphigenia, however, Jocasta does not arrive at a solution to the current crisis, and all of her ingenuity in the ensuing *agōn* fails to bring about reconciliation between her sons.[57] Rather, the overall progression of thought and mood in the monody is one of growing distress, as Jocasta's initial delight gives way to imprecation and sorrow: her last word, and the last word of lyric for nearly 200 lines, is "grief" (ἄχη, 354). She is eloquent but without the ability to influence her own situation. Where in *Iphigenia among the Taurians* solo song expresses deliberation and resourcefulness, here monody is used primarily as a vehicle for the futile emotions of a woman who has been stripped of her traditional role.

Jocasta sings alone. Often in tragedy, when a male and female character come together after an absence, the woman sings in lyric, while the man reassures her in iambic trimeter.[58] But Jocasta and Polyneices are conspicuously not brought together in an expression of shared emotion through song. Indeed, Jocasta's words are calculated to induce feelings of pity and shame in her son, whose absence has led to this situation.[59] Polyneices has abandoned his duty as a son and a leader, and in fact threatens the very city whose safety should be his hereditary concern. The ensuing *agōn* further dramatizes the selfishness of both brothers and their lack of civic and familial feeling. Jocasta's attempts to appeal to their better nature fail entirely. Despite the monody's rhetorical vigor, structural complexity, and emotional intensity, Jocasta cannot affect the course of events. Her song has fallen upon deaf ears.

3.5 Antigone's Monody (1485–1538)

More than 1,000 lines and the entire crisis of the play intervene between the monody of Jocasta and that of Antigone. After the paired speeches of the second messenger, which present the duel of Polyneices

---

[57] See Foley 2001: 280–283 on Jocasta as an arbitrator.

[58] Beverley 1997: 129. We have observed this type of lyrical reunion scene already between Creusa and Ion in *Ion* and between Iphigenia and Orestes in *Iphigenia among the Taurians*; it also occurs between Helen and Menelaus in *Helen* (625–697).

[59] Compare Foley 1985: 144, who comments, "in this play it is primarily the voices of women, of the very young and the very old, of those who stand outside or above the passions of politics, that remain in tune with the patterns of continuity in city and family life."

and Eteocles as well as their deaths and the suicide of their mother, Antigone returns from the battlefield, followed by a procession with the three corpses. The chorus indicate her entrance in five anapestic lines and then fall silent (1480–1485). The scene of solo actor's lyric that follows takes the place of the expected choral song: the role of reflecting upon the catastrophe of the house in lyric is filled not by the chorus but by Antigone in a monody.

The monody of Antigone (1485–1529) moves directly into her summoning of Oedipus (1530–1538) and their lyric exchange (1539–1581), in which Antigone sings the majority of the lines. Although the monody in this case cannot be separated entirely from the larger lyric system of which it forms a part, it is distinct from the duet in form and in content. Antigone's forty-five lines of solo song in this scene are focused almost exclusively on herself and her own grief, as she tries to make sense of this latest disaster in the history of the house's misfortune. The entrance of Oedipus marks an expansion of her awareness and suggests a purpose that will shape her future, as the two remaining members of the house are united in their shared suffering and in the necessity of exile.

Antigone's monody has not met with universal acclaim. For instance, Jane Beverley describes the progression of themes as "grief-by-numbers" and concludes that the piece is characterized throughout by a "flabby emptiness."[60] If there is an inadequacy to Antigone's lament, it is because she must alone communicate the grief of her entire family and, indeed, of her entire city. The expression of communal grief requires the preservation of communal structures; it is the loss of these very structures that Antigone mourns. Euripides represents the breakdown of the domestic and civil order through the broken meter and expression of the monody. Solo actor's lyric serves here better than choral lyric could in that it allows the expression of a point of view that is both more emotional and more disrupted.

But Beverley's charge of emptiness also passes over the careful formal integration of the monody into the larger movement of the drama. The monody and ensuing duet structurally balance the lyric scenes in the first part of the play. Antigone's monody engages directly with the vocabulary, imagery, and themes of Jocasta's monody. The exclamations and movements of joy and sorrow that marked Jocasta's monody (312–317) are countered in Antigone's monody by the language of unmixed grief, and

---

[60] Beverley 1997: 151.

3.5 Antigone's Monody (1485–1538)

the earlier gestural and visual symbols of mourning (322–326) are here presented in a new context as they are performed over visible, tangible corpses. The focus is again on Polyneices, whose body receives the most attention. Jocasta's mourning for her son was proleptic; Antigone laments deaths that have now occurred. Jocasta's opening monody, viewed in retrospect, emerges as a grim foreshadowing of the events to come, a threnody not only for Polyneices but also for herself and her whole family.

Where the metrical shape of Jocasta's monody is relatively simple, Antigone's monody employs varied and startlingly original rhythmical effects. The diversity of meters and the rapidity of rhythmic changes underscore the extremity of Antigone's emotional state. In fact, this is among the most metrically complex and heterogeneous monodies in extant Greek tragedy. The song begins with a dactylic passage as Antigone describes her own state of desperation and grief (1485–1507). As the content becomes even more passionate, the meter changes to include aeolic, choriambic, and iambic rhythms (1508–1529). In this central section, no single rhythm persists for more than three consecutive lines, and rhythmical changes frequently occur from one line to another. When Antigone turns away from her solitary lament to summon Oedipus, the meter becomes still more varied: dactyls return, along with new iambo-dochmiac and ionic elements (1530–1545). Antigone relates the news of the three deaths in a long passage that returns to the basically dactylic rhythm of the opening, with a strong admixture of anapests (1546–1581). If we look not simply at the specific meters used but more globally at their sheer number, we may ask ourselves if this is not a representation of the number of areas of breakdown in the family and in the community.

The first lines of the monody signal the connection to the song of Jocasta through specific verbal echoes, and by vivid visual evocations:

> οὐ προκαλυπτομένα βοτρυχώδεος ἁβρὰ παρηΐδος   1485/1486
> οὐδ' ὑπὸ παρθενίας τὸν ὑπὸ βλεφά-   1487
> ροις φοίνικ', ἐρύθημα προσώπου,
> αἰδομένα φέρομαι βάκχα νεκύ-
> ων, κράδεμνα δικοῦσα κόμας ἀπ' ἐ-
> μᾶς, στολίδα κροκόεσσαν ἀνεῖσα τρυφᾶς,
> ἁγεμόνευμα νεκροῖσι πολύστονον.   (1485–1492)

> Not veiling the delicate skin of my cheek, adorned with curls,
> or concealing in virginal modesty
> the crimson beneath my eyes, the reddening of my face,

> I rush forth as a bacchant of the dead,
> hurling the covering from my hair,
> unbinding my fine-woven saffron robe,
> an escort of the dead, filled with groans.

Where Jocasta identified herself as an old woman with trembling step (302–303), Antigone emphasizes her virginal status (παρθενίας, 1487). The description of Polyneices' cheeks and hair (308–309) are recalled by Antigone's reddened eyes, blushing cheeks, and loosened tresses and by the exact repetition of the words βόστρυχος (1485) and παρηίς (1486). The dark and light colors that were so pronounced in Jocasta's monody here become more vivid and violent: Antigone's eyes and face are red (φοίνικ', ἐρύθημα, 1488) and her robe is saffron, a color associated with festal activity and even marriage (κροκόεσσαν, 1491). Both women dance: Jocasta's dance around her son momentarily liberates her from age and grief (316–317), while Antigone's perversely solitary Bacchic dance, where she figures as the sole maenad, makes manifest in movement her agitation and distress.[61] Jocasta's image of the "reveling band" of disaster (κατεκώμασε, 352) is here grimly fulfilled by Antigone, the "bacchant of the dead" (βάκχα νεκύων, 1489–1490). The rush of words is conveyed through a fluid sequence of dactyls and creates a sense of agitation; we must imagine that the music and the movements of the actor added to this effect.

This opening exclamation is focused entirely on Antigone and takes the form of an asyndetic series of first-person verbs and nominative participles (προκαλυπτομένα, 1485; αἰδομένα, 1489; φέρομαι, 1489; δικοῦσα, 1490; ἀνεῖσα, 1491; ἁγεμόνευμα, 1492). Antigone's status as a distraught virgin, emphasized in her opening lines, places her in an unusual category as a monodist. Unlike the other virginal singers in extant Euripides, Electra and Iphigenia, Antigone is not joined by a sympathetic female chorus as she laments the downfall of her house.[62] As in Jocasta's monody, the distance of the chorus of Phoenician women helps to define Antigone's radical isolation from the traditions and rituals of her community. The absence of the expected antiphonal female exchange makes Antigone's musical appeal that Oedipus share her grief all the more striking.

---

[61] On the transgressive nature of a maenad who dances alone, see Olsen 2021: 129–138.

[62] In this way Antigone recalls Cassandra in Aeschylus' *Agamemnon*, whose increasingly explicit appeals the chorus cannot, and will not, share (1072–1330).

Antigone's isolation may also have been conveyed visually by the staging of the scene. It is possible that she entered first, followed by a funeral procession conveying the bodies of Jocasta, Polyneices, and Eteocles.[63] An unmarried woman, unaccompanied, pulling from her head the veil that marks her modesty, is shocking. As a maiden, Antigone normally would only display herself in the context of ritual occasions, in particular in festivals where she would participate in choral dances. The circumstances of the disaster at Thebes have forced the women of the house to act in ways that conflict with their usual societal roles. Just as in the *agōn* Jocasta takes on the male role of political mediator, Antigone must take on the responsibility of leading the dirge for the dead, which would ordinarily be filled by a mature wife or mother. When Jocasta calls Antigone to accompany her to the battlefield, she explicitly asks her to leave behind the dances of maidens (χορείας, παρθενεύμασιν, 1265). The exodus dramatizes the reversal of the motif of Antigone as a secluded maiden, as she abandons all hope of marriage and children and dedicates herself to a life of exile with her aged father.

To return to the text: the references to dead bodies (νεκύων, 1488; νεκροῖσι, 1492) draw Antigone's attention to the three corpses, and she turns from the description of her frenzied self to consider her own relation to the dead and to the ruin of the family. Like Jocasta, Antigone focuses on the bodies of her kinsmen, especially on that of Polyneices, and draws a causal connection between Polyneices, Thebes, and destructive strife (cf. 321, 351–353).[64] She cries:

> αἰαῖ, ἰώ μοι.
> ὦ Πολύνεικες, ἔφυς ἄρ' ἐπώνυμος· ὤμοι Θῆβαι·   1493/1494
> σὰ δ' ἔρις – οὐκ ἔρις, ἀλλὰ φόνῳ φόνος –   1495
> Οἰδιπόδα δόμον ὤλεσε κρανθεῖσ'
> αἵματι δεινῷ, αἵματι λυγρῷ.   (1492–1497)

Alas, ah me!
Oh Polyneices, your name was fitting. Alas, Thebes!
Your strife – not strife, but slaughter upon slaughter –
has destroyed the house of Oedipus,
brought to fulfillment in fearsome bloodshed,
in baneful bloodshed.

The aural impact of the passage depends on pathetic repetition and polyptoton (φόνῳ φόνος, 1493; αἵματι δεινῷ, αἵματι λυγρῷ, 1497). This technique

---

[63] Mastronarde 1994: ad 1492.

[64] The self-perpetuating force of the family's curse recurs as well outside of the two monodies; compare 70, 624, 765, 811–812, 1053, and 1255.

is parodied by Aristophanes in *Frogs* and seems to have been associated particularly with Euripidean monody. Repetition enhances Antigone's lament also in the next section (τίνα, τίνα, 1498–1499; δάκρυσι δάκρυσιν, 1500; ὦ δόμος, ὦ δόμος, 1500; δυσξυνέτον ξυνετὸς, 1506). The reoccurrence of significant words – home, tears, blood, slaughter – here emphasizes that the catastrophe is not single but multiple, affecting the younger generation as well as the older, the male line as well as the female.

As we observed earlier, Jocasta's monody moves from self-description through a series of questions as she describes Polyneices and the emotional effect that their reunion has upon her. Antigone also employs aporetic interrogatives (τίνα, τίνα, 1498–1499); but where Jocasta seeks to express delight through dance (314), Antigone searches instead for an appropriate song of mourning for her unparalleled situation, bereft at one stroke of three members of her family. The pleasure that Jocasta felt at seeing her son (χαρμονᾶν, 317) is darkly echoed by the pleasure (χάρματ', 1503) here taken by the Erinys:

> τίνα προσῳδὸν
> ἢ τίνα μουσοπόλον στοναχὰν ἐπὶ
> δάκρυσι δάκρυσιν, ὦ δόμος, ὦ δόμος,   1500
> ἀγκαλέσωμαι,
> τρισσὰ φέρουσα τάδ' αἵματα σύγγονα,
> ματέρα καὶ τέκνα, χάρματ' Ἐρινύος;   (1498–1503)

> What song,
> or what Muse-inspired groan
> with tears upon tears, oh house, oh house,
> shall I call upon for aid,
> bearing these three bloody corpses of my kin,
> mother and children, to charm the Erinys?

In the following lines Antigone describes the Sphinx, who throughout the play is considered one cause of the present evil and of the wholesale destruction of the house of Oedipus:[65]

> ἃ δόμον Οἰδιπόδα πρόπαρ ὤλεσε,
> τᾶς ἀγρίας ὅτε
> δυσξυνέτον ξυνετὸς μέλος ἔγνω
> Σφιγγὸς ἀοιδοῦ σῶμα φονεύσας.   (1504–1507)

---

[65] Compare 1689, 1728. The chorus at other points delve deeper into history to find the origin of the crime, following the line of violence to the serpent of Ares, killed by Cadmus. Antigone, focused on the immediate troubles of her natal family, looks no farther than her father's own deeds.

> She destroyed the house of Oedipus long ago,
> when he, intelligent, solved the unintelligible melody
> of the fierce Sphinx,
> slaying the body of the singer.

Why this comparison? Antigone progresses through a free association from her own song (προσῳδόν, 1498) and the riddling song of the Sphinx (μέλος, 1506) that long ago set Oedipus on the path to murder and incest. Antigone in the opening lines of the monody cast herself as the lone member of a Bacchic band; she is never joined in lamentation by the chorus; and she can find no example, either Greek or barbarian, for a woman who has suffered as she has. The only model she has for such a predicament is the monstrous Sphinx, the "singer" of others' destruction and, consequently, her own. Antigone puts herself in the place of the Sphinx, establishing music as a marker of both the beginning and the culmination of the house's woes.

The next lines are uncertain, both textually and metrically. There seems to be a transition from the primarily dactylic rhythm of the opening verses of monody to a more varied system of choriambs, iambs, and ionics. The content – the uniqueness of the present situation and of Antigone's fate – is thus echoed by the increasingly complex metrical effects:

> ἰώ μοί μοι·
> τίς Ἑλλὰς ἢ βάρβαρος ἢ
> τῶν προπάροιθ' εὐγενετᾶν
> ἕτερος ἔτλα κακῶν τοσῶνδ'
> αἵματος ἀμερίου
> τοιάδ' ἄχεα φανερά,
> τάλαιν' ὡς ἐλελίζω;   (1508-1514)[66]

> Alas, ah me, ah me!
> Who else, Greek or barbarian
> or descended from ancient nobility,

---

[66] In this passage I follow Mastronarde 1994: ad 1508-1514 in deleting πάτερ in 1508 and in preferring the first-person verb ἐλελίζω in 1514 to the second- or third-person verb transmitted in many manuscripts. It makes dramatic sense that Antigone continues to focus on herself in this passage, as she has until this point and as she continues to do until her explicit appeal to Oedipus in 1530. The verb ἐλελίζω may have two possible meanings: it is either a reduplicated form of ἑλίσσω, "I whirl around," or a derivative of ἐλελεῦ, "I cry in pain, I keen." Although the former seems to have been a favorite Euripidean word (cf. *Orestes* 358, 1432; *Bacchae* 569; *Iphigenia in Aulis* 1055; parodied by Aristophanes at *Frogs* 1314), in my translation I have chosen the second meaning, which better accommodates the direct object.

has endured so many evils
of mortal bloodshed,
such sorrows as are here made manifest,
such as you keen, wretched woman!

Antigone denies that any other mortal woman has endured what she has endured. The only creature that has felt comparable grief is the nightingale:

τίς ἄρ' ὄρνις, ἢ δρυὸς ἢ
ἐλάτας ἀκροκόμοις ἀμφὶ κλάδοις
μονομάτρος ὀδυρμοῖς
ἐμοῖς ἄχεσι συνῳδός;
αἴλινον αἰάγμασιν ἃ τοῦδε προκλαί-
ω μονάδ' αἰῶνα διάξουσα τὸν αἰ-   1520/1521
εἰ χρόνον ἐν λειβομένοισιν δάκρυσιν, ἰαχήσω.   1522/1523   (1515–1523)[67]

What bird, on the long-leaved branches
of an oak or a fir tree,
will sing her lonely mother's lamentation
to accompany my sorrows?
With cries of woe I lament, even before it comes,
the lonely life that I will live for the rest of time
amidst streaming tears, I will cry out!

As with her reference to the Sphinx, Antigone is searching for an analogue to her own situation, and can only find it in the artificial and inhuman world of literary *topos*. The nightingale, who sings alone and at night, is a traditional image dating back to Homer, receiving its fullest literary treatment in Euripides' *Helen* (1107–1121).[68] Antigone's reference to the nightingale may also here have a connection to the innovative musical effects of her lyrics. The musical ingenuity of the nightingale is described by Pliny in his *Natural History* as astonishing in its variety, characterized by a great range of pitch and volume, very long and very short notes, broken or prolonged bursts of music, and every effect that can be produced by man with a flute (*tibia*).[69] Here Antigone also draws upon the association between the nightingale and songs of mourning. But where the nightingale

---

[67] Text of de Poli 2011.
[68] Compare Homer, *Odyssey* 19.518–522; Aristophanes, *Birds* 210–216; Sophocles, *Oedipus at Colonus* 617–673; Euripides fr. 88. For discussion of the nightingale in contexts of mourning, see Weiss 2017. For the bird as a multivalent poetic symbol, see Weiss 2018a: 159–167 and LeVen 2021: 168–205.
[69] Pliny, *Natural History* x.43. See Chandler 1934 and Anhalt 2001–2.

is traditionally figured as a mother lamenting her child (μονομάτρος, 1517), Antigone laments her own mother and her brothers.

In the final lines of her monody, Antigone describes her inadequacy, as a sole mourner to lament the three corpses that lie before her. This *aporia* leads directly into her summoning of Oedipus, who will share her grief:

> τίν' ἐπὶ πρῶτον ἀπὸ χαί-
> τας σπαραγμοῖς ἀπαρχὰς βάλω;
> ματρὸς ἐμᾶς ἢ διδύμοις
> γάλακτὸς παρὰ μαστοῖς
> ἢ πρὸς ἀδελφῶν
> οὐλόμεν' αἰκίσματα νεκρῶν; (1524–1529)

> Over which of these
> shall I first cast my offerings,
> tearing out my hair?
> Beside the twin milk-bearing breasts of my mother,
> or the terrible wounds of my brothers' corpses?

We have observed that the main themes of Antigone's monody – her distress, the agents responsible for the destruction of the house, and the unique nature of her fate – recall and reverse the main themes of Jocasta's monody. In this way, Euripides uses the paired monodies, separated by almost the entire action of the play, to show the progression of the family's misfortunes. The monody also responds to Antigone's lyric lines in the *teichoskopia* and resembles the earlier passage in that it too takes the place that would usually be occupied by a choral song. Where the *teichoskopia* emphasized Antigone's modesty, curiosity, and naïveté, here her maidenly restraint has been definitely cast aside, and her youthful exuberance has turned to weighty sorrow, a burden that must be borne out of time and out of joint. On the level of formal craft, the agitated and broken music of the song expresses both grief for a personal loss and a pain, harder to articulate, for the destruction of domestic and social institutions.

3.6 Duet of Antigone and Oedipus (1539–1581)

We have seen that Antigone's monody both stands in for the expected choral song and recalls in structure and content the monody of Jocasta. In her monody, Antigone laments the unique nature of her fate (1508–1514) and explicitly calls for a fellow mourner who will sing in accompaniment to her woes (συνῳδός, 1518). The chorus of Phoenician women cannot join with her in lamentation; they remain outside the family's strife and their sorrow. The only other mortal alive who has suffered as Antigone has is Oedipus. Her shared song with her father in the *exodos* constitutes a long-awaited emotional union, but not one of joy; the scattered individual members of the house can only be brought together through grief. The lyric duet begins as a lament, with the innovation that Antigone's lines revisit the account of the second messenger from the previous episode. By combining elements of a messenger speech with those of a lament, Antigone uses narrative as a platform to reach a higher level of expression and emotion. Because her song constitutes a second treatment of the tragic event, she is granted a degree of freedom in her lyric departure from it.

Among modern scholars it has commonly been agreed that the *exodos* of *Phoenician Women* is riddled with later interpolations, some based upon other plays of the Theban cycle, that are inconsistent with one another and with other parts of the play. In the text as it stands, Antigone will defy Creon by burying the corpse of Polyneices; and she will go to Mount Cithairon and become a bacchant; and she will accompany her father into exile. Clearly, she cannot do all three. Yet the play as a whole is a pastiche of different versions of the Theban legend, and the process of identifying interpolations can be quite subjective as they tend to rely on considerations of literary taste. Elizabeth Craik has argued for the "fundamental integrity" of the *exodos*, marking only two lines in the entire final scene as spurious, while Francis Dunn proposes that the heterogeneity of the scene, the inclusion of its different and conflicting details, is in fact part of a larger narrative strategy and therefore genuine.[70] In what follows I use the text of Mastronarde, who accepts the entire scene until line 1736 as genuine.[71]

From a musical perspective, the lyric dialogue between Antigone and Oedipus is integrated into the larger formal design of the play by ring composition; the duet recalls and reverses the interaction between Antigone and the Old Servant in the *teichoskopia*. In the earlier scene, Antigone seeks the guidance, protection, and wisdom of the old man. Here it is she who knows what has happened on the battlefield, and who responds to the questions of her aged father with a new knowledge born

---

[70] Craik 1988 and Dunn 1996: 183. Mastronarde 1994 and de Poli 2011 offer detailed discussion of the authenticity of individual lines.
[71] Mastronarde 1994: ad 1736–1757.

of disaster. The themes of the duet also recall the monody of Jocasta: just as Jocasta moves from monody to attempted interaction in the political sphere, so Antigone takes on a new and successful role as guide to her father and, in the subsequent scene with Creon, as a decisive agent in shaping her own and her family's future.

Oedipus has been mentioned repeatedly during the play as secluded in the house and distraught by what is occurring onstage (cf. 66, 88, 327–336, 376–378, 611, 614, 873–877, 1088–1089). Lowell Edmunds has traced language in the play that describes Oedipus as a ghost or revenant, abject and weak but with the demonic power to do harm.[72] Now this shadowy figure is displayed before the audience. Oedipus is called forth by Antigone like a spirit from the Underworld in a combination of cretics, choriambs, dactyls, and dochmiacs.[73] The ensuing duet, which marks an emotional climax and a coming together of survivors, is also the most rhythmically inventive and complex passage in the play:

AV.	ὀτοτοτοῖ, λεῖπε σοὺς δόμους, ἀλάον ὄμμα φέρων, πάτερ γεραιέ, δεῖξον, Οἰδιπόδα, σὸν αἰῶνα μέλεον, ὃς ἐπὶ δώμασιν ἀέριον σκότον ὄμμασι σοῖσι βαλὼν ἕλκεις μακρόπνουν ζωάν. κλύεις, ὦ κατ' αὐλὰν ἀλαίνων γεραιὸν πόδ' ἢ δεμνίοις δύστανος ἰαύων;	(1530–1538)

AN. Otototoi, leave your house,
aged father, bearing your blinded sight,
reveal your miserable life,
you who have cast a dark mist over your eyes
and drag your deep-gasping life within the house.
Do you hear, wandering with aged step
across the court, or lying on your wretched bed?

Oedipus in his response compares himself to an invisible phantom (ἀφανὲς εἴδωλον, 1543), a ghost from below (νέκυν ἔνερθεν, 1544), or a winged dream (πτανὸν ὄνειρον, 1545). This tricolon presents Oedipus

---

[72] Edmunds 1981: 230–231.
[73] The vocabulary of these lines echoes the scene in Aeschylus' *Persians* where Darius is summoned from the Underworld (633–680).

as a being from another world, one who has transcended the three ages of man – infancy, maturity, and old age – dictated by the Sphinx's riddle:

Οι. τί μ', ὦ παρθένε, βακτρεύμασι τυφλοῦ
    ποδὸς ἐξάγαγες εἰς φῶς
    λεχήρη σκοτίων ἐκ θαλάμων οἰκ-
    τροτάτοισιν δακρύοισιν,
    πολιὸν αἰθέρος ἀφανὲς εἴδωλον ἢ
    νέκυν ἔνερθεν ἢ
    πτανὸν ὄνειρον;   (1539–1545)

Οε. Why, daughter, have you dragged me,
    supporting my blind footsteps with a staff,
    into the light by your pitiful tears,
    from the shadows of my chamber,
    bed-ridden, grey-haired, invisible
    as a phantom of the air, a spirit from below,
    or a winged dream?

The meter of the passage responds to the varied rhythms of Antigone's invocation and surpasses her verses in complexity.[74] Antigone in the *teichoskopia* was answered by the reserved trimeters of the Old Servant, and Jocasta in her monody sang without accompaniment from the chorus or response from Polyneices. Now for the first time in the play a lyric singer is able to find a partner at a matching level of intensity. Antigone is no longer a μονῳδός, a solo singer. She has found her συνῳδός at last.

That Antigone's partner in song – her συνῳδός – should be male is extraordinary. The *amoibaion* between Antigone and Oedipus in this play is the only instance of a shared lyric lament between a male and a female character in extant Euripides.[75] Is the effect to emphasize the distance between the two characters or to join them in a supreme moment of grief? Critics are divided. Helene Foley writes that "Antigone and Oedipus sing past each other,

---

[74] Oedipus' response contains a series of ionics, iambics, dochmiacs, dactyls, and paroemiacs.

[75] Chong-Gossard 2008: 58–61. In Euripides' *Electra* (1177–1237), Orestes and Electra sing in exchange with the chorus; the meter of the passage, which is predominantly lyric iambics, does not approach the complexity of this passage, and the presence of the chorus adds an additional element that sets the singers as a pair against an outside perspective. In Euripides' *Helen* (625–697), the recognition of Helen and Menelaus is capped by a duet, partly sung and partly spoken, in which the long-separated couple first celebrates their happiness and then Menelaus questions Helen about her disappearance. The shared lament of Oedipus and Antigone in *Phoenician Women* may be compared with the duet of Hecuba and Polyxena in *Hecuba* (154–215); there it is the parent who shares information and the child who reacts.

and at cross purposes," and that "the babbling old man has no interest in his daughter's attempts at heroics."[76] Monica Cyrino, by contrast, argues that the lament does bring the two figures together, and that the primary effect is to demonstrate their shared weakness. The status of Oedipus, Cyrino writes, is diminished by his participation in the lyric duet: his grief is represented as "an essentially feminine experience ... by allowing him the lyric expression normally reserved for the female character in an actors' duet."[77]

Many scholars have proposed that lament in tragedy is predominantly a female genre; men who participate in songs of mourning are thereby "feminized," shown to be weak and powerless.[78] The contrary position has also been voiced; Ann Suter has argued that men perform almost as many laments as women in tragedy, and that in fact a man's lament often leads to his redemption and reintegration into society.[79] In *Phoenician Women* the effect of the shared lament, it seems to me, is to reaffirm the weakness of Oedipus, which has already been established as a theme in the play; at the same time, and more importantly, the song demonstrates the paradoxical power of Antigone. She conveys information, gives comfort, and takes the lead in deciding how she and her father will leave the city. Her grief takes center stage.[80] Although her life will be one of sorrow and exile, through song she becomes mistress of her own fate.

If in her monody Antigone filled the role of the chorus, in her opening exchange with Oedipus she takes on the role of messenger (cf. ἀγγελίας, 1546):

AV. δυστυχὲς ἀγγελίας ἔπος οἴσῃ,
     πάτερ· οὐκέτι σοι τέκνα λεύσσει
     φάος οὐδ' ἄλοχος, παραβάκτροις
     ἃ πόδα σὸν τυφλόπουν θεραπεύμασιν αἰὲν ἐμόχθει,
     ⟨ὦ⟩ πάτερ, ὤμοι.   (1546–1550)

AN. You will endure the unfortunate utterance of my news,
     Father; no longer do your sons see the light,
     nor your wife, who would always tend and guide
     your blind footstep with a staff,
     Father, alas.

Antigone's lyrics recapitulate the content of the second messenger speech but in a more emotional, personal, and pathetic mode (1427–

---

[76] Foley 1985: 142.   [77] Cyrino 1998: 23–24.
[78] On lamentation in Greek culture and tragedy, see the Introduction, pp. 21–36.
[79] Suter 2008. Curiously, Suter does not include the scene under discussion in her appendix of the forty-two laments in extant tragedy. Compare also Chong-Gossard 2008 on men's song in Euripides.
[80] Lamari 2007: 21–22.

1479).[81] The second messenger, who reports the duel of the brothers and Jocasta's suicide to Creon and the chorus, identifies himself as a follower of Eteocles (1461). As a soldier and a Theban, his fate is tied up in the outcome of the battle, but he is not himself one of its principal players. Antigone is at once observer, participant, and narrator of the action she relates as well as the person most intimately affected by its outcome.

The emotional connection between Antigone and her father is underscored by the shared vocabulary of lamentation (especially the exclamation ὤμοι, which begins Oedipus' passage and concludes Antigone's) and by the repeated terms emphasizing their familial relationship (ὦ τέκνον, ὦ πάτερ):

Οι. ὤμοι ἐμῶν παθέων· πάρα γὰρ στενάχειν τάδ᾽, αὐτεῖν.
     τρισσαὶ ψυχαί· ποίᾳ μοίρᾳ
     πῶς ἔλιπον φάος; ὦ τέκνον, αὔδα.

Αν. οὐκ ἐπ᾽ ὀνείδεσιν οὐδ᾽ ἐπιχάρμασιν,
     ἀλλ᾽ ὀδύναισι λέγω· σὸς ἀλάστωρ
     ξίφεσιν βρίθων
     καὶ πυρὶ καὶ σχετλίαισι μάχαις ἐπὶ παῖδας ἔβα σούς,
     ὦ πάτερ, ὤμοι.   (1551–1559)

Οε. Alas for my sufferings! For I should groan, I should wail.
     Three lives! By what fate did they leave the light?
     My child, tell me.

Αν. I say this not to reproach or mock you,
     but with pain; your avenging curse,
     bristling with swords and fire and grievous battles,
     came down upon your sons.
     Father, alas.

In the next passage, the emotions of Oedipus and Antigone become even more closely interwoven, as they complete one another's lines, in principally dactylic meter:

Οι. αἰαῖ.   Αν. τί τάδε καταστένεις;
Οι. τέκνα.   Αν. δι᾽ ὀδύνας ἔβας·
     εἰ δὲ τέθριππά γ᾽ ἔθ᾽ ἅρματα λεύσσων
     ἀελίου τάδε σώματα νεκρῶν
     ὄμματος αὐγαῖς σαῖς ἐπενώμας;

---

[81] Euripides' experimentation with monody as messenger speech will be explored more fully in the monody of the Phrygian slave in *Orestes*, discussed in the next chapter.

3.6 Duet of Antigone and Oedipus (1539–1581)

Oi.   τῶν μὲν ἐμῶν τεκέων φανερὸν κακόν·
       ἁ δὲ τάλαιν' ἄλοχος τίνι μοι, τέκνον, ὤλετο μοίρᾳ;   (1560–1566)

Oe.   Ah me!   An.   Why do you groan?
Oe.   My children. An.   You go through pains;
       But what if, looking to the four-horsed chariot of the sun,
       you could cast the beams of your eyes
       upon the corpses of the dead!
Oe.   The evil fate of my sons is manifest;
       but my wretched wife, child, by what fate did she perish?

Antigone in her response narrates the suicide of Jocasta, describing her mother's death as a final act of solidarity with her sons. Because of its length, de Poli has classified this section as a self-contained monody.[82] However, Antigone's lines do form an essential part of the longer lyric system: her extended expository passage, couched in the highest poetic register, directly answers the question posed by Oedipus. She sings events that took place elsewhere, but whose physical, tangible results are present in the form of the corpses at her feet. Unlike her flights of song in the *teichoskopia*, which were increasingly detached from her onstage interlocutor, Antigone is now completely immersed in the relationship with Oedipus. This change underscores Antigone's journey from naïveté to full engagement with the fate of her family:

δάκρυα γοερὰ	1567a
φανερὰ πᾶσι τιθεμένα,	1567b
τέκεσι μαστὸν ἔφερεν ἔφερεν	1568
ἱκέτις ἱκέτιν ὀρομένα.	
ηὗρε δ' ἐν Ἠλέκτραισι πύλαις τέκνα	
λωτοτρόφον κατὰ λείμακα λόγχαις,	
κοινὸν ἐνυάλιον,	
μάτηρ, ὥστε λέοντας ἐναύλους,	
μαρναμένους ἐπὶ τραύμασιν, αἵματος	
ἤδη ψυχρὰν λοιβὰν φονίαν,	
ἂν ἔλαχ' Ἅιδας, ὤπασε δ' Ἄρης.	
χαλκόκροτον δὲ λαβοῦσα νεκρῶν πάρα φάσγανον εἴσω	
σαρκὸς ἔβαψεν, ἄχει δὲ τέκνων ἔπεσ' ἀμφὶ τέκνοισι.	
πάντα δ' ἐν ἄματι τῷδε συνάγαγεν,	

---

[82] De Poli 2011: 256–257.

ὦ πάτερ, ἁμετέροισι δόμοισιν ἄχη θεὸς
ὃς τάδε τελευτᾷ.   (1567–1581)

Her tears and wails
were manifest to all;
rushing forth the suppliant bore, she bore
her supplicant breast to her children.
But the mother found her sons
by the Electran gate,
in a meadow where the lotus blooms,
fighting with spears in a kindred battle,
like lair-dwelling lions, eager for wounds,
a murderous libation of blood already cold,
owed to Hades, poured out by Ares.
Then, taking from the corpses a sword of hammered bronze,
she thrust it into her flesh, and in grief for her children,
around her children she fell.
The god has brought together on this one day,
oh father, all pains for our house,
he who brings these things to completion.

If we compare Antigone's account of the action to that of the second messenger, emotionality and passion stand out in contrast to measured description. For example, in the messenger's version, Jocasta arrives in time to witness the last moments of her sons' lives and to take an emotional farewell from each. Here the messenger describes Jocasta's final actions, in iambic trimeter:

μήτηρ δ', ὅπως ἐσεῖδε τήνδε συμφοράν,
ὑπερπαθήσασ', ἥρπασ' ἐκ νεκρῶν ξίφος
κἄπραξε δεινά· διὰ μέσου γὰρ αὐχένος
ὠθεῖ σίδηρον, ἐν δὲ τοῖσι φιλτάτοις
θανοῦσα κεῖται περιβαλοῦσ' ἀμφοῖν χέρας.   (1455–1459)

But their mother, when she saw this disaster,
in grievous distress snatched a sword from the corpses
and did a dreadful deed. Through the middle of her throat
she thrust the iron blade, and now lies dead
among those she loved, having thrown her hands around both.

Jocasta's suicide is recounted in smooth, paratactic clauses, where aorist verbs follow each other in logical succession to convey as clearly as possible the sequence of events ("she saw," "she snatched," "she thrust," etc.). This use of "narrative verbs" in a secondary tense is typical of messenger speeches.[83] There are no descriptive adjectives, only participles or those adjectives commonly used as substantives (δεινά, 1457; τοῖσι φιλτάτοις, 1458; ἀμφοῖν, 1459). Although the content is shocking, the mode of delivery remains calm, balanced, chronological.

In Antigone's lyric, by contrast, words and sounds pile up to create an effect of chaos and disaster. For instance, Antigone's opening phrase is rendered almost incoherent through asyndeton, alliteration, and a lack of syntactical subordination, while the presence of the lyric alpha makes it at first difficult to distinguish between neuter plural and feminine singular or between Jocasta's action and its effects: δάκρυα γοερὰ φανερὰ πᾶσι τιθεμένα, literally "tears wails clear to all making," which only in retrospect can we understand as "she made tears and wails that were clear to all" (1567a–1567b).

In Antigone's next lines, one verb is repeated for aural effect and to add emotional weight (ἔφερεν ἔφερεν, 1568), while the polyptoton of the significant word "suppliant" emphasizes Jocasta's inability to save her sons (ἱκέτις ἱκέτιν, 1569). The alliteration of lambda in the phrase λωτοτρόφον κατὰ λείμακα λόγχαις (1571) draws attention to the pastoral setting in which Jocasta finds her sons; the poignancy of meadows and lotus flowers would be out of place within the plainer style of the messenger's speech. The simile of "mountain-dwelling lions," while not unconventional for fighting warriors, emphasizes the bestiality of the scene in contrast to the solemn, religious mood appropriate to the pouring of libations (ὥστε λέοντας ἐναύλους, 1573; ψυχρὰν λοιβὰν φονίαν, 1575). The actual act of Jocasta's suicide – the section of the narrative exactly parallel to the lines of the messenger, quoted earlier – through a rushing run of dactyls conveys the speed of Jocasta's final act, too swift for Antigone to stop. By having the same story related twice, first in spoken iambic trimeter by the messenger and then in solo song by Antigone, Euripides draws dramatic force from the difference in their perspectives. The second telling assumes the first, elaborating upon it in passionate variations; after the messenger has related the plain facts of the event, Antigone illustrates through her far-reaching song the terrible emotions that accompanied it.

3.7 Exchange with Creon (1582–1709) and Lyric Tailpiece (1710–1766)

The duet of Antigone and Oedipus is brought to an abrupt end by Creon, who calls for an end to piteous wailing (οἴκτων μὲν ἤδη λήγεθ', 1584). In the

---

[83] Dickin 2009.

iambic scene that follows, Antigone completes her transition from sheltered maiden to become the active and mature head of what remains of her family. Over the course of the play, attempts to confine Antigone to a traditional role have failed; here she definitively abandons the prospect of marriage to Haemon, competes with the king about questions of justice, and convinces her father to accept her help. Once she has taken upon herself the role of attendant and guide, her solidarity with Oedipus is expressed by a final return to lyric.

Oedipus, banished from Thebes, wonders who will guide him: the logical options, Jocasta, Eteocles, and Polyneices, all lie dead (1616–1618). He does not mention Antigone as a possibility. At this point, where resolution seems impossible, Antigone interrupts the conversation of the two men to express her own views. She challenges Creon's right to pass decrees on members of her family (1639–1645) and enters into an argument with him about the fate of her brother's corpse (1646–1682). The issue remains unresolved; when Creon departs, the focus shifts from the matter of burial to the more pressing question of whether Antigone will accompany Oedipus into exile. The ensuing conversation between father and daughter is accepted as genuine by almost all editors; we are therefore on surer ground in our interpretation. In iambic dialogue Antigone convinces Oedipus by degrees to accept her as his companion in exile. At first Oedipus tries to dissuade his daughter, saying that such an action would be shameful (αἰσχρά, 1691). She opposes him, contending that in fact if done with modesty, the action would be noble (γενναία, 1692). After he has physically acknowledged the dead, Oedipus at last openly asks Antigone to accompany him and minister to him in exile (1707–1709).

Once this conclusion has been reached, father and daughter sing a final duet in iambo-trochiac meter.[84] This song accompanies the characters from the stage and brings to a pathetic close the themes of exile, wandering, and weakness that have been prominent throughout the play. The song contains familiar motifs of mourning: Antigone urges her father to go forth into wretched exile (ἴθ'ἐσ φυγὰν τάλαιναν, 1710), while he refers to himself as "wandering in miserable exile" (δυστυχεστάτας φύγας ἀλαίνειν, 1723–1724); father and daughter are both "unhappy" (ἀθλία, 1715; ἄθλιοι, 1716) and have suffered terrible things (δεινὰ δείν', 1725); and Oedipus walks "like

---

[84] Mastronarde 1994: ad 1710–1766. A modulation from trimeter to a higher metrical register is not uncommon at the end of a tragedy; for example, Aeschylus' *Persians*, *Seven Against Thebes*, *Suppliants*, and *Eumenides* and Sophocles' *Antigone* and *Oedipus at Colonus*. To conclude other plays Euripides uses actor's anapests (*Medea*, *Electra*, *Orestes*, *Bacchae*), trochaic tetrameters (*Ion*), or solo actor's song in response with the chorus (*Hecuba*).

a dream in strength" (ὥστ' ὄνειρον ἰσχύν, 1722). These final lines of song complete the ring composition of the lyric scenes of the play, as Antigone, who entered by grasping the proffered hand of the Old Servant, here stretches forth her own hand to help her aged father (ὄρεγε χέρα φίλαν, 1710).

I am in agreement with the majority of editors who consider nearly the last twenty-five lines of the play to be spurious (1737–1763).[85] In the passage as it stands, Antigone again laments the maidenly pursuits she has left behind (ἀπαρθένευτ', 1739), declares that her loyalty to her father has given her glory (1741–1742), and predicts her own death as punishment for burying the body of Polyneices (1743–1746). Oedipus, in his lines, advises Antigone to go to the sacred precinct of Dionysus in the mountains (1751–1752) and mourns the fall of his fortunes (1758–1763). These sentiments, except for the novel suggestion that Antigone become a maenad, have been expressed already in the course of the *exodos*, and neither add to nor detract from the emotional impact of the scene. If genuine, they continue the theme of Antigone's maturation: she looks back to the life she has left behind and forward to her new role as the helper of her father. Yet for our purposes, the authenticity of these lines is of minimal consequence; whether at line 1736 or at line 1763, the play ends with actor's lyric.[86] The final scene belongs to Oedipus and Antigone, whose shared grief and shared strength in the face of that grief, expressed through song, brings the play to its intimate conclusion.

3.8 Conclusion

In this play, perhaps more than any other extant work, Euripides experiments with monody as a poetic form. Structurally and thematically, the four scenes of actor's lyric in *Phoenician Women* unify an intricate plot by marking the devolution of the play from anxiety and tentative hope to despair and mourning, and finally to a partial resolution founded on the shared suffering of Antigone and Oedipus. Each scene serves a discrete function as required by its particular context and expands the bounds of

---

[85] Mastronarde 1994: ad 1736–1757.
[86] Dunn 1996 has explored the ways in which Euripides in *Phoenician Women* becomes immersed in the difficulties of seeing or choosing an ending; the play lacks the gestures of closure familiar from Euripides' other works (e.g., a god or prophecy) and the final scene is open and inconclusive. What closure there is comes, I think, from the formal ring composition provided by the duet of father and daughter.

monody in new ways. In the *teichoskopia*, Euripides composes an epirrhematic dialogue that moves toward independent monody; the emotional state of Antigone in her innocence stands out against the backdrop of similar scenes in earlier literature, establishing an initial position of naïveté that will contrast with her suffering and knowledge in the *exodos*. Jocasta's monody raises hopes of a musical reunion scene only to disappoint them, leaving her isolated in fearful anticipation. Over 1,000 lines later, the fateful horror that Jocasta tried to ward off has come home at last; through comparison with mythological figures, Antigone in her monody declares herself to be unique in the nature and extent of her pain. Finally, in the paired duets of Antigone and Oedipus, the *disiecta membra* of the house are gathered together through shared song. Antigone steps beyond her sole suffering by taking upon herself the dual roles of messenger and comforter to her father. Thus, in giving voice to the disorder at the heart of the city, the four scenes of lyric by the actors paradoxically create a superordinate coherence within the play itself.

4 | Orestes

Monody As Messenger Speech

Orestes, produced in 408 BCE, further expands the boundaries of monody as a versatile dramatic form.[1] The percentage of song delivered by actors in *Orestes* is the highest for all extant Greek tragedy.[2] In a play of 1,693 lines, the chorus sing only two brief odes (316–347, 807–843). By contrast, nearly three quarters of the music of the play is delivered by actors, culminating in an extended monody by an anonymous, enslaved Phrygian.[3] The Phrygian's monody is the longest in extant tragedy, covering 133 lines of text in six astrophic sections.[4] This monody, I will argue, overturns the expectations of the audience through its unprecedented combination of the traditionally antithetical genres of monody and messenger speech. Operating as a virtual microcosmic play-within-a-play, the song creates an atmosphere within which themes of pervasive uncertainty and unease will flower. Accordingly, it is to the Phrygian's monody that this chapter will devote most of its attention.

As Peter Euben has written, the plot of *Orestes* "develops with explosive shifts of mood and attitude. So discordant are the episodes in themselves and in relation to one another, and so agitated are the speeches and the speakers, that the play threatens to disintegrate entirely."[5] In a play that consistently violates conventions and expectations of dramatic form, the monody of the Phrygian constitutes a crisis. As I will demonstrate, Euripides has primed the audience to expect a messenger speech. Accordingly, they come to the scene with specific expectations about what type of information it will contain and about the manner in which this information will be conveyed, only to find that the Phrygian is

---

[1] For dating, see Willink 1986: xxii.
[2] Csapo 1999–2000: 413; 68.2 percent of the music in the play is delivered by the actors or 72.6 percent if recitative is included. The play is quite long, but the total percentage that is in lyric (22.9 percent, or 31.1 percent including recitative) is on par with Euripides' other works of this period.
[3] If we accept Electra's monody as genuine; discussed further on pp. 159–160.
[4] The Phrygian's song is interrupted six times by one-line interjections in iambic trimeter from the chorus, but because of the continuity between the different sections I follow de Poli 2011: 293–316 in classifying it as a single monody rather than an *epirrhematic* dialogue.
[5] Euben 1986: 237–238.

completely unsuited to filling this role. By combining the *Bauformen* of monody and messenger speech, the playwright sets up a number of obstacles that prevent knowledge of "the facts" of what happened. Any desire for a straightforward progression, for the presentation of information in a satisfactory and unified way, is denied. Seen in this light, the disjointed, aporetic monody is of a piece with the rest of the play; it exposes more clearly than any other scene the widening gap between words and their meanings. The whole play thus emerges as deeply "polyphonic," a set of contradictions that defy simple resolution. By removing the omniscience of the spectators, the playwright draws the audience together with the characters of the tragedy in their groping search for purpose, coherence, and understanding.

Much criticism of *Orestes* has focused on the divided nature of the plot.[6] The first third of the play (1–724) describes an attempted rescue: Orestes and Electra wait as suppliants for their expected savior, Menelaus. When Menelaus proves unable to stay the execution of his niece and nephew, the middle of the play (725–1097) constitutes a second major dramatic movement, developing by contrast an example of loyal friendship, as Pylades pledges his support to the siblings. The opening two thirds of the play – or the long first half – thus present an unorthodox version of the aftermath of Orestes' killing of his mother Clytemnestra. However, after Orestes is sentenced to death by the Argive assembly at the beginning of the fourth episode, the plot takes an unexpected turn, introducing a completely different movement, the plan for revenge (1098–1690). Orestes, Pylades, and Electra resolve on desperate, violent action: to kidnap and kill Helen or die trying. This chain of events appears to be completely Euripides' invention.[7] As Froma Zeitlin has written, here the play "attempts to escape its mythic frame and freely formulate its own actions and reactions."[8] It is at this climactic moment of tension and uncertainty that Euripides introduces the singing Phrygian.

Whereas in *Phoenician Women* the placement of solo actor's lyric lent shape and unity to an apparently disordered plot, in *Orestes* Euripides skillfully plays upon the precedent built up by the music in the first portion of the play to make the tour de force of the Phrygian's monody all the more shocking. In the scenes antecedent to the Phrygian's appearance, the use of

---

[6] Conacher 1967: 213–214 argues for a tripartite division, as does Mastronarde 2010: 83–85. By contrast, Wright 2008, Encinas Reguero 2011, and Wohl 2015: 118–120 trace a two-part structure, with a transition marked by the plan to kill Helen.
[7] On originality, see Winnington-Ingram 1969; Arnott 1973 and 1983; Fuqua 1978.
[8] Zeitlin 1980: 53.

familiar musical forms sets up a contrast with the monody that will follow. The chorus of Argive women reflect on the history and sufferings of the royal house, following the example of the female choruses of many of Euripides' earlier plays.[9] Their two odes are extremely short; in total, the songs of the chorus make up only sixty-seven lines, half the length of the Phrygian's monody. In the first ode, the chorus pray that the Erinyes will be appeased, while in the second they comment on the instability of human fortune as illustrated by the Tantalids. Despite their poetic beauty and thematic import, these songs hardly present a novel understanding of the house's calamity.[10]

The scenes where the actor playing Electra sings also conform to a recognizable pattern. The *parodos* takes the form of an *amoibaion* between Electra and the chorus (140–207). In her monody, assuming that it is genuine, Electra mourns her own and the house's woes (960–1012).[11] This arrangement, where a female figure sings first in alternation with a sympathetic female chorus and then later delivers a monody of lament, is recognizable from other plays and matches almost exactly the pattern we observed in the previous chapter on *Iphigenia among the Taurians*. Indeed, a lyric role of lamentation seems to be typical of Electra as a figure on the stage; Electra sings in every one of her appearances in extant tragedy, always early in the play and in alternation with a female chorus.[12] In

---

[9] For instance, those of *Medea, Hippolytus, Trojan Women, Andromache, Hecuba, Electra, Helen,* and *Phoenician Women*.

[10] Critics have tended to dismiss the relevance of the choral odes to the main action of the drama, beginning with the declaration of Verrall 1905: 216 that "of the Chorus we need say little, and would gladly say nothing." An important reevaluation of the odes may be found in Fuqua 1978, who explores the ways in which the choral songs are integrated with the main action of the drama through their sophisticated mythological references.

[11] Some scholars have argued that the lyric lines assigned to Electra at 960–1012 are not in fact a monody but a choral ode adapted for a solo singer at a later date. Biehl 1965, West [1987] 2007, and Damen 1990 consider the passage a choral song, while de Poli 2012: 28–29 treats the song as a monody, supported by Raffa 2016. On actors' interpolations in tragedy, compare Page 1934 and Hamilton 1974. The argument for a choral attribution is well supported but does not vitiate our major point: all possible assignations of the song – to Electra, to the chorus, or to both – resemble traditional musical structures. If the song were a monody, it would be familiar because of Electra's role as a singer of lamentations in the plays of Aeschylus, Sophocles, prior Euripides, and, presumably, other fifth-century tragedians. If the song were a choral ode, it would be orthodox in its position as an act-dividing song, in its metrical structure of strophe, antistrophe, and epode, and in its dependence on tropes of lamentation (960–970), the workings of divine envy (φθόνος, 974), and longed-for escape (982–986). Finally, if the song were a duet shared by Electra and the chorus, it would mirror the pattern of the *parodos* in this very play, where the heroine and the women of the house also bewail in alternation the woes of the royal family. In all three cases the song would be of a piece with the earlier lyric scenes in defining a traditional structure for the opening two thirds of *Orestes*.

[12] Compare Hall 1999: 115–116 on figures who are "pre-programmed" to sing in tragedy and Loraux [1999] 2002 on Electra as a mourner in the plays of Aeschylus and Sophocles. In

Orestes, then, Electra's opening *amoibaion* with the chorus and subsequent monody of lament would conform to an audience's expectation of her role.

The *parodos*, the first stasimon, and the monody of Electra constitute the entire musical contribution of the first two thirds of the play. Thus far, Euripides has hewed to predictable musical forms. But after Electra's monody, at the beginning of the fourth episode, all expectations are overturned. As Zeitlin writes, in the last movement of the play, the characters, "casting about for a totally novel device to break the claustrophobic deadlock of their earlier efforts to cope with the stubborn refusal of circumstances to conform to the mythic paradigm, resort to a series of other scripts."[13] This is true especially for the musical scripts of the tragedy: the usually mournful Electra takes on a new role as a vengeful Fury, calling down destruction upon her own house and family in song; and the monody of the Phrygian is a *coup de théâtre* unparalleled by anything in the extant tragic corpus. What, given this radical shift in register, knits together the tonally and formally disparate elements of the play?

4.1 The Monody of the Phrygian (1369–1502)

In an influential chapter, Shirley Barlow proposes that the dramatic modes of monody and messenger speech are diametrically opposed. Monody, Barlow argues, conveys through lyric the inner emotional state of a single figure, while in a messenger speech the personality of the speaker is suppressed in the service of a clear account of fact. Barlow finds this difference articulated in particular through imagery:

> Where imagery in monody conveys the irrational and subjective attitudes which characterize the singer of that monody, that of the messenger must seem to convey a rational account of objective fact, the existence of which has nothing to do with him personally, except in the sense that he happened to observe it .... Stylistically, [the mode of the messenger speech] bears the same relation to lyric imagery as a black and white etching to a painting.[14]

Sophocles' *Electra*, Electra sings an opening monody (86–120) and then a lyric *amoibaion* with the chorus (121–125). Perhaps it is no coincidence that this play featuring Electra has the highest percentage of music delivered by actors in the extant works of Sophocles, given by Csapo 1999–2000 as 5.2 percent. Similarly, in Euripides' *Electra*, Electra sings first by herself (112–167) and then in alternation with the chorus (167–212) in the *parodos*.

[13] Zeitlin 1980: 58. See Hall 1993 on the political and cosmic turbulence of the play.
[14] Barlow 1971: 61.

What is the effect, then, when we encounter a monody that is simultaneously a messenger speech? The impact of the Phrygian's monody depends first on its similarity to traditional messenger speeches; against this backdrop, the differences inherent in the lyric mode stand out more clearly. This hybrid – of speech and song, narration and emotion, objectivity and subjectivity – has profound implications for our understanding of the play as a whole. The composite of monody and messenger speech temporarily stops the urgent, accelerating plot in its tracks. The levels of irony thus created force the audience into an active position, where they must decide for themselves which, if any, of the play's competing voices can claim authority.

The monody of the Phrygian has been criticized for its "outlandish novelty" and, on the other hand, defended as a carefully structured and coherent scene.[15] I hope to show that any reading of the monody is enriched by exploring the ways in which Euripides self-consciously engages with conventions of messenger speeches elsewhere in Greek tragedy including in his own works. There are approximately thirty-six messenger speeches in the extant tragic corpus.[16] Every play by Euripides – with the exception of *Trojan Women* – contains at least one messenger speech, while several contain two or more.[17] Some scholars, such as J. M. Bremer and Malcolm Heath, have expanded upon Barlow's view of the messenger speech as an impartial means of conveying information that the audience is meant to accept as true.[18] Others, such as Irene de Jong and James Barrett, have sought to complicate this picture.[19] De Jong, a narratologist, argues against functionalist views and posits that messenger speeches subtly characterize the figures who deliver them; the speeches are produced by individuals, all of whom have loyalties and judgments that are evident in their words and influence the way in which they convey their news.[20] For de Jong, "No narrative is ever objective."[21]

---

[15] Porter 1994: 173–213.
[16] On messengers, see di Gregorio 1967, Bremer 1976, Heath 1987, de Jong 1991, Barrett 2002, and Dickin 2009.
[17] Barrett 2002: 223–224. The plays containing multiple messenger speeches are Sophocles' *Antigone* and *Trachiniae* and Euripides' *Bacchae*, *Helen*, *Iphigenia among the Taurians*, *Orestes*, *Phoenician Women*, and *Rhesus*.
[18] Bremer 1976; Heath 1987.
[19] De Jong 1991; Barrett 2002. Yoon 2012 in her work on anonymous figures in tragedy omits discussion of messengers entirely; her analysis of the Phrygian focuses on the stichomythic scene with Orestes, where she sees the slave as a foil who calls into question the morality and heroism of the protagonist: "It is the state of the tormenter, not the victim, that is of interest" (82). Yet Yoon's analysis of figures who are free of determination by the mythical tradition may be brought to bear on the question of the messenger's perceived objectivity.
[20] De Jong 1991: 29–40. Her remarks are especially pertinent in the case of "false" messengers, such as Lichas in *Trachiniae* and the Paidagogos in Sophocles' *Electra*.
[21] De Jong 1991: 60.

Barrett has proposed that the narrative voice of the messenger closely resembles that of the epic poet, and that this appropriation of Homeric form conveys powerful authority upon the speaker.[22] As messenger speeches constitute tragedy's most sustained employment of extended narrative, Barrett suggests, they engage with contemporary philosophical discourse on language, persuasion, rhetoric, and truth.

All these scholars agree that a messenger speech in tragedy has certain defining features as a *Bauform*: it is a long, continuous speech in iambic trimeter, in which a figure who does not feature prominently in other scenes of the play reports as a witness on events that have taken place offstage. Messenger speeches contain a high proportion of third-person "narrative verbs" in the aorist, imperfect, and pluperfect tenses; usually, iambic dialogue involving the messenger precedes the speech itself. Both de Jong and Barrett include the monody of the Phrygian in appendices listing all the messenger speeches in Greek tragedy, but neither discusses the scene in any detail. Barrett acknowledges that as a messenger the Phrygian "hardly performs according to conventional expectations."[23] This is an understatement: the Phrygian contradicts in almost every particular Barrett's theory of the messenger as an omniscient and emotionally detached epic narrator embedded in the tragic text.[24] And of course the Phrygian violates the central tenet of the definition of the *Bauform* in that he delivers in place of a speech in iambic trimeter a long, semicontinuous *song* in an unparalleled variety of lyric meters.

It is this very refusal to conform to expectations, this violation of formal constraints, I suggest, that constitutes the "message" of this unconventional messenger. The monody of the Phrygian derives its dramatic power from the conflict between narrative objectivity and the subjectivity of lyric. The Phrygian conveys essential information, but in an emotional, agitated, disorganized, and distorted manner; his wishes and fears are overlaid upon the bare facts of what happened. Thus he tells two tales simultaneously, and the audience must look through one properly to decipher the other. Throughout the monody we are led to seek beyond the words of the Phrygian for an account that is different and less prejudiced.

---

[22] Barrett 2002: xvii.
[23] Barrett 2002: 223. Similarly, Perris 2011: 2 writes that "perhaps the main barrier to [the Phrygian's] fully-fledged membership in the messenger's club is his rather *outré* decision to sing."
[24] Seidensticker 1982: 114 sees the scene as a caricature of a messenger speech; to me, Euripides' handling of the conventions does not seem purely parodic in intention or effect.

Yet this less prejudiced account never appears. What really happened to Helen? The monodic messenger speech of the Phrygian instantiates in lyric form the radical critique of objectivity and truth that has marked the play from its opening scenes. As Victoria Wohl has described, "there is an air of hallucinatory madness to the entire play: here all the characters are weak or hateful; the gods are absent or unjust; the ideals of Athenian society debased and perverted."[25] In line with these other ambiguities, the playwright leaves the audience in doubt as to Helen's fate for more than 300 lines, from the moment when her cries are heard from within the house at line 1296 until the epiphany of Apollo at line 1625. And when Apollo appears on high at the end of the play to announce Helen's deification, the mystery remains. If Helen is now a goddess, as Apollo declares, then she is no longer "alive," no longer among mortals as the wife of Menelaus and the mother of Hermione. She is both dead and not dead. In retrospect, the Phrygian's report approaches the truth more nearly than Euripides led the audience to believe. The Phrygian is in this way akin to a riddling oracle, directing and misdirecting the attention of the spectators through the competing voices at work in his monody.

Euripides' use of the form of monody is all the more unsettling because the Phrygian does conform to many of the conventions associated with messengers elsewhere in the corpus of Euripides. He is enslaved and a member of the royal retinue, which places him in the company of the messengers of, for instance, *Medea, Ion, Helen, Bacchae*, and *Iphigenia among the Taurians*.[26] He is anonymous and appears only in this scene. He declares that he has been an eyewitness to the events he now relates and explains his position vis-à-vis the action.[27] He reiterates his claim to autopsy through first-person verbs and vocabulary emphasizing sight and vision. He reports action that has taken place offstage to ignorant listeners who are eager to hear the outcome of his story. With the glaring exceptions of his mode of delivery and his failure to declare plainly what actually happened, he fulfills the expected role of messenger.

Euripides has carefully crafted the circumstances that precede the monody so that the audience will anticipate a messenger speech. Orestes and Pylades enter the palace, intent upon the murder of Helen (1216–1245). Electra and the chorus are stationed outside as guards (1246–1295). Then, from within the house, the voice of Helen is heard: she twice cries out that

---

[25] Wohl 2015: 119.   [26] Barrett 2002: 99.   [27] Barrett 2002: 74.

she is being murdered, in words that suggest a violent death: "I am terribly destroyed" (ὄλλυμαι κακῶς, 1296) and, even more explicitly, "I am dying" (θνῄσκω, 1301). In other tragedies, most famously at the moment when the king is murdered in Aeschylus' *Agamemnon*, such cries faithfully convey what is happening offstage.[28] Electra's short, savage song of triumph encourages Orestes and Pylades in their bloody work (1302–1310). A potential obstacle appears in the form of Hermione, but, deceived by Electra, she too walks into the snare (1313–1335).

All these details indicate that the conspirators stand victorious: Helen is dead, Hermione taken prisoner. In a short strophe, the chorus hope that none of the Argives will arrive before they receive conclusive proof of what has happened:

πρὶν ἐτύμως ἴδω τὸν Ἑλένας φόνον
καθαιμακτὸν ἐν δόμοις κείμενον,
ἢ καὶ λόγον του προσπόλων πυθώμεθα· (1357–1359)

Before I truly see the slaughter of Helen
lying bloody within the house,
or even hear the speech of one of the servants.

The words of the chorus virtually promise one of two possibilities: either the corpse of Helen will be displayed on the *ekkyklema*, the wheeled platform used to reveal interior scenes in tragedy ("before I see the slaughter of Helen/lying bloody within the house"), or an attendant will shortly appear to deliver a messenger speech ("or even hear the speech of one of the servants"). The impression that the climactic event has already taken place is reinforced by the last lines of the song, where the chorus declare that justice has been served, using a verb in a past tense (ἔβα, 1361):

διὰ δίκας ἔβα θεῶν
νέμεσις ἐς Ἑλέναν.
δακρύοισι γὰρ Ἑλλάδ' ἅπασαν ἔπλησε,
διὰ τὸν ὀλόμενον ὀλόμενον Ἰδαῖον
Πάριν, ὃς ἄγαγ' Ἑλλάδ' εἰς Ἴλιον. (1361–1365)

By justice the vengeance
of the gods has come upon Helen;
for she filled all of Hellas with tears,
through the accursed, accursed Paris of Ida,
who led Hellas to Ilion.

---

[28] Aeschylus, *Agamemnon* 1343, 1345. In Euripides' *Hecuba*, the cries of the king Polymestor as he is blinded may recall these well-known lines (1035–1038); see Collard 1991a and 1991b.

4.1 The Monody of the Phrygian (1369–1502)

Their song seemingly complete, the chorus anticipate a new scene: "What are the doors about to disclose?" (1366). But there is no tableau on the *ekkyklema* or trustworthy messenger in the style of the peasant who appears earlier in the play. Instead, a nameless, terrified barbarian emerges suddenly from the palace. In his agitated solo song and dance he tantalizingly promises and delays the true account that the chorus, Electra, and the audience await.

The monody begins *in medias res*, the Phrygian still fearing for his life:

> Ἀργεῖον ξίφος ἐκ θανάτου
> πέφευγα βαρβάροις ἐν εὐμάρισιν,
> κεδρωτὰ παστάδων ὑπὲρ τέραμνα
> Δωρικάς τε τριγλύφους,
> φροῦδα φροῦδα, Γᾶ Γᾶ,
> βαρβάροισι δρασμοῖς.
> αἰαῖ· πᾷ φύγω, ξέναι, πολιὸν αἰθέρ' ἀμπτάμενος ἢ   1375/1376
> πόντον, Ὠκεανὸς ὃν
> ταυρόκρανος ἀγκάλαις
> ἑλίσσων κυκλοῖ χθόνα;   (1369–1379)

> I have fled from the death of an Argive sword
> in barbarian slippers of deerskin,
> above the cedar beams of the porch
> and the Doric cornices,
> gone, gone, Earth, Earth,
> in barbarian escapes.
> Alas!
> Where may I flee, foreign women, flying up to the bright air
> or to the sea, which bull-headed Ocean
> encircles, whirling the land in his embraces?

As we have seen, the last lines of the chorus in the previous scene set up a series of expectations associated with the messenger speech as a *Bauform* of tragedy.[29] The abrupt appearance of the Phrygian strikes the first blow against these expectations. The exact manner of his entrance has been the subject of much debate.[30] Certainly its main effect is to shock and amaze.[31]

---

[29] Perris 2011: 4 summarizes the conventional format for introducing a messenger speech: "the reporter announces his arrival, sometimes asking the whereabouts of his intended addressee; the reporter makes a general statement of affairs; the addressee asks what has happened; the speaker sums up the specific event, often in a stichomythic exchange; and the addressee requests a detailed description, often with a πῶς question."

[30] See Dale 1969: 268–269; Willink 1986: ad 1366–1368; West [1987] 2007: ad 1366–1368; Porter 1994: 192–199.

[31] Halleran 1985: 48 n. 18.

Does the Phrygian enter at a run from the palace doors or daringly leap from the roof of the *skene* building? There is an apparent contradiction: the words of the chorus (1366–1368) indicate that the doors of the palace are rattling, and that someone will soon open them and emerge, but the Phrygian seems to say that he has escaped by way of the roof, not by the front door (1371–1372). An ancient scholiast maintains that in the original production the Phrygian jumped from the roof of the *skene* but that later actors inserted the explanatory lines of the chorus to avoid the hazard of this unconventional entrance; other ancient commentators argue that the Phrygian's words should be interpreted differently, and that he refers to a roof inside the palace that is not visible to the audience.[32] Modern scholars have defended both positions.[33] My own view is that the entrance indeed takes place via the roof of the *skene* building; an ingenious theatrical professional, as Euripides certainly was, could contrive technical means to ensure the safety of the actor.[34] Like the appearance of Medea on the chariot of the Sun in Euripides' *Medea*, the effect of such an unconventional entrance would be powerful and would immediately signal that this messenger is in a class of his own.

The first section of the monody serves to establish immediately some basic features of the singer, chief among them his subjectivity as a narrator. Euripides combines conventions drawn from three areas: the stereotypical portrait of a cowardly and deceitful barbarian, the poetic inventiveness of a lyric singer, and the presumed objectivity of a messenger. In performance, the costume, mask, and gestures of the actor would offer immediate clues as to the rank, ethnicity, and emotional state of this unnamed figure. He is a foreigner, enslaved, and a eunuch, a character marked as "queer" who subverts many institutionalized forms and categories.[35] In the vocabulary, imagery, and diction of his opening passage, the Phrygian conforms to many of the conventional features of barbarians on the Greek tragic stage.[36]

---

[32] For the *scholion* and other ancient testimony, see Porter 1994: 193.

[33] West [1987] 2007: ad 1366–1368 and Mastronarde 1990 offer some suggestions.

[34] When I directed this play in 2018, the actor playing the Phrygian leapt from the very low wall of a garden, only to boast of its great height, to general laughter; see Catenaccio 2019.

[35] This may be inferred from Orestes' comment that he is neither a woman nor a man (1528). The explicit term εὐνοῦχος is nowhere used. A possible model for Euripides' choice here may be found in Phrynicus' lost play *Phoenician Women* (476 BCE), which was set in Persia and dealt with the aftermath of the battle of Salamis; the Persian defeat was reported in the first scene by a eunuch. Compare TrGF I F 8–12 and Garvie 2009: ix–xii. On the "queerness" of the Phrygian, see Youd 2022.

[36] The concept of the barbarian as "other" on the Greek stage has been discussed in particular by Hall 1989: 121–133, who argues that the tragic "discourse of the barbarian" was essential to the formation of civic ideology in Athens in the fifth century. The topic is revisited in Hall 2006:

His barbarian slippers (βαρβάροις ἐν εὐμάρισιν, 1370) and his barbarian flight (βαρβάροισι δρασμοῖς, 1374) typify him as luxury-loving, effeminate, and cowardly.[37] The term εὔμαρις denotes an Asiatic shoe made of deerskin and gives an exotic flavor to his opening lines.[38] The repetition of individual words (φροῦδα φροῦδα, Γᾶ Γᾶ, 1373) and extrametrical cry (αἰαῖ, 1375) emphasize his excessive emotionality.[39] The meter – a complex mixture of dactylic, iambic, bacchic, cretic, and ithyphallic elements – conveys his extreme agitation.[40] The initial impression is of a figure completely overwhelmed by terror and unable to deliver a clear account of what has happened.

Yet the very urgency of the Phrygian's opening words is undercut by descriptive detail. In eleven lines he uses only one verb to describe an actual event (πέφευγα, 1370), surrounded by seven adjectives and a metaphor personifying the ocean that surrounds the earth. As I noted earlier, a high frequency of "narrative verbs" (third-person verbs in the aorist, imperfect, and pluperfect tenses) is a defining feature of the conventional messenger speech; their absence here signals that the Phrygian is not performing his expected role.[41] A wish to escape the present situation is a familiar *topos* from Euripidean lyric, in all other cases delivered by a female singer or a female chorus, further aligning the Phrygian with women rather than men.[42] Such elaborate descriptive language is unprecedented for a messenger and unusual even for a monodist. Unlike, for instance, Creusa's vivid evocation of Apollo in her monody in *Ion*, where the precise and personally meaningful image of the god's shining hair conveys the mixture of awe and horror that she felt at the time of his attack, here the Phrygian's desire to escape is expressed in conventional and ornamental terms drawing on the language of choral lyric.

184–224. On barbarians and alterity in Greek literature, see also Bacon 1961; Seidensticker 1982; Saïd 1984; Long 1986; de Romilly 1993; Harrison 2002 and 2020; Lefkowitz 2022; and Papadodima 2022.

[37] On the Phrygian's gender, see line 1528. A female messenger would be highly unusual: among tragic messengers, only the Nurse in Sophocles' *Trachiniae* and the servant in Euripides' *Alcestis* are female. The cowardice of barbarians was a popular *topos* in comedy; see Long 1986: 141.

[38] Darius' ghost wears yellow sandals in Aeschylus' *Persians* (εὐμάριδες, 660). On Dorian dress in tragedy, see Battezzato 1999.

[39] Hall 1989: 119 comments that this is the most extensive use of lyric repetition by a barbarian in tragedy.

[40] For metrical analysis, see de Poli 2011: 293–316. Holzman 2016 describes the mixture of rhythms, styles, and instruments typical of actual Phrygian music during this period.

[41] Dickin 2009.

[42] For example, *Hippolytus* 732–741, *Iphigenia among the Taurians* 1138–1142, and *Bacchae* 402–416; compare *Orestes* 982–987.

In addition to the confluence of roles, in the Phrygian's opening lines we are confronted with several anomalous features that at times reinforce and at times subvert the conventions associated with a messenger speech. First, the Phrygian does not come out of the palace with the intention of relating the news of Helen's disappearance; he must be guided into the role of messenger by the chorus. After his first lyric passage, the chorus interrupt to ask for clear information (τί δ' ἔστιν, Ἑλένης πρόσπολ', Ἰδαῖον κάρα; 1380). As he continues in his song, they again request a narrative that is "clear" and moves through "each thing" in sequence (σαφῶς λέγ' ἡμῖν αὖθ' ἕκαστα τἀν δόμοις, 1393). The chorus is as frustrated as the audience in their expectations: the Phrygian refuses to conform to a standard pattern.

Second, the principal news that the Phrygian reports, the mysterious disappearance of Helen, is withheld until the very end of his song. In all other messenger speeches in extant tragedy, the outcome of events is made known to the spectators in advance of the messenger's extended account.[43] The punchline comes first. In this same play, for instance, the peasant who delivers the first messenger speech at once declares to Electra and the chorus, who are waiting anxiously for news, that the Pelasgians have voted for a penalty of death (857–858). The exchange is explicit, using programmatic words that identify the *Bauform* that is about to take place, for example "messenger" (ἄγγελος) and "speech, account" (λόγος), here emphasized in bold:

Χορός	Πυλάδης, ἔοικε δ' οὐ μακρὰν **ὅδ' ἄγγελος λέξειν** τὰ κεῖθεν σοῦ κασιγνήτου πέρι.
Ἄγγελος	ὦ τλῆμον, ὦ δύστηνε τοῦ στρατηλάτου Ἀγαμέμνονος παῖ, πότνι' Ἠλέκτρα, **λόγους** ἄκουσον οὕς σοι δυστυχεῖς ἥκω φέρων.
Ἠλέκτρα	αἰαῖ, διοιχόμεσθα: δῆλος εἶ **λόγῳ**. κακῶν γὰρ ἥκεις, ὡς ἔοικεν, **ἄγγελος**.
Ἄγγελος	ψήφῳ Πελασγῶν σὸν κασίγνητον θανεῖν καὶ σέ, ὦ τάλαιν', ἔδοξε τῇδ' ἐν ἡμέρᾳ. (850–858)

---

[43] De Jong 1991: 32.

4.1 The Monody of the Phrygian (1369–1502)

Chorus: Pylades, it seems that **this messenger** will soon
report what took place there concerning your brother.

Messenger: Wretched woman, unhappy daughter of the general
Agamemnon, my lady Electra, hear the unhappy **report**
that I have come to bring you.

Electra: Alas! We are ruined. You are clear **in your report**.
For you are a **messenger**, it seems, of evil tidings.

Messenger: It has been decided by the vote of the Pelasgians
that you and your brother are to die on this day.

The basic news is delivered in a straightforward couplet at the end of the exchange: the Pelasgians have decided that the two children of Agamemnon must die, at once. The rustic messenger then explains and elaborates on this central point. Not so with the Phrygian. The crucial piece of information – that Helen has inexplicably vanished – is not disclosed until the final lines of the monody. And until this revelation, it is impossible to separate extraneous details in the Phrygian's account from the item of greatest consequence for the action of the play.

A third incongruous element is that the song of the Phrygian presents information that is not already known from another source. This is typical of a messenger, but not of a monodist. In other plays, monodists sing of their woes and relate in detail the history of their sorrows, often including a degree of narrative. Usually, however, the audience is already familiar with the general outline of events from a prologue or from another earlier scene in the play. Again, the parallel case of Creusa's monody in *Ion* is instructive: there, Creusa in her monody recapitulates information already conveyed by Hermes in the prologue. As we saw in Chapter 1, Creusa's account does provide new details, but the song's principal contribution lies in its expression of Creusa's emotional torment, both at the time of the rape and in her present moment of grief. Here the Phrygian relates information that is new to the chorus, new to Electra, new to the audience, and, it turns out, new even to Orestes, who in the next scene seems to think that he has actually succeeded in killing Helen (1512, 1354). The onstage and offstage audiences are united in their ignorance of what is presented in the monody, making the frustrating delays, inconsistencies, and misdirection of the Phrygian's song a matter of the utmost importance.

To sum up the discussion thus far, the lines preceding the entrance of the Phrygian set up the expectation of a messenger speech; instead, the first passage of the monody is an elaborate song that displays the excessive emotionality of a barbarian, the lyrical ingenuity of a monodist, and the traditional *topoi* of a choral singer. Once he has taken his place on the stage, the Phrygian's aria extends over 133 lines of text, divided into six astrophic sections by the one-line interruptions of the chorus in iambic trimeter.[44] The first two passages of lyric borrow from the language, imagery, and metrical forms of other genres, combining conventions of monody, choral lyric, lament, and epic. These passages establish the identity of the singer and his multiple voices as a narrator. In the subsequent four passages of lyric, the Phrygian relates the events that took place inside the palace. By this point, however, the information that he presents has already been called into question; he is sympathetic to Helen and portrays Orestes and Pylades as military heroes, views in tension with earlier scenes in the play. The choice of narrator and of mode is inseparable from Euripides' decision that the deceptive, yet true, account of Helen's "death" should culminate in a cryptic "disappearance."[45] By undermining the clarity of the Phrygian's report from the beginning of the monody, Euripides contributes to the confusion surrounding the fate of Helen. What has happened, and how much can be believed?

In the second passage of the monody, Euripides departs still more from the conventions of the messenger speech by introducing elements drawn from lament, epic, and earlier tragedy. Shifts of tone are rapid: in a short space the song is charged with several attitudes, applicable to several subjects, and bearing the different weights of various allusions. For example, the Phrygian conflates his fear in the present crisis with grief for the homeland he has left behind:

> Ἴλιον Ἴλιον, ὤμοι μοι,
> Φρύγιον ἄστυ καὶ καλλίβωλον Ἴ-
> δας ὄρος ἱερόν, ὥς σ' ὀλόμενον στένω
> ἁρμάτειον ἁρμάτειον μέλος

---

[44] The chorus interject at 1380, 1393, 1425, 1453, and 1473. I follow West 2007 [1987] in marking line 1394, which is absent from many ancient copies of the play, as spurious. The six lyric passages of the Phrygian increase and then decrease in length: ten lines, eleven lines, twenty-nine lines, thirty-four lines, twenty-six lines, twenty-eight lines. Detailed discussion of the text and meters of the monody can be found in Biehl 1965 and de Poli 2011: 293–316. Several critics protest against the tendency to exaggerate the frenzy of the monody; compare Webster 1967: 17–20, Willink 1986: ad 1366–1502, and Porter 1994: 178–183.

[45] Given the multitude of myths that surround Helen, the audience could accept that she would in fact be saved by the gods, spirited away as her *eidolon* is in Euripides' *Helen*. The existence of the *eidolon* myth would further complicate expectations about Helen's fate in this play; see Wright 2006.

4.1 The Monody of the Phrygian (1369–1502)

> βαρβάρῳ βοᾷ διὰ τὸ τᾶσδ' ὀρνι-
> θόγονον ὄμμα κυκνοπτέρου
> καλλοσύνας, Λήδας σκύμνον, Δυσελένας Δυσελένας,
> ξεστῶν περγάμων Ἀπολλωνίων Ἐρινύν.   1388/1389a
> ὀττοτοῖ   1389b
> ἰαλέμων ἰαλέμων
> Δαρδανία τλάμων, Γανυμήδεος ἱπποσύ-
> να, Διὸς εὐνέτα.   (1381–1393)

> Ilion, Ilion, alas for me,
> the Phrygian city and the holy mountain
> of Ida with its lovely soil,
> how I groan for you, destroyed,
> – a chariot, chariot melody –
> with the barbarian cry
> because of the bird-begotten face
> of swan-plumed beauty,
> the cub of Leda,
> evil Helen, evil Helen,
> for the polished Apollonian towers
> an Erinys. *Ottotoi!*
> Wretched Dardania of dirges, of dirges,
> for the horsemanship of Ganymede,
> the bedfellow of Zeus.

Lamentation in tragedy is often figured as an act proper to barbarians and to women.[46] The features of lament in this passage align the Phrygian with other Trojan mourners in Greek literature, both monodic and choral. Solo singers include Andromache and Hecuba in the *Iliad* and Hecuba, Polyxena, and Cassandra in earlier tragedy. In this play there is no woman who could express the sorrow of the captured city; Helen, the only woman of Troy in Argos, is also the cause of the disaster, as the Phrygian acknowledges. Troy's sole mourner is an enslaved eunuch whose disjointed song is a far cry from the laments of previous monodic mourners, all female and all royal. Trojan choruses are featured in eleven of the surviving tragedies from the fifth century; in *Orestes*, the Phrygian takes on this choral role, but as a monodist.

This anonymous barbarian becomes the voice of grief for the loss of Troy, an event that has been in the background of the play but never before addressed directly and with sympathy. In this passage traditional aural

---

[46] See discussion in the Introduction, pp. 21–36. On lamentation and barbarians, see in particular Hall 1989: 83–84, 121–133; Foley 1993 and 2001: 21–29; Suter 2003 and 2008; Dué 2006: 30–56; Swift 2010: Nooter 2011; 298–367; and Weiss 2017.

features of lamentation are especially pronounced, particularly anadiplosis ("Ἴλιον Ἴλιον, 1381; ἁρμάτειον ἁρμάτειον, 1384; Δυσελένας Δυσελένας, 1387; ἰαλέμων ἰαλέμων, 1390) and pathetic exclamation (ὤμοι μοι, 1381; ὀττοτοῖ, 1389b).[47] There is only one verb, a first-person indicative in the present tense, explicitly establishing the context of mourning (στένω, 1383). The "chariot melody" (ἁρμάτειον μέλος, 1384) that the Phrygian claims to be singing is a traditional lyric form used by Stesichorus, delivered in a high register and associated with the music of the pipe; here the introduction of the technical term draws attention to the mode of the song and to the certain accompaniment of the *aulos*.[48] Euripides emphasizes simultaneously the matter expressed and the means of expression, generating a sense of estrangement through the shifts of tone, genre, and attitude within this single passage.

Some scholars have argued that meter, form, and content here come together to create an allusion to Cassandra in Aeschylus' *Agamemnon*.[49] The two figures are juxtaposed in various ways: like Cassandra, the Phrygian is a foreigner and enslaved, recently arrived from Troy, and both figures sing, predominantly in dochmiacs, to a frustrated and initially uncomprehending chorus.[50] But whereas Cassandra enters the palace to face certain death, the Phrygian has just escaped from the palace with his life; the riddling knowledge of the prophetess is countered by the account of the Phrygian, who cannot or will not see beyond his own fear. Cassandra's prophecies look back in time to past crimes and forward to her own death and the cycle of vengeance that will consume the house; the Phrygian knows nothing beyond what has just happened, and even about these events his testimony is uncertain. The evocation of Aeschylus' earlier play therefore creates a double effect: it connects the monody to other canonical

---

[47] Electra in the prologue discusses the Trojan War and the resentment it has occasioned among the Argives, mentioning Helen's reluctance to show herself before the fathers of those who died at Troy (56–62, 98).

[48] West 1987: ad 1384, with a longer treatment of Stesichorus in West 1971: 309–311. The *aulos* in tragedy has various associations ranging from sweet and joyous to mournful (cf. *Bacchae* 380 and 127–128, *Electra* 879, *Trojan Women* 126). The instrument is called Phrygian at *Bacchae* 127–128 and both Phrygian and barbarian at *Iphigenia in Aulis* 576–577. On the *aulos*, see Martin 2003; Wilson 1999; LeVen 2010 and 2014; Power 2010; and Holzman 2016.

[49] Zeitlin 1980: 59, Marshall 1996: 94, and Encinas Reguero 2011, contested by Porter 1994: 174 n. 4. Zeitlin 1980: 63 suggests that at the same time the Phrygian is "the inversion of Aeschylus' androgynous Clytemnestra."

[50] After the varied meters of his first lyric passage, the Phrygian settles into a principally dochmiac rhythm. For metrical analysis, see de Poli 2011: 293–316. The introduction of a dactylic rhythm emphasizes the epic resonances of lines 1381 (Ἴλιον Ἴλιον, ὤμοι μοι) and 1392–1393 (Δαρδανία τλάμων, Γανυμήδεος ἱπποσύνᾳ), with their Asiatic place-names and proper names.

narratives of the fall of Troy, while simultaneously emphasizing the break with tradition represented by this singer and his song.

The first two passages of lyric thus establish the Phrygian as the antithesis of the detached, objective messenger that the audience has been led to expect. In the subsequent four passages of lyric, the Phrygian describes what happened within the palace. Although the monody from this point on is predominantly narrative, the Phrygian never lays aside his subjectivity as a monodist. Indeed, this subjectivity is constantly emphasized by discrepancies, contradictions, and linguistic signals of prejudice and misprision. The orderly succession of events is interrupted by allusions to other genres and other myths. The seeming chaos that ensues creates a space where meaning can be created, not directly from the Phrygian's words but indirectly, through the tension between the different tones, references, and points of view in the passage.

After another interjection from the chorus, who again ask for a straightforward account of what took place in the house (1393–1394), the Phrygian begins his third passage of lyric:

> αἴλινον αἴλινον ἀρχὰν θανάτου
> βάρβαροι λέγουσιν,
> αἰαῖ, Ἀσιάδι φωνᾷ, βασιλέων
> ὅταν αἷμα χυθῇ κατὰ γᾶν ξίφεσιν
> σιδαρέοισιν Ἅιδα.
> ἦλθον ἐς δόμους,   1400a
> ἵν' αὖθ' ἕκαστά σοι λέγω,   1400b
> λέοντες Ἕλλανες δύο διδύμω·
> τῷ μὲν ὁ στρατηλάτας πατὴρ ἐκλῄζετο,
> ὁ δὲ παῖς Στροφίου, κακόμητις ἀνήρ,
> οἷος Ὀδυσσεύς, σιγᾷ δόλιος,
> πιστὸς δὲ φίλοις, θρασὺς εἰς ἀλκάν,
> ξυνετὸς πολέμου, φόνιός τε δράκων.
> ἔρροι τᾶς ἡσύχου
> προνοίας κακοῦργος ὤν.
> οἳ δὲ πρὸς θρόνους ἔσω μολόντες ἃς
> ἔγημ' ὁ τοξότας Πάρις
> γυναικός, ὄμμα δακρύοις
> πεφυρμένοι, ταπεινοί,
> ἕζονθ', ὁ μὲν τὸ κεῖθεν, ὁ δὲ
> τὸ κεῖθεν, ἄλλος ἄλλοθεν πεφραγμένοι.
> περὶ δὲ γόνυ χέρας ἱκεσίους
> ἔβαλον ἔβαλον Ἑλένας ἄμφω.

ἀνὰ δὲ δρομάδες ἔθορον ἔθορον
ἀμφίπολοι Φρύγες·
προσεῖπε δ' ἄλλος ἄλλον
πεσὼν ἐν φόβῳ,
μή τις εἴη δόλος.
κἀδόκει τοῖς μὲν οὔ,
τοῖς δ' ἐς ἀρκυστάταν
μηχανὰν ἐμπλέκειν
παῖδα τὰν Τυνδαρίδ' ὁ   1424a
μητροφόντας δράκων.   1424b   (1395–1424)

A cry of woe, a cry of woe,
the barbarians call the beginning of death, *aiai*,
in an Asiatic tone,
whenever the blood of kings is poured
upon the earth with iron blades
for Hades.
They came into the house –
so that I may tell each thing to you –
two twin lions of Hellas;
as for the one, a general was called his father,
as for the other, the son of Strophius,
an evil-plotting man, like Odysseus,
deceitful in silence,
trusty to his friends, bold for the fight;
intelligent in war, a deadly serpent.
May he be cursed for his quiet preparation,
the evil-doer.
Coming in toward the throne
of the wife of Paris the archer,
their faces befouled with tears,
they sat down, abasing themselves,
one on this side, one on that,
each fencing her in from another direction.
And around the knees of Helen
they cast, they cast their suppliant hands.
Up they sprang, up they sprang, the frantic
Phrygian attendants;
and one would speak to another, falling in fear,
that this was some deceit.
To some there seemed to be none;
to others it seemed that
the mother-slaying snake

>   was weaving the daughter of Tyndareus
>   into his plot, hemmed in with nets.

This section is longer than the first two and more complex in its blend of motifs, conventions, and genres. The passage opens with poetic features familiar from the previous lyric sections: anadiplosis (αἴλινον αἴλινον, 1395), alliteration and assonance (αἴλινον αἴλινον ἀρχὰν, 1394), pathetic exclamation (αἰαῖ, 1397), and references to the Phrygian's foreignness (βάρβαροι, 1396; Ἀσιάδι φωνᾷ, 1397). The opening cry of woe (αἴλινον αἴλινον, 1395) and the reference to the death of kings (1397–1399) continue the impression that Helen has been killed and that the Phrygian is the singer of her lament. The main item of news seems clear. The Phrygian now undertakes to tell "each thing" to the eager chorus (ἕκαστά σοι λέγω, 1400b), a transition marked formally by the prominent placement of a narrative verb in the third person (ἦλθον, 1400a) and metrically by the shift to a more regular iambic meter.[51] The Phrygian seems to have stepped into his role as messenger at last.

Euripides has the Phrygian further conform to the conventions of a messenger speech by establishing at the outset the spatial relationship of the principals, a typical feature of "scene-setting" in narrative. The central tableau comprises Helen on her throne, with Orestes and Pylades kneeling in supplication on either side.[52] Around these three static figures the other enslaved Phrygians are scattered in frantic motion. Their actions are conveyed through a rush of verbs and participles: they run, cluster in confusion, spring up, address one another, and fall in fear (δρομάδες, 1416; ἔθορον ἔθορον, 1416; προσεῖπε, 1418; πεσών, 1419). Lines 1414–1416, with their two anadiploses, one describing the three Greeks, one the Phrygians (ἔβαλον ἔβαλον, 1415; ἔθορον ἔθορον, 1416), are rendered in a sudden rush of resolved short syllables. These lines emphasize the pictorial contrast between Helen, Orestes, and Pylades, on the one hand, and the Phrygians on the other, rendering the scene as vivid and dynamic as a described dance.

Throughout the passage the Phrygian's words echo against the backdrop of earlier literature, creating a disjunction between what he says and what the audience can accept as plausible. The Phrygian at first does not name Orestes and Pylades but describes them obliquely with animal similes drawn from the world of epic: together they are "two twin lions" (λέοντες δύο διδύμω, 1401) and Pylades is a "deadly snake" (φόνιός τε δράκων,

---

[51] In particular, lines 1408–1413 are in a fairly regular iambic meter.
[52] Barlow 1971: 63. In this play, we may compare this passage to the similar "scene-setting" in the earlier messenger speech (879–883).

1406).⁵³ He explicitly compares Pylades to Odysseus in his deceit and his silence (οἷος Ὀδυσσεύς, σιγᾷ δόλιος, 1404) and refers to Helen as the wife of Paris (ὁ τοξότας Πάρις γυναικός, 1409).⁵⁴ The Phrygian presumably means these comparisons sincerely; he fears the two Greeks, and his recent experience merits the curse against Pylades' "quiet preparation." More cunningly, he may be painting Orestes and Pylades in flattering terms to win the sympathy of Electra and the chorus. Yet for the audience, the epic resonances of the passage throw into relief the absurdity and cowardice of Orestes and Pylades' attack. As Victoria Wohl has described, the sharp changes in action and tone that punctuate *Orestes* significantly complicate any sympathy on the part of the audience for the plays' aristocratic protagonists; in the second half of the play, Electra, Orestes, and Pylades are rapidly transformed "from victims of a corrupt society into agents of sacrilege, bloodshed, and chaos."⁵⁵ The monody of the Phrygian is crucial to the complication of sympathy that Wohl identifies. Against the invoked background of the *Iliad*, the *aristeia* of the would-be warriors Orestes and Pylades, whose opponents are a woman and her unarmed barbarian retinue, emerges as distinctly unheroic.⁵⁶ The deeds of these warriors – if locking people in a closet constitutes a "deed" – are immortalized in song not by an epic bard and his accompanying Muse but by one of their confused and cringing victims.

If the audience is unable to accept the heroism ascribed to Orestes and Pylades, they may also doubt the virtue that the Phrygian attributes to his mistress. In the fourth passage of lyric, the Phrygian describes the tranquil domestic scene of Helen spinning wool, fanned by his fellow enslaved Phrygians:

> Φρυγίοις ἔτυχον Φρυγίοισι νόμοις
> παρὰ βόστρυχον αὔραν αὔραν
> Ἑλένας Ἑλένας εὐπαγεῖ κύκλῳ
> πτερίνῳ πρὸ παρηίδος ἀίσσων
> βαρβάροις νόμοισιν.
> ἁ δὲ λίνον ἠλακάτᾳ

---

⁵³ De Jong 1991: 84–91 writes that a messenger's use of epithets, adjectives, and brief similes may reveal his incredulity at the enormity of the events he is watching, and mentions in this context the Phrygian's words describing Orestes and Pylades.

⁵⁴ Zeitlin 1980: 60–61 comments that the reference to Odysseus also establishes a connection to the *Odyssey*, which creates a new series of palimpsestic allusions.

⁵⁵ Wohl 2015: 124.

⁵⁶ Compare Euben 1986: 231, who writes, "The play not only reduces the heroic ethic to malevolent triviality, it parodies the greatness of the Trojan War." On comedic aspects, compare Seidensticker 1982: 108 and Lazarus 2005.

δακτύλοις ἔλισσε.
νήματα δ' ἵετο πέδῳ,
σκύλων Φρυγίων ἐπὶ τύμβον ἀγάλ-
ματα συστολίσαι χρῄζουσα λίνῳ,
φάρεα πορφύρεα,
δῶρα Κλυταιμήστρᾳ.   (1426–1437)

> With the Phrygians in Phrygian custom
> I happened to be wafting
> around the locks of Helen, of Helen
> the breeze, the breeze, with a round feathered fan,
> before her cheeks, in barbarian custom.
> And she with her fingers
> was twisting the thread on her distaff,
> but she put her yarn down on the ground,
> wishing to make with her thread
> purple cloths from Phrygian spoils,
> adornments for the tomb, a gift for Clytemnestra.

Here again the Phrygian's words allude to earlier literature: the scene of Helen at her loom is taken from the *Iliad*, while the theme connects her also with Penelope, the virtuous weaver of the *Odyssey*. The narrative unwinds at a leisurely pace: the main verb "she put her yarn down" (νήματα ἵετο, 1433) is nestled between two descriptive passages so that Helen's action seems to take place without haste or fear. Yet the anadiploses convey excitement and agitation, in seeming contrast to the peaceful and luxurious atmosphere of the chamber (Φρυγίοις ... Φρυγίοισι, 1426; αὔραν αὔραν, 1427; Ἑλένας Ἑλένας, 1428). Helen's calm, virtuous action, weaving a gift for her sister's grave, is rendered sinister by the detail that she uses the spoils of Phrygia, the land destroyed for her sake (σκύλων Φρυγίων, 1434). Throughout the play Helen has been vilified by Electra, Pylades, Orestes, and Tyndareus. The slave seems to be the only figure who does not hate her. The sympathetic description of Helen in the monody invites the audience to contrast what the Phrygian says with what has already been said by other figures in the play. For the first time the possibility arises that Helen is, like the Phrygian, a victim of fortune.[57] In this passage the two views of Helen exist awkwardly side by side, forcing the audience to make their own judgment about this mysterious and contested figure.

---

[57] For a thought-provoking defense of Helen as a sympathetic figure in this play, see Vellacott 1975. This interpretation was explored as a rehearsal exercise in the production of *Orestes* that I directed in 2018; see Catenaccio 2019.

An explicit admission of bias comes in the Phrygian's words about his own countrymen:

προσεῖπε δ' Ὀρέστας	
Λάκαιναν κόραν· Ὦ Διὸς παῖ,	
θὲς ἴχνος πέδῳ δεῦρ' ἀποστᾶσα κλισμοῦ,	
Πέλοπος ἐπὶ προπάτορος ἕδραν παλαιᾶς	
ἑστίας, ἵν' εἰδῇς λόγους ἐμούς.	1442/1443
ἄγει δ' ἄγει νιν· ἁ δ' ἐφεί-	
πετ', οὐ πρόμαντις ὦν ἔμελ-	
λεν. ὁ δὲ συνεργὸς ἀλλ' ἔπρασσ'	1446a
ἰὼν κακὸς Φωκεύς·	1446b
Οὐκ ἐκποδὼν ἴτ'; ἀλλ' ἀεὶ κακοὶ Φρύγες.	
ἔκλῃσε δ' ἄλλον ἄλλοσ' ἐν	
στέγαις, τοὺς μὲν ἐν σταθμοῖ-	
σιν ἱππικοῖσι, τοὺς δ' ἐν ἐξέδραισι, τοὺς δ'	1450a
ἐκεῖσ' ἐκεῖθεν ἄλλον ἄλ-	140b
λοσε διαρμόσας ἀποπρὸ δεσποίνας.	(1438–1451)

Orestes addressed the woman of Sparta:
"Child of Zeus, arising from your chair
place your footstep here on the ground,
toward the seat of the ancient hearth
of Pelops, my ancestor,
so that you may know what I have to say."
He led, he led her; and she followed,
no prophet of what was to come;
but his accomplice, the evil man from Phocis,
went away and did other things:
"Won't you get out of my way?" But Phrygians are always base.[58]
He shut them up, one here, one there, in the house;
some in the stables of the horses, some in the halls,
hither and thither, here and there,
dispersing them far from their mistress.

Parallel construction juxtaposes Pylades and the Phrygians, playing on the multiple meanings of the adjective κακός (κακὸς Φωκεύς, 1446b; κακοὶ Φρύγες, 1447). In both cases the term has a moral force, but with a different valence: applied to Pylades, it carries the sense of "evil, pernicious, destructive," while as an epithet of the Phrygians it connotes baseness and

---

[58] West 1987: ad 1447 comments that the translation "but Phrygians are always cowards" does not make sense, but this pronouncement seems to me subjective. I follow de Poli 2011 in accepting the manuscript reading of ἀεί.

cowardice. Why does the Phrygian admit his own lack of courage in this way? Or – if the phrase is articulated by the Phrygian not in his own voice but still reporting the speech of Pylades – why does he bring this charge forward? One reason, perhaps, is to disarm the hostile Greeks onstage, Electra and the chorus. In his later stichomythic scene with Orestes, the Phrygian similarly emphasizes his cowardice in order to save his life (1507, 1517).[59] He begs, pleads, flatters, and lies. The Phrygian is willing to do and say anything to protect himself, which brands him as κακός. But throughout the play Orestes, joined by Electra and Pylades, has been engaged in the same quest, struggling to save his life in a series of increasingly desperate ploys. Only Orestes' lofty rhetoric of justice, along with his aggressiveness, distinguishes him from the Phrygian. If the desire to live at all costs is κακός, then the Greeks are little better than this barbarian.

The fifth passage of lyric, like the second, begins with a lamentation; the Phrygian then resumes a more orderly account of events:

Ἰδαία μᾶτερ μᾶτερ	1454a
ὀβρίμα ὀβρίμα, αἰαῖ,	1454b
φονίων παθέων ἀνόμων τε κακῶν	1455
ἅπερ ἔδρακον ἔδρακον	1456a
ἐν δόμοις τυράννων.	1456b
ἀμφιπορφυρέων πέπλων ὑπὸ σκότου	
ξίφη σπάσαντες ἐν χεροῖν ἄλλος ἄλλοσε	
δίνασεν ὄμμα, μή τις παρὼν τύχοι.	
ὡς κάπροι δ' ὀρέστεροι	
γυναικὸς ἀντίοι σταθέν-	
τες ἐννέπουσι· Κατθανῇ κατθανῇ·	
κακὸς σ' ἀποκτείνει πόσις, κασιγνή-	
του προδοὺς ἐν Ἄργει θανεῖν γόνον.	
ἃ δ' ἀνίαχεν ἴαχεν· ὤμοι μοι.	
λευκὸν δ' ἐμβαλοῦσα πῆχυν στέρνοις	
κτύπησε κρᾶτα μέλεον πλαγάν.	
φυγᾷ δὲ ποδὶ τὸ χρυσεοσάνδαλον ἴχνος	
ἔφερεν ἔφερεν· ἐς κόμας δὲ δακτύλους	
δικὼν Ὀρέστας, Μυκηνίδ' ἀρβύλαν	
προβάς, ὤμοις ἀριστεροῖσιν ἀνακλάσας δέρην,	
παίειν λαιμῶν ἔμελλεν εἴσω μέλαν ξίφος.	(1454a–1472)

---

[59] The scholiast comments that the ensuing scene is "unworthy of tragedy and of Orestes' situation," Σ ad 1512: ἀνάξια καὶ τραγῳδίας καὶ τῆς Ὀρέστου συμφορᾶς τὰ λεγόμενα. See further Seidensticker 1982: 109, who examines comic and "burlesque" aspects in interaction between Orestes and the Phrygian, as well as Gregory 1999–2000.

> Mother Ida,
> mighty, mighty mother,
> *aiai* for the murderous sufferings
> and the lawless evils which I have seen, I have seen
> in the palace of the kings.
> Drawing swords from beneath the darkness
> of their purple cloaks,
> each one darted his eye in a different direction,
> lest someone should happen to be present.
> Like mountain-dwelling boars,
> standing opposite the woman they addressed her:
> "You will die, you will die,
> your base husband kills you,
> having betrayed the son of his brother
> to die in Argos."
> And she screamed, she screamed, *omoi moi*.
> Hurling her white arm against her breast
> she beat her wretched head with blows;
> then she brought, she brought the golden-sandaled
> track of her foot in flight;
> but Orestes, thrusting his fingers into her hair,
> getting in front of her with his Mycenean boot,
> bending back her neck to the left shoulder,
> was about to plunge the black sword
> into her neck.

The Phrygian reports the words first of Orestes and Pylades, in unison, and then of Helen. Direct quotation is a feature found in many of Euripides' messenger speeches, and the assumption in all other cases is that the messenger faithfully reports the words of the absent speaker.[60] But here a verbatim account would seem to be impossible: at the very least, the prosody and tone must be different since the Phrygian is singing, while Orestes, Pylades, and Helen presumably were not. In the report of the Phrygian, the Greeks use the same anadiplosis that has been typical of his own language throughout the monody (e.g., κατθανῇ κατθανῇ, 1462), while Helen echoes the Phrygian's previous cries of distress (ὤμοι μοι, 1465). We may imagine that the actor at this point would enhance his performance by mimicking the voices of the principals, exploiting the difference between the threatening tone of the men and the high-pitched, terrified scream of Helen for dramatic effect. Events, actions, and even the direct speech of

---

[60] Compare Bers 1997: 65–68 on *oratio recta* in the report of the messenger earlier in the play.

other characters are filtered through the Phrygian's own emotional and poetic perspective.

In addition to recalling other tragic messengers, the inclusion of direct speech in this passage may recall the conventions of kitharoidic song – that is, music composed for performance on the *kithara*, or concert lyre – in the late fifth century. As Pauline LeVen has shown with reference to Timotheus' *Persians*, direct speech within a third-person narrative account creates a sense of immediacy that may also be disorienting.[61] Timotheus of Miletus was an infamous practitioner of the New Music in the late fifth century, linked in ancient biography to Euripides as a friend and collaborator.[62] His *Persians* is a *nomos*, or astrophic narrative song, for performance by a single musician with a *kithara*, describing the Greek victory at the naval battle of Salamis mainly from a Persian point of view. It was probably composed several years later than Euripides' *Orestes*, although the exact chronology is frustratingly uncertain.[63] Approximately 240 lines of verse are preserved on one fragmentary papyrus found in Abusir, Egypt in 1902, part of an original composition that may have been two or three times this length. The *nomos* includes four passages of direct speech by different individuals and groups involved in the battle of Salamis: a Persian nobleman; a group of Mysians; a man from Celaenae, a city in Phrygia; and the Great King Xerxes.

As LeVen demonstrates, the passages of intertextual speech in Timotheus' *Persians* emphasize the relationship between poet, audience, and the world created through the processes of "mental transport" and "displaced consciousness."[64] The foreigners whose words are quoted in the *nomos* evoke a self-contained and vicariously close world. Timotheus portrays these barbarians suffering and dying, even ventriloquizing one man in the process of drowning in the Hellespont. The song focuses sequentially on the experiences of individual figures overwhelmed by the disaster, in each case creating a visually and aurally colorful vignette to dramatize the last, miserable minutes of the lives of these various barbarians. Unlike the Phrygian in *Orestes*, Timotheus' characters speak garbled Greek, a linguistic caricature avoided in Greek tragedy.[65] But like Euripides' monody, the *Persians* of Timotheus is a hybrid song that draws on many different genres including tragedy, comedy, and epic.[66] The style of the *nomos* is purposely combinatory and alludes to an array of earlier texts. By its inclusion of direct speech, the monody of the

---

[61] LeVen 2014: 193–220.   [62] Hordern 2002: 4.
[63] Hordern 2002: 1–16; Budelmann 2018: 230–236.   [64] LeVen 2014: 209.
[65] Hall 2006: 279; Gurd 2016: 114–123.   [66] Hall 2006: 255–287.

Phrygian may have reminded spectators not only of epic and earlier tragedy but of the popular mimetic genre of kitharoidic song as well.

Turning back to the text of the monody, the Phrygian's sixth and final passage of lyric concludes the account of events within the palace. Omitting the final rout in battle of the Phrygian servants, here are the last lines of the song:

ἄθυρσοι δ' οἷά νιν δραμόντε Βάκχαι	1492
σκύμνον ἐν χεροῖν	1493a
ὀρείαν ξυνήρπασαν·	1493b
πάλιν δὲ τὰν Διὸς κόραν	1494a
ἐπὶ σφαγὰν ἔτεινον· ἃ δ' ἐκ θαλάμων	1494b
ἐγένετο διαπρὸ δωμάτων ἄφαντος,	1495
ὦ Ζεῦ καὶ Γᾶ καὶ Φῶς καὶ Νύξ,	1496
ἤτοι φαρμάκοισιν	1497a
ἢ μάγων τέχναις ἢ θεῶν κλοπαῖς.	1497b
τὰ δ' ὕστερ' οὐκέτ' οἶδα· δραπέταν γὰρ ἐξ-	1498
έκλεπτον ἐκ δόμων πόδα.	1499
πολύπονα δὲ	1500a
πολύπονα πάθεα Μενέλαος ἀνασχόμενος	1500b
ἀνόνητον ἀπὸ Τροίας ἔλαβε	1501
τὸν Ἑλένας γάμον. 1502	(1492–1502)

These two, just like running Bacchants without *thyrsoi*,
snatched her up, a mountain cub, in their hands.
Then they advanced again toward the daughter of Zeus,
to slay her; but she was gone from the chamber,
and vanished throughout the house,
Zeus and earth and light and night,
whether truly by drugs or the arts of magicians
or the thefts of the gods.
What happened next I do not know,
for I stole out of the house with a runaway foot.
Menelaus, having endured many terrible, many terrible sufferings
took back his wife Helen from Troy to no purpose.

This concluding section is the most heterogeneous of all, its disordered language matching the disordered action within the house. The total defeat of the Phrygians is conveyed in one virtuosic line of iambic trimeter, an unexpected return to the usual meter of a messenger speech (νεκροὶ δ' ἔπιπτον, οἱ δ' ἔμελλον, οἱ δ' ἔκειντ', 1489). The attackers are described in similes drawn from both epic and tragedy: Pylades is like Hector or Ajax, while the two men together, incongruously, are likened to Bacchants, which heightens the sense of frenzy (ἄθυρσοι δ' οἷά νιν δραμόντε Βάκχαι, 1492).⁶⁷ In the midst of this confusion, the Phrygian finally reveals the arrival of Hermione and the disappearance of Helen. The account is maddeningly unclear: he reports that Helen was gone "out of the chamber" (ἐκ θαλάμων ἐγένετο, 1494b–1495) and was "unseen throughout the house" (διαπρὸ δωμάτων ἄφαντος, 1495), but he does not describe the manner of her disappearance and can only speculate as to its cause. Finally, he admits what the audience has suspected all along: he does not know what happened next (τὰ δ' ὕστερ' οὐκέτ' οἶδα, 1498).

I have suggested that the narrative style of the Phrygian is unique among messengers in Greek tragedy. This is not simply because he sings, or even because of the heterogeneous nature of his song, but because his knowledge of events is in doubt. In other tragedies, we encounter figures who lie and whose lies are known in advance by the audience, such as the messenger in Sophocles' *Electra*; or there are figures who lie and whose lies are revealed subsequently, such as Lichas in Sophocles' *Trachiniae*. Messengers may adapt their words to different interlocutors, as when the solider in Sophocles' *Antigone* is reluctant to speak openly in front of Creon, or when the herald in Aeschylus' *Agamemnon* announces the triumph of the army to Clytemnestra, revealing only to the chorus the suffering entailed by the war and the journey home. In each of these cases, the messenger delivers a false or partial report because of concerns clearly articulated by the action of the play, of which the audience is fully aware; the messenger's actual awareness of what has happened is not called into question.

The monody of the Phrygian, by contrast, is deeply ambiguous. Does he set out to deceive, to obscure and conceal information? When he appears onstage, the Phrygian is in flight for his life, and imagines Orestes and Pylades in hot pursuit. Electra and the hostile chorus surround the palace, blocking all routes of escape. The subsequent scene with Orestes reveals that the Phrygian is willing to say whatever is necessary; his twisting monody, then, may be an attempt to distract the Greeks long enough to win their sympathy and save himself – at least, this would be one plausible way to play the scene on the modern stage.

Another possibility is that the Phrygian simply does not know what has happened. Is he "unreliable," and, if so, in what sense? Most scholarship on

---

⁶⁷ *Orestes* barely predates Euripides' *Bacchae*; the language may also have drawn on plays about the birth and exploits of Dionysus by Aeschylus, Sophocles, or other playwrights.

reliable and unreliable narrators focuses on works of modern prose fiction; the term was coined in 1961 by Wayne C. Booth, a critic of American literature, and is defined by M. H. Abrams as a narrator "whose perception, interpretation, and evaluation of the matters he or she narrates do not coincide with the opinions and norms implied by the author, which the author expects the alert reader to share."[68] This is clearly insufficient to describe the Phrygian. In ancient drama, the competing voices of the various figures onstage make the "opinions and norms" of an author difficult, even impossible, to identify; the audience must judge whether an internal narrator, such as a messenger, is reliable by comparing his account to information gleaned from other scenes and characters, and draw their own conclusions. If the term "unreliable" cannot be applied to the Phrygian, how may we describe the style of his narrative? The inconsistencies in the Phrygian's song, its abrupt shifts of tone, are part of a larger strategy by the playwright. The overall effect of such an eclectic construction, beyond unsettling or even incongruous, is to frustrate any hope the audience may have in the possibility of learning the truth from the Phrygian as a reliable source. If most figures in tragedy have one voice, one claim to authority, I suggest that the style of the Phrygian might be termed "polyphonic." His song contains multiple systems of meaning that are by convention self-sufficient, self-contained, and mutually exclusive: as we have seen, his language is at times epic, tragic, comic, choral, and monodic. The coexistence of these forms leads to a clash between the opposing forces of objectivity and subjectivity, even truth and falsehood.

The monody is histrionic: that is, the Phrygian's narrative is disrupted by emotion and yet artfully shaped toward the desired impact upon his onstage audience. What I call his resultant "polyphonic" voice as a narrator is conveyed through several synergistic techniques, both rhetorical and dramatic. The wishes and fears that color his song are expressed by direct avowal and would have been enhanced in performance by mimetic show. They are also expressed by extra-syntactical means through pauses, exclamatory breaks, and forays into unexpected meters and genres. In its abrupt and forceful juxtaposition of different elements, the monody combines lamentation with reminiscences of epic, comedy, *nomos*, and earlier tragedy. Through the unprecedented combination of monody and messenger speech the poet foregrounds the competing voices of the

---

[68] Booth 1961; Abrams and Harpham 2014: 235. For an overview of theories of the unreliable narrator, see Olson 2003 and Nünning 2005. For narrators in Euripides (with a short section on messengers, not mentioning the Phrygian), see Lowe 2004.

Phrygian's song. Indeed, Euripides contrives to make this implicit competition, this battle at the level of dramatic form, the center of interest in the scene.

4.2 Conclusion

We have seen that Euripides has constructed the monody of the Phrygian to draw attention to the disparity between this atypical messenger's report and what the audience would expect to hear in this dramatic situation. Aurally, the song is characterized by apostrophe, asyndeton, alliteration, assonance, internal rhyme, compound adjectives, interjections, and pathetic exclamations – that is, upon the formal hallmarks of lyric verse. The Phrygian's language repeatedly makes reference to his outlandish appearance, his excitable nature, his foreignness, and his cowardice. In fact, given the conventions of tragedy, such outlandish and unheroic utterances could only have been put into the mouth of an outsider. These poetic devices, no doubt originally enhanced by virtuosic vocal delivery and musical accompaniment, establish a sense of emotionality and agitation that are substituted for an orderly progression of narrative.

The content of the song, as well as its form, unsettles the expectations of the audience by at times following and at other times frustrating the conventions of the messenger speech. Ethical allegiances are also called into question: whom should we trust, care about, admire, or execrate? The Phrygian begins *in medias res* without first stating the principal item of news that he has come to report. He has of course not come in order to report anything at all, but has escaped from the house in fear of his life, and knows himself to be in danger throughout his exposition. His actual account of events is apparently confused and does not proceed in an ordered chronological sequence or according to a conventional hierarchy of importance. Instead of a distanced and objective narrative, he offers above all a personal commentary on events, in a course still unfolding, which he barely has the presence of mind to share, or perhaps the desire to do so. His description is rich in sensory detail, but the information he presents appears distorted by his own fear. This sense of confusion and disorientation is compounded by a complex mixture of generic styles, drawn from the conventions of monody, choral lyric, lament, kitharoidic *nomos*, and epic.

The effect of what I have termed the "polyphonic" narration of the Phrygian is to draw attention to the uneasy coexistence of illusion and reality in the world of the play. In addition, because the Phrygian's narrative cannot be taken at face value, events and their motivations are called into question. The result is an elaborate structure of ironies. The polyphony of this narrator demands that we question the other narrators within the play, in particular Orestes, whose protestations of justice and manly heroism ring hollow. In the final scene of the play, these competing mortal voices are silenced by the epiphany of Apollo, but the sense of unease initiated by the monody remains, undercutting the god's attempts to solve the crisis of the play.[69] On a stage crowded with self-interested, erratic, and unappealing characters, there appears to be no one with whom the audience can easily sympathize for long.

Form and content work together in the monody to open an ironic distance between the words of the Phrygian and any possible consistent construction we may put upon them. Here there are no facts, only interpretations; and Euripides constantly blocks attempts at interpretation. Everything the Phrygian relates is filtered through his compromised, fractured point of view, his words competing with what has already been established by earlier scenes in the play as well as with the implications of his own tale. He says that Helen is virtuously weaving grave-gifts for Clytemnestra; but Electra in the prologue accuses Helen of making only a token offering to honor her sister's death. He pronounces Orestes and Pylades fierce and brave, like the warriors of the Trojan War; but in his account these "heroes" triumph over defenseless women and terrified enslaved barbarians. He admits that he and his fellow Phrygians are κακοί, base; but this moral charge simultaneously implicates Orestes, Pylades, and Electra. He declares, finally, that Helen has not died but mysteriously disappeared – yet here the audience has no external knowledge that could contradict this revelation. Attention is directed to figures of speech in an empty space. The whole monody has built up to this final point. There is no information in which we can put our trust.

---

[69] The concluding pronouncements of Apollo have struck many critics of the play as deeply unsatisfying. Verrall 1905: 257 declares the epiphany "absurd, unreal, meaningless, impossible," and modern scholars have tended to agree with this view. (An exception is the spirited defense of Papadimitropoulos 2011.) Burkert 1974 finds the entire play deeply pessimistic. Euben 1986: 242 writes that "the very arbitrariness of the ending, together with the idealized unity it contrives to establish, only emphasizes the impossibility of harmony and order." Dunn 1996: 171 comments that the god "imposes a 'resolution' that resolves nothing." Seidensticker 1996: 392 concurs, arguing that Apollo's intervention "has no meaningful connection with the dramatic action that precedes it" and that its "glaring absurdity ... only serves to intensify the general impression of senselessness and futility." Wohl 2015: 128 writes that the ending "seems to make a mockery of the play's fraught politics and to retroactively vitiate all its human dilemmas and decisions, stripping them of consequence and meaning."

Conclusion

Freedom and Form

It has been the aim of the last four chapters to show that monody is an essential part of Euripides' mature dramatic art. Through a series of close readings, we have examined who sings and when, how, and why. The first two questions can be approached directly; I have suggested answers that may illuminate the means of Euripides' stagecraft and go part of the way toward explaining why his work was so disruptive in his time, both formally and socially. It is perhaps not so surprising, after all, that he was not awarded as many prizes in his lifetime as his later reputation might seem to warrant. The third question, the "how" of the songs, has necessitated examination in detail. Monody has long resisted critical efforts because we lack a record of the melodies; nonetheless, there is much in the words and in the meter to guide us, situated in the context of theatrical and musical innovation in the last decades of the fifth century. Lastly, the question of why a song appears calls for an accounting both of what has led up to it and to what purpose or effect the dramatist has employed it. This has of necessity led to some speculation on my part, signaled as such. I hope my reader has followed me, but I do not anticipate universal assent.

My first argument concerns dramatic form: Euripides, as we have seen, experiments with monody through the self-conscious combination of the different poetic building blocks of tragedy. By 415 BCE, when Euripides was at the height of his career, various formal features of tragedy, including monody, had become highly conventionalized. All the surviving examples of actor's lyric by Aeschylus and Sophocles are songs of lamentation, where the use of solo song emphasizes the relationship between the isolated singer and the larger group. Reacting against this tradition, in his late plays Euripides successively redefines monody: each song takes over a traditional *Bauform* of tragedy and expands upon it. These reconfigurations, or "liberations," as I have termed them, are signaled so that attention is drawn in each case to the poet's formal ingenuity. Euripides uses the paired monodies of *Ion* to pose a conflict of ideas that might otherwise be conveyed through an *agōn*. In *Iphigenia among the Taurians*, the heroine's crisis and its resolution are presented in lyric song rather than as a deliberative *rhesis*. In *Phoenician Women*, Antigone, Jocasta, and Oedipus take over the musical role of the chorus in lamenting the fall of the royal house of Thebes. Finally, the enslaved Phrygian in *Orestes* sings a monody explicitly marked as a messenger speech that inverts literary conventions to raise questions about objectivity and truth in a disordered world. In the passages of actor's lyric in each play, several forms are folded together into one, as the playwright joins these simpler elements within the emotive matrix of song.

In addition to Euripides' flexible handling of monody as a *Bauform*, a second theme in this book has been the relationship between solo song, emotion, and the development of character in late fifth-century tragedy. Monody is a privileged vehicle for emotion because of the heightened expressivity inherent in song. Beyond that, the fact that actor's lyric is sung by a single person makes a decisive difference. It is the solo voice, not the collective chorus, that can best give expression to the disrupted, shifting perspective of a human mind in turmoil. Madness, love, accusation, ecstasy, despair: monody as Euripides envisioned it encompassed extreme and varied emotional states. Nonetheless, in attempting to distinguish the potential inherent in solo song from that of choral song, certainly I do not mean to suggest that monody has a greater force of expressivity. Most strongly and originally in Euripides, the two musical formats may be set in counterpoise; the individual voice of a monodist in any play always resonates against the background of collective choral song. As we have seen, Euripides particularly favors arrangements where a female figure, closely tied to the chorus at the outset of the play, moves toward greater independence through monody as the tragedy progresses; this is the case with Creusa, with Iphigenia, with Helen, and with Antigone.

In each monody we have examined, the singer focuses on his or her own mental processes: joy and fear, wish and memory. Poetically, this subjectivity is manifest in the predominance of first-person verbs, adjectives expressing the perception of sight and sound, and vocabulary emphasizing the processes of recollection and imagination, all distinctive features of tragic monody. In most cases, the complex rhythmic and sonic effects possible in monody underscore this personal point of view, an impression that would no doubt have been enhanced in performance by virtuosic vocal delivery and accompaniment on the *aulos*. The aporetic monody of the Phrygian in *Orestes* represents an extreme example. By contrast, when a monodist adheres to the predictable strophic patterns of a choral ode, the effect is equally striking; in the case of the opening song in *Ion*, for instance, the young man is distinguished by his state of ordered, pious calm.

Personal experience of the world as conveyed through the senses is a hallmark of solo song in Euripides. Singers often dwell impressionistically on sights, sounds, smells, and feelings. "The dark, curling locks of your hair cast their shadow on my neck," sings Jocasta in *Phoenician Women*, embracing Polyneices. "She found her sons by the Electran gate, in a meadow where the lotus blooms," sings Antigone later in the same play, remembering her mother's death and relating it with the specificity of an eyewitness. Of course, terrible misunderstandings may arise when singers grant such importance to their own subjective judgments, as in *Ion* when Creusa's error leads her to plot the death of her long-lost son, a crime only averted by the timely intervention of the gods. The pervasive dramatic irony in Euripides' late tragedies, with their intertwined plots, mistaken identities, and failures to connect, stages a world where the multiple solitary perspectives of individual characters fail to cohere in any tidy or predictable way.

In the late plays of Euripides, experience and emotion assume great importance as driving forces in human action. There is a new significance granted to the way in which men and women themselves interpret what they see around them and what they feel inside. Euripides' characters are the artificers of their own lives, for better or worse. The daily task of sweeping the temple steps, the recollection of sexual trauma, the fraught decision over which course of action to take, the glittering sight of an army arrayed on the plain – all are developed because they are central to Euripides' total conception of dramatic character, and all are highlighted through the marked use of solo song. Through monody, Euripides explores a new assessment of the human mind that privileges individual perception and emotion. The monodies of his late plays are vivid, playful, audacious, and dramatically effective. The concentration of strong emotion and its expression through solo song is at once a formal experiment in lyric poetry, a central component of Euripides' tragic realism, and a radically autonomous reconception of character on the late fifth-century stage.

Appendix | Actor's Song in the Extant Plays of Aeschylus, Sophocles, and Euripides

Playwright	Play	Date (BCE)	Verses	Singer
Aeschylus	*Persians*	472	907–1077	Xerxes (with chorus)
	Agamemnon	458	1072–1177	Cassandra (with chorus)
	Choephoroi	458	306–480	Electra, Orestes (with chorus)
(?)	*Prometheus Bound*	c. 430s (?)	88–127	Prometheus
			561–608	Io
Sophocles	*Trachiniae*	c. 440s	983–1043	Heracles (with Hyllus and Old Man)
	Ajax	c. 440s	394–472	Ajax (with Tecmessa and chorus)
	Electra	c. 420s	86–120	Electra
	Philoctetes	409	1081–1217	Philoctetes (with chorus)
	Oedipus at Colonus	401	237–253	Antigone
Euripides	*Alcestis*	438	244–272	Alcestis (with Admetus)
			393–415	Eumelus
	Hippolytus	428	669–679	Phaedra
			817–851	Theseus
			1347–1388	Hippolytus
	Hecuba	c. 425	59–97, 154–176	Hecuba
			197–215	Polyxena
			1056–1106	Polymestor
	Andromache	c. 425	103–116	Andromache
			846–865	Hermione
			1173–1196	Peleus
	Suppliant Women	c. 422	990–1030	Evadne

(cont.)

Playwright	Play	Date (BCE)	Verses	Singer
	Electra	c. 420	112–166	Electra
			175–189, 198–212	Electra
	Trojan Women	415	98–152	Hecuba
			278–291	Hecuba
			308–340	Cassandra
	Ion	c. 414	82–183	Ion
			859–922	Creusa
	Iphigenia among the Taurians	c. 412	143–178, 203–235	Iphigenia
***			869–899	Iphigenia
	Helen	412	164–178, 191–210, 229–252	Helen
			348–385	Helen
	Phoenician Women	c. 410	182–192	Antigone
			301–354	Jocasta
			1485–1538, 1567–1581	Antigone
			1732–1746	Antigone
	Orestes	408	174–186, 195–207	Electra
			960–1011	Electra
			1369–1502	Phrygian
	Iphigenia in Aulis	405	1279–1335	Iphigenia
			1475–1496	Iphigenia
(?)	Rhesus	(?)	895–914	Muse

References

Abrams, M. H. and G. G. Harpham, eds. 2014. *A Glossary of Literary Terms*. 11th ed. South Melbourne: Cengage Learning.

Alden, M. 2000. *Homer beside Himself: Para-narratives in the* Iliad. Oxford: Oxford University Press.

Alexiou, M. 1974. *The Ritual Lament in the Greek Tradition*. Cambridge: Cambridge University Press.

Allan, W. 2008. *Euripides:* Helen. Cambridge: Cambridge University Press.

Altena, H. 1999-2000. "Text and Performance: On Significant Actions in Euripides' *Phoenissae*." *Illinois Classical Studies* 24-25: 303-323.

Andújar, R. forthcoming. *Playing the Chorus in Greek Tragedy*. Cambridge: Cambridge University Press.

Andújar, R., T. R. P. Coward, and T. A. Hadjimichael, eds. 2018. *Paths of Song: The Lyric Dimension of Greek Tragedy*. Berlin: De Gruyter.

Anhalt, E. K. 2001-2. "A Matter of Perspective: Penelope and the Nightingale in *Odyssey* 19.512-534." *Classical Journal* 97: 145-159.

Aretz, S. 1999. *Die Opferung der Iphigeneia in Aulis: Die Rezeption des Mythos in antiken und modernen Dramen*. Stuttgart: Teubner.

Arnott, W. G. 1973. "Euripides and the Unexpected." *Greece & Rome* 20: 49-64.

— 1983. "Tension, Frustration, and Surprise: A Study of Theatrical Techniques in Some Scenes from Euripides' *Orestes*." *Antichthon* 17: 13-28.

Arthur, M. 1977. "The Curse of Civilization: The Choral Odes of *Phoenissae*." *Harvard Studies in Classical Philology* 81: 163-185.

Bacon, H. H. 1961. *Barbarians in Greek Tragedy*. New Haven: Yale University Press.

Barker, A. 1984. *Greek Musical Writings*, vol. 1: *The Musician and His Art*. Cambridge: Cambridge University Press.

Barlow, S. A. 1971. *The Imagery of Euripides: A Study in the Dramatic Use of Pictorial Language*. London: Methuen.

— 1986. "The Language of Euripides' Monodies." In Betts, J. H., J. T. Hooker, and J. R. Green, eds. *Studies in Honour of T.B.L. Webster*. Bristol: Bristol Classical Press. 10-22.

Barner, W. 1971. "Die Monodie." In Jens, W., ed. *Die Bauformen der griechischen Tragödie*. Munich: Wilhelm Fink Verlag. 277-320.

Barrett, D. 2010. *Supernormal Stimuli: How Primal Urges Overran Their Evolutionary Purpose*. New York: W. W. Norton.

Barrett, J. 2002. *Staged Narrative: Poetics and the Messenger in Greek Tragedy.* Berkeley: University of California Press.

Basta-Donzelli, G. 2010. "La Parodo dello *Ione* di Euripide." In Belloni, L., ed. *Le Immagini nel Testo.* Trento: Università degli studi di Trento. 141–167.

Battezzato, L. 1999. "Dorian Dress in Greek Tragedy." *Illinois Classical Studies* 24: 343–362.

  2009. "Metre and Music." In Budelmann, F., ed. *The Cambridge Companion to Greek Lyric.* Cambridge: Cambridge University Press. 130–146.

  2018. *Euripides:* Hecuba. Cambridge: Cambridge University Press.

Bees, R. 1993. *Zur Datierung des* Prometheus Desmotes. Stuttgart: Teubner.

Bélis, A. 2001. "Euripide Musicien." In Pinault, G. J., ed. *Musique et Poésie dans l'antiquité.* Clermont-Ferrand: Presses Universitaires Blaise Pascal. 27–51.

Bers, V. 1997. *Speech in Speech: Studies in Incorporated* Oratio Recta *in Attic Drama and Oratory.* Lanham: Rowman & Littlefield.

Beverley, E. J. 1997. The Dramatic Function of Actors' Monody in Later Euripides. Dissertation. Oxford University.

Bicknell, J. 2009. *Why Music Moves Us.* Basingstoke: Palgrave Macmillan.

Biehl, W. 1965. *Euripides:* Orestes. Berlin: Akademie-Verlag.

Billings, J. 2021. *The Philosophical Stage: Drama and Dialectic in Classical Athens.* Princeton: Princeton University Press.

Billings, J., F. Budelmann, and F. Macintosh, eds. 2013. *Choruses, Ancient and Modern.* Oxford: Oxford University Press.

Blok, J. H. 2001. "Virtual Voices: Toward a Choreography of Women's Speech in Classical Athens." In Lardinois, A. and L. McClure, eds. *Making Silence Speak: Women's Voices in Greek Literature and Society.* Princeton: Princeton University Press. 95–116.

Booth, W. 1961. *The Rhetoric of Fiction.* Chicago: University of Chicago Press.

Bosher, K., ed. 2012. *Theater Outside Athens: Drama in Greek Sicily and South Italy.* Cambridge: Cambridge University Press.

Bremer, J. M. 1976. "Why Messenger-Speeches?" In Radt, S. L., J. M. Bremer, and C. J. Ruijgh, eds. *Miscellanea Tragica in Honorem J.C. Kamerbeek.* Amsterdam: Hakkert. 29–48.

Bremmer, J. N. 2013. "Human Sacrifice in Euripides' *Iphigenia in Tauris*: Greek and Barbarian." In Bonnechere, P. and R. Gagné, eds. *Sacrifices humains: Perspectives croisées et representations.* Liège: Presses Universitaires de Liège. 87–100.

Brinkema, E. 2014. *The Forms of the Affects.* Durham: Duke University Press.

Brown, A. L. 1977. "Eteocles and the Chorus in the *Seven against Thebes.*" *Phoenix* 31: 300–318.

Brown, S. G. 1972. Metrical Studies in the Lyrics of Euripides' Late Plays. Dissertation. University of Michigan.

Bruit-Zaidman, L. 1991. "La Voix des femmes: Les femmes et la guerre dans *Les Sept Contra Thebes.*" *Annales littéraires de l'Université de Besançon* 444: 43–54.

Budelmann, F., ed. 2009. *The Cambridge Companion to Greek Lyric*. Cambridge: Cambridge University Press.

Budelmann, F. 2018. *Greek Lyric: A Selection*. Cambridge: Cambridge University Press.

Budelmann, F. and P. Easterling. 2010. "Reading Minds in Greek Tragedy." *Greece & Rome* 57: 289–303.

Burgess, D. L. 1988. "The Authenticity of the Teichoskopia of Euripides' *Phoenissae*." *Classical Journal* 83: 103–113.

Burian, P. 2009. "City, Farewell! *Genos, Polis*, and Gender in Aeschylus' *Seven against Thebes* and Euripides' *Phoenician Women*." In McCoskey, D. E. and E. Zakin, eds. *Bound by the City: Greek Tragedy, Sexual Difference, and the Formation of the Polis*. Albany: State University of New York Press. 15–45.

Burkert, W. 1966. "Greek Tragedy and Sacrificial Ritual." *Greek, Roman, and Byzantine Studies* 7: 87–121.

1974. "Die Absurdität der Gewalt und das Ende der Tragödie: Euripides' *Orestes*." *Antike und Abendland* 20: 97–109.

Burnett, A. P. 1962. "Human Resistance and Divine Persuasion in Euripides' *Ion*." *Classical Philology* 57.2: 89–103.

1971. *Catastrophe Survived: Euripides' Plays of Mixed Reversal*. Oxford: Oxford University Press.

Butler, S. 2015. *The Ancient Phonograph*. New York: Zone Books.

Byrne, L. 1997. "Fear in the *Seven against Thebes*." In Deacy, S. and K. Peirce, eds. *Rape in Antiquity*. London: Duckworth. 143–162.

Cairns, D. L. 1993. *Aidōs: The Psychology and Ethics of Honour and Shame in Ancient Greek Literature*. Oxford: Oxford University Press.

Cairns, D. L., ed. 2019. *A Cultural History of the Emotions in Antiquity*. London: Bloomsbury.

Calame, C. 1994–5. "From Choral Poetry to Tragic Stasimon: The Enactment of Women's Song." *Arion* 3: 136-154.

1997. *Choruses of Young Women in Ancient Greece: Their Morphology, Religious Role, and Social Function*. Trans. D. Collins and J. Orion. Lanham: Rowman & Littlefield.

Caldwell, R. 1973. "The Misogyny of Eteocles." *Arethusa* 6: 197–231.

1974–5. "Tragedy Romanticized: The *Iphigenia Taurica*." *Classical Journal* 70: 23–40.

Catenaccio, C. 2017. "Sudden Song: The Musical Structure of Sophocles' *Trachiniae*." *Arethusa* 50: 1–33.

2019. "Teaching *Orestes* through Performance." *Classical World* 113: 87–100.

Chandler, A. R. 1934. "The Nightingale in Greek and Latin Poetry." *Classical Journal* 30: 78–84.

Chiu, A. 2005. "Caught in Time: Creusa, Iphigenia, and Resolving the Past in Euripides' *Ion* and *Iphigenia in Tauris*." In Constantinidis, S., ed. *Text and*

Presentation: Papers of the Comparative Drama Conference. Jefferson: McFarland. 5–19.

Chong-Gossard, J. H. K. O. 2003. "Song and the Solitary Self: Euripidean Women Who Resist Comfort." *Phoenix* 57: 209–231.

2008. *Gender and Communication in Euripides' Plays: Between Song and Silence.* Leiden: Brill.

Collard, C. 1975. "Formal Debates in Euripides' Drama." *Greece & Rome* 22: 58–71.

1991a. *Euripides:* Hecuba. Warminster: Aris & Phillips.

1991b. "Euripides, *Hecuba* 1056–1106: Monody of the Blinded Polymestor." In López Férez, J. A., ed. *Estudios Actuales sobre Textos Griegos.* Madrid: Universidad Nacional de Educación a Distancia. 161–173.

Conacher, D. J. 1967. *Euripidean Drama: Myth, Theme, and Structure.* Toronto: University of Toronto Press.

1981. "Rhetoric and Relevance in Euripidean Drama." *American Journal of Philology* 102: 3–25.

Conomis, N. C. 1964. "The Dochmiacs of Greek Drama." *Hermes* 92: 23–50.

Conser, A. 2020. "Pitch Accent and Melody in Aeschylean Song." *Greek and Roman Musical Studies* 8: 254–278.

Cousland, J. R. C. and J. R. Hume, eds. 2009. *The Play of Texts and Fragments: Essays in Honour of Martin Cropp.* Leiden: Brill.

Craik, E. 1988. *Euripides:* Phoenician Women. Warminster: Aris & Phillips.

Cropp, M. J. 2000. *Euripides:* Iphigenia in Tauris. Warminster: Aris & Phillips.

2004. "Euripides' *Hypsipyle*." In Collard, C., M. J. Cropp, and J. Gibert, eds. *Euripides: Selected Fragmentary Plays*, vol. 2. Warminster: Aris & Phillips. 169–258.

Cropp, M. J. and G. Fick. 1985. *Resolutions and Chronology in Euripides: The Fragmentary Tragedies.* London: Institute of Classical Studies.

Cropp, M. J., K. Lee, and D. Sansone, eds. 1999–2000. *Euripides and Tragic Theater in the Late Fifth Century* (= *Illinois Classical Studies* 24–25, 1999–2000). Champaign: Stipes Publishing.

Cross, I. 1999. "Is Music the Most Important Thing We Ever Did? Music, Development and Evolution." In Yi, S. W., ed. *Music, Mind and Science.* Seoul: Seoul National University Press. 10–39.

Csapo, E. 1999–2000. "Later Euripidean Music." *Illinois Classical Studies* 24–25: 399–426.

2002. "Kallipides on the Floor-Sweepings: The Limits of Realism in Classical Acting and Performance Styles." In Easterling, P. E. and E. Hall, eds. *Greek and Roman Actors: Aspects of an Ancient Profession.* Cambridge: Cambridge University Press. 127–147.

2004. "The Politics of the New Music." In Murray, P. and P. Wilson, eds. *Music and the Muses: The Culture of "Mousikē" in the Classical Athenian City.* Oxford: Oxford University Press. 207–248.

2010. *Actors and Icons of the Ancient Theater*. Chichester: Wiley-Blackwell.
Csapo, E. and W. J. Slater, eds. 1994. *The Context of Ancient Drama*. Ann Arbor: University of Michigan Press.
Curtis, L. and N. Weiss, eds. 2021. *Music and Memory in the Ancient Greek and Roman Worlds*. Cambridge: Cambridge University Press.
Cyrino, M. S. 1998. "Sex, Status and Song: Locating the Lyric Singer in the Actors' Duets of Euripides." *Quaderni Urbinati di Cultura Classica* 60: 81–101.
D'Angour, A. 2006. "The New Music: So What's New?" In Goldhill, S. and R. Osbourne, eds. *Rethinking Revolutions through Ancient Greece*. Cambridge: Cambridge University Press. 264–283.
    2017. "Euripides and the Sound of Music." In McClure, L., ed. *A Companion to Euripides*. Malden: John Wiley & Sons. 428–443.
    2021. "Recreating the Music of Euripides' *Orestes*." *Greek and Roman Musical Studies* 9: 175–190.
Dale, A. M. 1968. *The Lyric Meters of Greek Drama*. Cambridge: Cambridge University Press.
    1969. *Collected Papers*. Cambridge: Cambridge University Press.
Damen, M. 1990. "Electra's Monody and the Role of the Chorus in Euripides' *Orestes* 960–1012." *Transactions of the American Philological Association* 120: 133–145.
Dawe, R. D. 1967. "The End of *Seven against Thebes*." *The Classical Quarterly* 17: 16–28.
de Jong, I. J. F. 1991. *Narrative in Drama: The Art of the Euripidean Messenger-Speech*. Leiden: Brill.
de Jong, I. J. F., R. Nünlist, and A. Bowie, eds. 2004. *Narrators, Narratees, and Narratives in Ancient Greek Literature*. Leiden: Brill.
de Oliveira Pulquério, M. 1967–8. "Características métricas das monódias de Eurípides." *Humanitas* 19–20: 87–168.
de Poli, M. 2011. *Le Monodie Di Euripide: Note Di Critica Testuale e Analisi Metrica*. Padova: S.A.R.G.O.N.
    2012. *Monodie Mimetiche e Monodie Diegetiche: i Canti a Solo Di Euripide e La Tradizione Poetica Greca*. Tübingen: Narr.
de Romilly, J. 1993. "Les Barbares Dans le Pensée de la Grèce Classique." *Phoenix* 47: 283–292.
de Temmerman, K. and E. van Emde Boas, eds. 2018. *Characterization in Ancient Greek Literature*. Studies in Ancient Greek Narrative, vol. 4. Leiden: Brill.
Delcourt, M. 1938. "La pureté des éléments et l'invocation de Créuse dans *Ion* (870sqq.)." *Revue Belge de Philologie et d'Histoire* 17: 195–203.
di Benedetto, V. 1971. *Euripide: teatro e società*. Turin: Giulio Einaudi.
di Gregorio, L. 1967. *Le Scene d'Annuncio nella Tragedia Greca*. Milan: Società Editrica Vita e Pensiero.
Dickin, M. 2009. *A Vehicle for Performance: Acting the Messenger in Greek Tragedy*. Lanham: University Press of America.

Diggle, J. 1981. *Studies on the Text of Euripides:* Supplices, Electra, Heracles, Troades, Iphigenia in Tauris, Ion. Oxford: Oxford University Press.

Dillon, M. 2002. *Girls and Women in Classical Greek Religion.* London: Routledge.

Dover, K. J. 1993. *Aristophanes:* Frogs. Oxford: Oxford University Press.

Dowden, K. 1989. *Death and the Maiden: Girls' Initiation Rites in Greek Mythology.* London: Routledge.

Dubischar, M. 2001. *Die Agonszenen bei Euripides: Untersuchungen zu ausgewählten Dramen,* vol. 13. Stuttgart: Metzler.

  2017. "Form and Structure." In Mclure, L., ed. *A Companion to Euripides.* Chichester: Wiley-Blackwell. 367–389.

Duchemin, J. 1968 [1945]. *L'ἀγών dans la tragédie grecque.* Paris: Les Belles Lettres.

Dué, C. 2006. *The Captive Woman's Lament in Greek Tragedy.* Austin: University of Texas Press.

Duncan, A. 2011. "Nothing to Do with Athens? Tragedians at the Courts of Tyrants." In Carter, D. M., ed. *Why Athens? A Reappraisal of Tragic Politics.* Oxford: Oxford University Press. 69–84.

Dunn, F. 1990. "The Battle of the Sexes in Euripides' *Ion.*" *Ramus* 19: 130–142.

  1996. *Tragedy's End: Closure and Innovation in Euripidean Drama.* Oxford: Oxford University Press.

Easterling, P. E. 1973. "Presentation of Character in Aeschylus." *Greece and Rome* 20: 3–19.

  1990. "Constructing Character in Greek Tragedy." In Pelling, C. B. R., ed. *Characterization and Individuality in Greek Literature.* Oxford: Oxford University Press. 83–99.

  2002. "Actor As Icon." In Easterling, P. E. and E. Hall, eds. *Greek and Roman Actors: Aspects of an Ancient Profession.* Cambridge: Cambridge University Press. 327–341.

Easterling, P. E. and E. Hall, eds. 2002. *Greek and Roman Actors: Aspects of an Ancient Profession.* Cambridge: Cambridge University Press.

Edmunds, L. 1981. "The Cults and Legend of Oedipus." *Harvard Studies in Classical Philology* 85: 221–238.

  2002. "Sounds Off Stage and On Stage in Aeschylus, *Seven against Thebes.*" In Aloni, A., E. Berardi, G. Besso, and S. Cecchin, eds. *I Setti a Tebe: Dal mito alla letturatura.* Patron Editore: Bologna. 105–115.

Elderkin, G. W. 1940. "The Sacred Doves of Delphi." *Classical Philology* 35: 49–52.

Emerson, M. 2007. *Greek Sanctuaries: An Introduction.* London: Bristol Classical Press.

Encinas Reguero, M. C. 2011. "La estructura del *Orestes* de Eurípides y el enigmático relato del frigio." *Cuadernos de Filología Clásica* 21: 119–133.

Euben, J. P. 1986. "Political Corruption in Euripides' *Orestes.*" In Euben, J. P., ed. *Greek Tragedy and Political Theory.* Berkeley: University of California Press. 222–251.

Farmer, M. C. 2016. *Tragedy on the Comic Stage.* Oxford: Oxford University Press.

Farrington, A. 1991. "ΓΝΩΘΙΣΑΥΤΟΝ: Social Self-Knowledge in Euripides' *Ion*." *Rheinisches Museum für Philologie* 134: 120–136.

Ferrante, D. 1996. *Euripide:* Le Fenice. Naples: Edizioni Danilo.

Finglass, P. 2011. *Sophocles:* Ajax. Cambridge: Cambridge University Press.

Finkelstein, N. 2010. Unmentionables: The Erinyes As the Culmination of Alpha Privative and Negated Language in Aeschylus' *Oresteia*. Dissertation. Columbia University.

Fleming, T. J. 1977. "The Musical Nomos in Aeschylus' *Oresteia*." *The Classical Journal* 72: 222–233.

Flintoff, E. 1980. "The Ending of the *Seven against Thebes*." *Mnemosyne* 33: 244–271.

Folch, M. 2016. *The City and the Stage: Performance, Genre, and Gender in Plato's Laws*. Oxford: Oxford University Press.

Foley, H. P. 1981. "The Conception of Women in Athenian Drama." In Foley, H. P., ed. *Reflections of Women in Antiquity*. London: Routledge. 127–168.

1985. *Ritual Irony: Poetry and Sacrifice in Euripides*. Ithaca: Cornell University Press.

1993. "The Politics of Tragic Lamentation." In Sommerstein, A., ed. *Tragedy, Comedy, and the Polis: Papers from the Greek Drama Conference: Nottingham, 18–20 July 1990*. Bari: Levante Editori. 101–143.

2001. *Female Acts in Greek Tragedy*. Princeton: Princeton University Press.

2003. "Choral Identity in Greek Tragedy." *Classical Philology* 98: 1–30.

Foucault, M. 2001. *Fearless Speech*. Pearson, J., ed. Cambridge, MA: MIT Press.

Fowler, R. L. 1987. "The Rhetoric of Desperation." *Harvard Studies in Classical Philology* 91: 5–38.

Fraenkel, E. 1950. *Aeschylus:* Agamemnon. 3 vols. Oxford: Oxford University Press.

Franklin, J. C. 2016. *Kinyras: The Divine Lyre*. Washington, DC: Center for Hellenic Studies.

2019. "Behind the Schemes: UVM's Production of Euripides' *Helen* (March 22–25, 2018)." *Didaskalia* 15.

Fuqua, C. 1978. "The World of Myth in Euripides' *Orestes*." *Traditio* 34: 1–28.

Furley, W. D. 1999–2000. "Hymns in Euripidean Tragedy." *Illinois Classical Studies* 24–25: 183–197.

Gagné, R. and M. G. Hopman, eds. 2013. *Choral Mediations in Greek Tragedy*. Cambridge: Cambridge University Press.

Garvie, A. F. 2009. *Aeschylus:* Persae. Oxford: Oxford University Press.

Gellie, G. 1984. "Apollo in the *Ion*." *Ramus* 13: 93–101.

Giannopoulou, V. 1999–2000. "Divine Agency and 'Tyche' in Euripides' *Ion*: Ambiguity and Shifting Perspectives." *Illinois Classical Studies* 24–25: 257–271.

Gibert, J. 1999–2000. "Falling in Love with Euripides (*Andromeda*)." *Illinois Classical Studies* 24–25: 75–91.

2019. *Euripides:* Ion. Cambridge: Cambridge University Press.

Gill, C. 1986. "The Question of Character and Personality in Greek Tragedy." *Poetics Today* 7: 251–273.

Giordano-Zecharya, M. 2006. "Ritual Appropriateness in *Seven against Thebes*: Civic Religion in a Time of War." *Mnemosyne* 59: 53–74.

Giraud, M. H. 1987. "Les Oiseaux Dans l'*Ion* d'Euripide." *Revue de Philologie* 61: 83–94.

Goff, B. 1988. "The Shields of *Phoenissae*." *Greek, Roman, and Byzantine Studies* 29: 135–152.

　1995. "The Women of Thebes." *Classical Journal* 90: 353–365.

　1999. "The Violence of Community: Ritual in the *Iphigenia in Tauris*." In Padilla, M. W., ed. *Rites of Passage in Ancient Greece: Literature, Religion, Society*. Lewisburg: Bucknell University Press. 109–125.

Goldhill, S. 1986. *Reading Greek Tragedy*. Cambridge: Cambridge University Press.

　1987. "The Great Dionysia and Civic Ideology." *Journal of Hellenic Studies* 107: 58–76.

　2007. "What's in a Wall?" In Kraus, C., S. Goldhill, H. P. Foley, and J. Elsner, eds. *Visualizing the Tragic: Drama, Myth, and Ritual in Greek Art and Literature*. Oxford: Oxford University Press. 127–147.

Goldhill, S. and R. Osborne, eds. 1999. *Performance Culture and Athenian Democracy*. Cambridge: Cambridge University Press.

Gould, J. 1978. "Dramatic Character and 'Human Intelligibility' in Greek Tragedy." *Proceedings of the Cambridge Philological Society* 24: 43–67.

Green, R. 2002. "Towards a Reconstruction of Performance Style." In Easterling, P. E. and E. Hall, eds. *Greek and Roman Actors: Aspects of an Ancient Profession*. Cambridge: Cambridge University Press. 93–126.

Gregg, M. and G. J. Seigworth, eds. 2010. *The Affect Theory Reader*. Durham: Duke University Press.

Gregory, J. W. 1999. *Euripides: Hecuba*. Atlanta: Scholars Press.

　1999–2000. "Comic Elements in Euripides." In Cropp, M., K. Lee, and D. Sansone, eds. *Euripides and Tragic Theater in the Late Fifth Century* (= *Illinois Classical Studies* 24–25, 1999–2000). Champaign: Stipes Publishing. 59–74.

Griffith, M. 1977. *The Authenticity of the Prometheus Bound*. Cambridge: Cambridge University Press.

　1995. "Brilliant Dynasts: Power and Politics in the *Oresteia*." *Classical Antiquity* 14: 62–129.

　2000 [1983]. *Aeschylus*: Prometheus Bound. Cambridge: Cambridge University Press.

　2017. "The Music of War in Aeschylus' *Seven against Thebes*." In Torrance, I., ed. *Aeschylus and War: Comparative Perspectives on* Seven against Thebes. London: Routledge. 114–149.

　2021. "Music, Memory, and the (Ancient Greek) Imagination." In Curtis, L. and N. Weiss, eds. *Music and Memory in the Ancient Greek and Roman Worlds*. Cambridge: Cambridge University Press. 25–62.

Grimaldi, W. M. A. 1988. *Aristotle,* Rhetoric *II: A Commentary*. New York: Fordham University Press.

Gurd, S. A. 2016. *Dissonance: Auditory Aesthetics in Ancient Greece*. New York: Fordham University Press.

Hagel, S. 2010. *Ancient Greek Music: A New Technical History*. Cambridge: Cambridge University Press.

Haldane, J. A. 1965. "Musical Themes and Imagery in Aeschylus." *Journal of Hellenic Studies* 85: 33–41.

Hall, E. 1989. *Inventing the Barbarian: Greek Self-Definition through Tragedy*. Oxford: Oxford University Press.

　1993. "Political and Cosmic Turbulence in Euripides' *Orestes*." In Sommerstein, A. H., ed. *Tragedy, Comedy and the Polis*. Bari: Levante Editori. 263–285.

　1996. *Aeschylus:* Persians. Warminster: Aris & Phillips.

　1997. "The Sociology of Athenian Tragedy." In Easterling, P. E., ed. *The Cambridge Companion to Greek Tragedy*. Cambridge: Cambridge University Press. 93–126.

　1999. "Actor's Song in Tragedy." In Goldhill, S. and O. Robin, eds. *Performance Culture and Athenian Democracy*. Cambridge: Cambridge University Press. 96–122.

　2006. *The Theatrical Cast of Athens: Interactions between Ancient Greek Drama and Society*. Oxford: Oxford University Press.

　2012. "The Politics of Metrical Variety in Classical Athenian Drama." In Yatromanolakis, D., ed. *Music and Cultural Politics in Greek and Chinese Societies*. London: Routledge. 1–28.

　2013. *Adventures with* Iphigenia in Tauris: *A Cultural History of Euripides' Black Sea Tragedy*. Oxford: Oxford University Press.

Halleran, M. R. 1985. *Stagecraft in Euripides*. London: Croom Helm.

Halliwell, S. 2011. *Between Ecstasy and Truth: Interpretations of Greek Poetics from Homer to Longinus*. Oxford: Oxford University Press.

Hamilton, R. 1974. "Objective Evidence for Actors' Interpolations in Greek Tragedy." *Greek, Roman, and Byzantine Studies* 15: 387–402.

Hanink, J. and A. S. Uhlig. 2016. "Aeschylus and His Afterlife in the Classical Period: 'My Poetry Did Not Die with Me.'" In Constantinidis, S. E., ed. *The Reception of Aeschylus' Plays through Shifting Models and Frontiers*. Leiden: Brill. 51–79.

Harrison, T., ed. 2002. *Greeks and Barbarians*. New York: Routledge.

Harrison, T. 2020. "Reinventing the Barbarian." *Classical Philology* 115: 139–163.

Hartigan, K. 1986. "Salvation via Deceit: A New Look at the *Iphigeneia in Tauris*." *Eranos* 84: 119–125.

　1991. *Ambiguity and Self-Deception: The Apollo and Artemis Plays of Euripides*. Frankfurt am Main: P. Lang.

Hawley, R. 1998. "The Male Body As Spectacle in Attic Drama." In Foxhall, L. and J. Salmon, eds. *Thinking Men: Masculinity and Its Self-Representation in the Classical Tradition*. London: Routledge. 83–99.

Heath, M. 1987. *The Poetics of Greek Tragedy*. London: Duckworth.
Hoffer, S. 1996. "Violence, Culture, and the Workings of Ideology in Euripides' Ion." *Classical Antiquity* 15: 289–318.
Holmes, B. 2008. "Euripides' Heracles in the Flesh." *Classical Antiquity* 27: 231–281.
Holzman, S. 2016. "Tortoise-Shell Lyres from Phrygian Gordion." *American Journal of Archeology* 120: 537–564.
Hordern, J. H. 2002. *Fragments of Timotheus of Miletus*. Oxford: Oxford University Press.
Hose, M. 1990. *Studien zum Chor bei Euripides*. Stuttgart: Teubner.
Hughes, D. D. 1991. *Human Sacrifice in Ancient Greece*. London: Routledge.
Hunter, R. 2009. *Critical Moments in Classical Literature: Studies in the Ancient View of Literature and Its Uses*. Cambridge: Cambridge University Press.
  2011. "Apollo and the *Ion* of Euripides: Nothing to Do with Nietzsche?" *Trends in Classics* 3: 18–37.
Hutchinson, G. O. 1985. *Aeschylus: Septem Contra Thebas*. Oxford: Oxford University Press.
Ieranò, G. 2002. "La Cittàtta delle Donne: Il sesto canto dell'*Iliade* e i *Sette contro Tebe* di Eschilo." In Aloni, A., E. Berardi, G. Besso, and S. Cecchin, eds. *I Setti a Tebe. Dal mito alla letturatura*. Bologna: Patron Editore. 73–92.
Imhof, M. 1966. *Euripides' Ion: Eine Literarische Studie*. Bern: Francke Verlag.
Jackson, L. C. M. M. 2020. *The Chorus of Drama in the Fourth Century BCE: Presence and Representation*. Oxford: Oxford University Press.
Jens, W., ed. 1971. *Die Bauformen der griechischen Tragödie*. Munich: Wilhelm Fink Verlag.
Kambitsis, J. 1972. *L'Antiope d'Euripide*. Athens: Élie Hourzamanis.
Kannicht, R. 2004. *Tragicorum Graecorum Fragmenta*, vol. 5. Göttingen: Vandenhoeck & Ruprecht.
Käppel, L. 1992. *Paian: Studien zur Geschichte einer Gattung*. Berlin: De Gruyter.
Karanika, A. 2014. *Voices at Work: Women, Performance, and Labor in Ancient Greece*. Baltimore: Johns Hopkins University Press.
Kárpáti, A. 2012. "A Satyr-Chorus with Thracian Kithara: Toward an Iconography of the Fifth-Century New Music Debate." *Phoenix* 66: 221–246.
Kassel, R. 1976. *Aristotelis* Ars Rhetorica. Berlin: De Gruyter.
Kassel, R. and C. Austin. 1983. *Poetae Comici Graeci*. Berlin: De Gruyter.
Kearns, E. 2013. "Pindar and Euripides on Sex with Apollo." *The Classical Quarterly* 63: 57–67.
Klimek-Winter, R. 1993. *Andromedatragödien: Sophokles, Euripides, Livius Andronikos, Ennius, Acciuss*. Stuttgart: Teubner.
Knox, B. 1964. *The Heroic Temper: Studies in Sophoclean Tragedy*. Berkeley: University of California Press.
Koelsch, S. 2012. *Music and Brain*. New York: Wiley-Blackwell.
Konstan, D. 2006. *The Emotions of the Ancient Greeks: Studies in Aristotle and Classical Literature*. Toronto: University of Toronto Press.

Kowalzig, B. 2007. *Singing for the Gods: Performance of Myth and Ritual in Archaic and Classical Greece*. Oxford: Oxford University Press.

Kranz, W. 1933. *Stasimon: Untersuchungen zu Form und Gehalt der griechischen Tragödie*. Berlin: Weidmann.

Kyriakou, P. 2006. *A Commentary on Euripides'* Iphigenia in Tauris. Berlin: De Gruyter.

Lamari, A. A. 2007. "Aeschylus' *Seven against Thebes* vs. Euripides' *Phoenissae*: Male vs. Female Power." *Wiener Studien* 120: 5–24.

2010. *Narrative, Intertext, and Space in Euripides'* Phoenissae. New York: De Gruyter.

Landels, J. G. 1999. *Music in Ancient Greece and Rome*. London: Routledge.

LaRue, J. 1963. "Creusa's Monody: *Ion* 859–922." *Transactions of the American Philological Association* 94: 126–136.

Lazarus, B. 2005. "Parodies and Breakdowns in Euripides' 'More Comic' *Orestes*." *Iris* 18: 2–12.

Lech, M. L. 2008. "A Possible Date of the Revival of Aeschylus' *The Seven against Thebes*." *The Classical Quarterly* 58: 661–664.

Lee, K. H. 1969. "Two Illogical Expressions in Euripides." *The Classical Review* 19: 13–14.

1996. "Shifts of Mood and Concepts of Time in Euripides' *Ion*." In Silk, M. S., ed. *Tragedy and the Tragic*. Oxford: Oxford University Press. 85–109.

1997. *Euripides: Ion*. Warminster: Aris & Phillips.

Lefkowitz, M. 2016. *Euripides and the Gods*. Oxford: Oxford University Press.

2022. "The Phrygian Slave in Euripides' *Orestes*." In Papadodima, E., ed. *Ancient Greek Literature and the Foreign: Athenian Dialogues II*. Berlin: De Gruyter. 99–118.

LeVen, P. A. 2010. "New Music and Its Myths: Athenaeus' Reading of the Aulos Revolution (*Deipnosophistai* 14.616E–617F)." *Journal of Hellenic Studies* 130: 35–48.

2014. *The Many-Headed Muse: Tradition and Innovation in Late Classical Greek Lyric Poetry*. Cambridge: Cambridge University Press.

2021. *Music and Metamorphosis in Graeco-Roman Thought*. Cambridge: Cambridge University Press.

Levin, F. R. 2009. *Greek Reflections on the Nature of Music*. Cambridge: Cambridge University Press.

Levine, C. 2015. *Forms: Whole, Rhythm, Hierarchy, Network*. Princeton: Princeton University Press.

Lloyd, M. A. 1986. "Divine and Human Action in Euripides' *Ion*." *Antike und Abendland* 32: 33–45.

1992. *The Agon in Euripides*. Oxford: Oxford University Press.

Long, T. 1986. *Barbarians in Greek Comedy*. Carbondale: Southern Illinois University Press.

Loraux, N. 1987. *Tragic Ways of Killing a Woman*. Trans. A. Foster. Cambridge, MA: Harvard University Press.
  2002 [1999]. *The Mourning Voice: An Essay on Greek Tragedy*. Trans. E. T. Rawlings. Ithaca: Cornell University Press.
Lourenço, F. 2011. *The Lyric Metres of Euripidean Drama*. Coimbra: Centro de Estudos Clássicos e Humanísticos.
Lowe, N. 2004. "Euripides." In de Jong, I. J. F., R. Nünlist, and A. Bowie, eds. *Narrators, Narratees, and Narratives in Ancient Greek Literature*. Leiden: Brill. 269–280.
Lübeck, M. H. 1993. *Iphigeneia, Agamemnon's Daughter: A Study of Ancient Conceptions in Greek Myth and Literature Associated with the Atrides*. Stockholm: Almqvist & Wiksell International.
Ludwig, W. 1954. Sapheneia: Ein Beitrag zur Formkunst im Spätwerk des Euripides. Dissertation. Tübingen University.
Lynch, T. A. C. and E. Rocconi, eds. 2020. *A Companion to Ancient Greek and Roman Music*. Chichester: Wiley-Blackwell.
MacInnes, D. 2007. "Gainsaying the Prophet: Jocasta, Tiresias, and the Lille Stesichorus." *Quaderni Urbinati di Cultura Classica* 86: 95–108.
Mannsperger, B. 1971. "Die Rhesis." In Jens, W., ed. *Die Bauformen der griechischen Tragödie*. Munich: Wilhelm Fink Verlag. 143–181.
March, J. 1987. *The Creative Poet: Studies on the Treatment of Myth in Greek Poetry* [BICS Suppl. 49]. London: Institute of Classical Studies.
Margulis, E. H. 2019. *The Psychology of Music: A Very Short Introduction*. Oxford: Oxford University Press.
Marshall, C. W. 1996. "Literary Awareness in Euripides and His Audience." In Worthington, I., ed. *Voice into Text: Orality and Literacy in Ancient Greece*. Leiden: Brill. 81–98.
  2009. "Sophocles' *Chryses* and the Date of *Iphigenia in Tauris*." In Cousland, J. R. C. and J. R. Hume, eds. *The Play of Texts and Fragments: Essays in Honour of Martin Cropp*. Leiden: Brill. 141–156.
  2014. *The Structure and Performance of Euripides'* Helen. Cambridge: Cambridge University Press.
Martin, G. 2018. *Euripides:* Ion. Berlin: De Gruyter.
Martin, R. P. 2003. "The Pipes Are Brawling: Conceptualizing Musical Performance in Athens." In Dougherty, C. and L. Kurke, eds. *The Cultures within Ancient Greek Culture: Contact, Conflict, Collaboration*. Cambridge: Cambridge University Press. 153–180.
  2008. "Keens from the Absent Chorus: Troy to Ulster." In Suter, A., ed. *Lament: Studies in the Ancient Mediterranean and Beyond*. Oxford: Oxford University Press. 118–138.
Mastronarde, D. J. 1975. "Iconography and Imagery in Euripides' *Ion*." *California Studies in Classical Antiquity* 8: 163–176.

1990. "Actors on High: The Skene-Roof, the Crane, and the Gods in Attic Drama." *Classical Antiquity* 9: 247–294.

1994. *Euripides:* Phoenissae. Cambridge: Cambridge University Press.

2002. *Euripides:* Medea. Cambridge: Cambridge University Press.

2010. *The Art of Euripides: Dramatic Technique and Social Context.* Cambridge: Cambridge University Press.

McClure, L. 1995. "Female Speech and Characterization in Euripides." In de Martino, F. and A. H. Sommerstein, eds. *Lo Spettacolo delle Voci.* Bari: Levante Editori. 35–60.

1999. *Spoken Like a Woman: Speech and Gender in Athenian Drama.* Princeton: Princeton University Press.

McClure, L., ed. 2017. *A Companion to Euripides.* Malden: John Wiley & Sons.

Medda, E. 2005. "Il coro straniato: considerazioni sulla voce corale nella *Fenicie* di Euripide." *Prometheus* 31: 119–131.

Melidis, K. 2020. "The Vocal Art in Greek and Roman Antiquity." In Lynch, T. A. C. and E. Rocconi, eds. *A Companion to Ancient Greek and Roman Music.* Hoboken: Wiley. 201–212.

Michaelides, S. 1978. *The Music of Ancient Greece: An Encyclopaedia.* London: Faber & Faber.

Mikalson, J. D. 1991. *Honor Thy Gods: Popular Religion in Greek Tragedy.* Chapel Hill: University of North Carolina Press.

Minchin, E. 2021. "Visualizing the Shield of Achilles: Approaching Its Landscapes via Cognitive Paths." *Classical Quarterly* 70: 473–484.

Mirto, M. S. 1995. "Salvare il γένος e riformare il culto: Divinazione et razionalità nell' *Ifigenia Taurica.*" *MD* 32: 55–98.

2009. *Euripide:* Ione. Milan: RCS Libri, S.p.A.

Moore, T. J. 2022. "Ancient Plays: Are They Musicals?" *Greek and Roman Musical Studies* 11: 1–21.

Mossman, J. 1995.*Wild Justice: A Study of Euripides'* Hecuba. Oxford: Oxford University Press.

2005. "Women's Voices." In Gregory, J., ed. *A Companion to Greek Tragedy.* Oxford: Blackwell. 352–365.

Mueller, M. 2010. "Athens in a Basket: Naming, Objects, and Identity in Euripides' *Ion.*" *Arethusa* 43: 365–402.

2016. *Objects As Actors: Props and the Poetics of Performance in Greek Tragedy.* Chicago: University of Chicago Press.

2018. "Dreamscape and Dread in Euripides' *Iphigenia among the Taurians.*" In Felton, D., ed. *Landscapes of Dread in Classical Antiquity: Negative Emotion in Natural and Constructed Spaces.* London: Routledge. 77–94.

Mueller-Goldingen, C. 1985. *Untersuchungen zu den Phönissen des Euripides.* Palingenesia 22. Stuttgart: F. Stiener Verlag Wiesbaden.

Murnaghan, S. 1999. "The Poetics of Loss in Greek Epic." In Beissinger, M., J. Tylus, and S. Wofford, eds. *Epic Traditions in the Contemporary World: The Poetics of Community*. Berkeley: University of California Press. 203–220.

2005. "Women in Groups: Aeschylus' *Suppliants* and the Female Choruses of Greek Tragedy." In Pedrick, V. and S. M. Oberhelman, eds. *The Soul of Tragedy: Essays on Athenian Drama*. Chicago: University of Chicago Press. 183–198.

2011. "*Choroi achoroi*: The Athenian Politics of Tragic Choral Identity." In Carter, D. M., ed. *Why Athens? A Reappraisal of Tragic Politics*. Oxford: Oxford University Press. 245–267.

2013. "The Choral Plot of Euripides' *Helen*." In Gagné, R. and M. G. Hopman, eds. *Choral Mediations in Greek Tragedy*. Cambridge: Cambridge University Press. 155–177.

Murray, G. 1965 [1913]. *Euripides and His Age*. Oxford: Oxford University Press.

Murray, P. and P. Wilson, eds. 2004. *Music and the Muses: The Culture of "Mousikē" in the Classical Athenian City*. Oxford: Oxford University Press.

Natanblut, E. 2009. "Amphion in Euripides' *Antiope*." *Rheinisches Museum für Philologie* 152: 133–140.

Nooter, S. 2011. "Language, Lamentation, and Power in Sophocles' *Electra*." *Classical World* 104: 399–417.

2012. *When Heroes Sing: Sophocles and the Shifting Soundscape of Tragedy*. Cambridge: Cambridge University Press.

2017. *The Mortal Voice in the Tragedies of Aeschylus*. Cambridge: Cambridge University Press.

Nordheider, H. W. 1980. *Chorlieder des Euripides in ihrer dramatischen Funktion*. Frankfurt am Main: Lang.

Nünning, A. 2005. "Reconceptualizing Unreliable Narration: Synthesizing Cogitive and Rhetorical Approaches." In Phelan, J. and P. L. Rabinowitz, eds. *A Companion to Narrative Theory*. Malden: Wiley-Blackwell. 89–107.

Nussbaum, M. C. 2001. *Upheavals of Thought: The Intelligence of Emotions*. Cambridge: Cambridge University Press.

O'Brien, M. J. 1988. "Pelopid History and the Plot of *Iphigenia in Tauris*." *The Classical Quarterly* 38: 98–115.

O'Bryhim, S. 2000. "The Ritual of Human Sacrifice in Euripides." *Classical Bulletin* 76: 29–38.

O'Connor-Visser, E. A. M. E. 1987. *Aspects of Human Sacrifice in the Tragedies of Euripides*. Amsterdam: B. R. Grüner.

Olsen, S. 2021. *Solo Dance in Archaic and Classical Greek Literature: Representing the Unruly Body*. Cambridge: Cambridge University Press.

Olsen, S. and M. Telò, eds. 2022. *Queer Euripides: Re-readings in Greek Tragedy*. London: Bloomsbury.

Olson, G. 2003. "Reconsidering Unreliability: Fallible and Untrustworthy Narrators." *Narrative* 11: 93–109.

Orwin, C. 1980. "Feminine Justice: The End of the *Seven against Thebes*." *Classical Philology* 75: 187–196.

Owen, A. S. 2003 [1939]. *Euripides, Ion*. Oxford: Oxford University Press.

Page, D. L. 1934. *Actors' Interpolations in Greek Tragedy, Studied with Special Reference to Euripides'* Iphigenia in Aulis. Oxford: Oxford University Press.

  1972. *Aeschyli: Septem Quae Supersunt Tragoedias*. Oxford: Oxford University Press.

Papadimitropoulos, L. 2011. "On Apollo's Epiphany in Euripides' *Orestes*." *Hermes* 139: 501–506.

Papadodima, E. 2016. "The Rhetoric of Fear in Euripides' *Phoenician Women*." *Antichthon* 50: 33–49.

Papadodima, E., ed. 2022. *Ancient Greek Literature and the Foreign: Athenian Dialogues II*. Berlin: De Gruyter.

Parker, L. P. E. 2016. *Euripides'* Iphigenia in Tauris. Oxford: Oxford University Press.

Parker, R. 1983. *Miasma: Pollution and Purification in Early Greek Religion*. Oxford: Oxford University Press.

Parry, H. 1978. *The Lyric Poems of Greek Tragedy*. Toronto: Samuel Stevens.

Pedrick, V. 2007. *Euripides, Freud, and the Romance of Belonging*. Baltimore: Johns Hopkins University Press.

Pellegrino, M. 2004. *Euripide: Ione*. Bari: Palomar.

Pelling, C., ed. 1990. *Characterization and Individuality in Greek Literature*. Oxford: Oxford University Press.

Peponi, A.-E. 2012. *Frontiers of Pleasure: Models of Aesthetic Response in Archaic and Classical Greek Thought*. Oxford: Oxford University Press.

Peponi, A.-E., ed. 2013. *Performance and Culture in Plato's* Laws. Cambridge: Cambridge University Press.

Perris, S. 2011. "What Maketh the Messenger: Reportage in Greek Tragedy." In Mackey, A., ed. *Australia Society for Classical Studies 32 Proceedings*. ascs.org.au/news/ascs32/Perris.pdf.

Phillips, T. 2015. "Echo in Euripides' *Andromeda*." *Greek and Roman Musical Studies* 3: 53–66.

Pintacuda, M. 1978. *La Musica Nella Tragedia Greca*. Cefalù: L. Misuraca.

Podlecki, A. J. 1962. "Some Themes in Euripides' *Phoenissae*." *Transactions and Proceedings of the American Philological Association* 93: 355–373.

  2005. *Aeschylus: Prometheus Bound*. Oxford: Phillips.

Pöhlmann, E. and G. Heldmann. 2008. *Gegenwärtige Vergangenheit: Ausgewählte Kleine Schriften*. Berlin: De Gruyter.

Pöhlmann, E. and M. L. West. 2001. *Documents of Ancient Greek Music: The Extant Melodie and Fragments*. Oxford: Oxford University Press.

Porter, J. R. 1994. *Studies in Euripides'* Orestes. *Mnemosyne* Supp. 128. Leiden: Brill.

Power, T. C. 2010. *The Culture of Kitharôidia*. Washington, DC: Center for Hellenic Studies.

Prodi, E. E. 2018. "Dancing in Delphi, Dancing in Thebes: The Lyric Chorus in Euripides' *Phoenician Women*." In Andújar, R., T. Coward, and T. Hadjimichael, eds. *Paths of Song: The Lyric Dimension of Greek Tragedy*. Berlin: De Gruyter. 291–314.

2022. "Tragic Hexameters and Generic Archeology: Hera's Hymn to the Nymphs (Aesch. Frags. 168–168B Radt)." *Classical Philology* 117: 234–258.

Purves, A. C. 2010. *Space and Time in Ancient Greek Narrative*. Cambridge: Cambridge University Press.

Rabinowitz, N. S. 1993. *Anxiety Veiled: Euripides and the Traffic in Women*. Ithaca: Cornell University Press.

Radding, J. 2017. "Paeanic Crises: Eurpides' *Ion* and the Failure to Perform Identity." *American Journal of Philology* 138: 393–434.

Raffa, M. 2016. "Performance corale ed emissione vocale nella parodo dell'*Oreste* di Euripide: evidenza testuale ed esegesi antica." *Quaderni Urbinati di Cultura Classica* 112: 121–135.

Rawson, E. 1970. "Family and Fatherland in Euripides' *Phoenissae*." *Greek, Roman, and Byzantine Studies* 11: 109–127.

Revermann, M. 1999–2000. "Euripides, Tragedy, and Macedon: Some Conditions of Reception." In Cropp, M., K. Lee, and D. Sansone, eds. *Euripides and Tragic Theatre in the Late Fifth Century* (= *Illinois Classical Studies* 24–25, 1999–2000). Champaign: Stipes Publishing. 451–467.

2016. "The Reception of Greek Tragedy from 500 to 323 B.C." In van Zyl Smit, B., ed. *A Handbook to the Reception of Greek Drama*. Chichester: Wiley-Blackwell. 13–28.

Rose, P. W. 1992. *Sons of the Gods, Children of Earth: Ideology and Literary Form in Ancient Greece*. Ithaca: Cornell University Press.

Rosenbloom, D. 2006. *Aeschylus: Persians*. London: Duckworth.

Rosivach, V. 1977. "Earthborns and Olympians: The Parodos of the *Ion*." *The Classical Quarterly* 27: 284–294.

Rutherford, I. 1994–5. "Apollo in Ivy: The Tragic Paean." *Arion* 3: 112–135.

2001. *Pindar's Paeans: A Reading of the Fragments with a Survey of the Genre*. Oxford: Oxford University Press.

Rutherford, R. B. 2012. *Greek Tragic Style: Form, Language, and Interpretation*. Cambridge: Cambridge University Press.

Rynearson, N. 2014. "Creusa's Palinode: Gender, Genealogy, and Intertextuality in the *Ion*." *Arethusa* 47: 39–69.

Sacks, O. 2007. *Musicophilia: Tales of Music and the Brain*. New York: Knopf.

Saïd, S. 1984. "Grecs et Barbares dans les tragédies d'Euripide: La fin des différence?" *Ktèma* 9: 27–53.

Sansone, D. 1975. "The Sacrifice-Motif in Euripides' *Iphigenia in Tauris*." *Transactions of the American Philological Association* 105: 283–295.

1981. *Euripides:* Iphigenia in Tauris. Leipzig: Teubner.

2016. "The Size of the Tragic Chorus." *Phoenix* 70: 233–254.

Saxonhouse, A. W. 2005. "Another Antigone: The Emergence of the Female Political Actor in Euripides' *Phoenician Women.*" *Political Theory* 33: 472–494.

Scafuro, A. 1990. "Discourses of Sexual Violation in Mythic Accounts and Dramatic Versions of 'The Girl's Tragedy'." *Differences* 2: 126–159.

Schadewaldt, W. 1926. *Monolog und Selbstgespräch*. Berlin: Weidmannsche Buchhandlung.

Scharffenberger, E. 1995. "A Tragic Lysistrata? Jocasta in the 'Reconciliation Scene' of Euripides' *Phoenician Women.*" *Rheinisches Museum für Philologie* 138: 312–326.

Schmidt, H. W. 1971. "Die Struktur des Eingangs." In Jens, W., ed. *Die Bauformen der griechischen Tragödie*. Munich: Wilhelm Fink Verlag. 1–46.

Scodel, R. 1997. "Teichoskopia, Catalogue, and the Female Spectator in Euripides." *Colby Quarterly* 33: 76–93.

Scott, W. C. 1984. *Musical Design in Aeschylean Theater*. Hanover: University Press of New England.

1996. *Musical Design in Sophoclean Theater*. Hanover: University Press of New England.

Seaford, R. 1987. "The Tragic Wedding." *Journal of Hellenic Studies* 107: 106–130.

Segal, C. 1989. "Song, Ritual, and Commemoration in Early Greek Poetry and Tragedy." *Oral Tradition* 4.3: 330–359.

1993. *Euripides and the Poetics of Sorrow: Art, Gender, and Commemoration in* Alcestis, Hippolytus, *and* Hecuba. Durham: Duke University Press.

1999. "Euripides' *Ion*: Generational Passage and Civic Myth." In Padilla, M., ed. *Rites of Passage in Ancient Greece*. Lewisburg: Bucknell University Press. 67–108.

Seidensticker, B. 1982. *Palintonos Harmonia: Studien zu komischen Elementen in der griechischen Tragödie*. Hypomnemata 72. Göttingen: Vandenhoeck und Ruprecht.

1996. "*Peripeteia* and Tragic Dialectic in Euripidean Tragedy." In Silk, M. S., ed. *Tragedy and the Tragic: Greek Theatre and Beyond*. Oxford: Oxford University Press. 377–396.

Shisler, F. L. 1942. "The Technique of the Portrayal of Joy in Greek Tragedy." *Transactions of the American Philological Association* 73: 277–292.

Silk, M., ed. 1996. *Tragedy and the Tragic: Greek Theater and Beyond*. Oxford: Oxford University Press.

Simone, C. 2020. "The Music One Desires: Hypsipyle and Aristophanes' 'Muse of Euripides'." In Finglass, P. J. and L. Coo, eds. *Female Characters in Fragmentary Greek Tragedy*. Cambridge: Cambridge University Press. 162–178.

Sinos, S. 1982. "Characterization in the *Ion*: Apollo and the Dynamism of the Plot." *Eranos* 80: 129–134.

Slater, N. W. 1990. "The Idea of the Actor." In Winkler, J. J. and F. I. Zeitlin, eds. *Nothing to Do with Dionysus? Athenian Drama in Its Social Context.* Princeton: Princeton Univeristy Press. 385–395.

Smith, D. G. 2018. "The Reception of Aeschylus in Sicily." In Kennedy, R. F., ed. *Brill's Companion to the Reception of Aeschylus.* Leiden: Brill. 9–53.

Sommerstein, A. H. 1985. *Aristophanes:* Peace. Warminster: Aris & Phillips.

2006. "Rape and Consent in Athenian Tragedy." In Cairns, D. and V. Liapis, eds. *Dionysalexandros: Essays on Aeschylus and His Fellow Tragedians in Honour of Alexander F. Garvie.* Swansea: Classical Press of Wales. 233–252.

Spira, A. 1960. *Untersuchungen zum Deus ex machina bei Sophokles und Euripides.* Kallmünz: M. Lassleben.

Stehle, E. 2005. "Prayer and Curse in Aeschylus' *Seven against Thebes.*" *Classical Philology* 100: 101–122.

Steiner, D. T. 2021. *Choral Constructions in Greek Culture: The Idea of the Chorus in the Poetry, Art, and Social Practices of the Archaic and Early Classical Period.* Cambridge: Cambridge University Press.

Stieber, M. C. 2011. *Euripides and the Language of Craft.* Leiden: Brill.

Stinton, T. C. W. 1990. *Collected Papers on Greek Tragedy.* Oxford: Oxford University Press.

Storey, I. C. 2011. *Fragments of Old Comedy*, vol. 1. Cambridge, MA: Harvard University Press.

Sultan, N. 1993. "Private Speech, Public Pain: The Power of Women's Laments in Ancient Greek Poetry and Tragedy." In Marshall, K., ed. *Rediscovering the Muses: Women's Musical Traditions.* Boston: Northeastern University Press. 92–110.

Suter, A. 2003. "Lament in Euripides' *Trojan Women.*" *Mnemosyne* 56: 1–28.

Suter, A., ed. 2008. *Lament: Studies in the Ancient Mediterranean and Beyond.* Oxford: Oxford University Press.

Swift, L. A. 2008. *Euripides:* Ion. London: Duckworth.

2009. "Sexual and Familial Distortion in Euripides' *Phoenissae.*" *Transactions of the American Philological Association* 139: 53–87.

2010. *The Hidden Chorus: Echoes of Genre in Tragic Lyric.* Oxford: Oxford University Press.

Synodinou, K. 1988. "Electra in the *Orestes* of Euripides: A Case of Contradictions." *Métis* 3: 305–320.

Taplin, O. 1977. *The Stagecraft of Aeschylus: The Dramatic Use of Entrances and Exits in Greek Tragedy.* Oxford: Oxford University Press.

1980. "The Shield of Achilles within the *Iliad.*" *Greece and Rome* 27: 1–21.

Taplin, O. and R. Wyles, eds. 2010. *The Pronomos Vase and Its Context.* Oxford: Oxford University Press.

Thalmann, W. G. 1978. *Dramatic Art in Aeschylus'* Seven against Thebes. New Haven: Yale University Press.

Thompson, W. F. 2014. *Music, Thought, and Feeling: Understanding the Psychology of Music*. Oxford: Oxford University Press.

Thorburn, J. E. 2000. "Euripides' *Ion*: The Gold and the Darkness." *Classical Bulletin* 76: 39–49.

Torrance, I. 2007. *Aeschylus:* Seven against Thebes. London: Bloomsbury.

  2013. *Metapoetry in Euripides*. Oxford: Oxford University Press.

Torrance, I., ed. 2017. *Aeschylus and War: Comparative Perspectives on* Seven against Thebes. London: Routledge.

Trieschnigg, C. 2008. "Iphigenia's Dream in Euripides' *Iphigenia Taurica*." *The Classical Quarterly* 58: 461–478.

  2016. "Turning Sound into Sight in the Chorus' Entrance Song of Aeschylus' *Seven against Thebes*." In Cazzato, V. and A. Lardinois, eds. *The Look of Lyric: Greek Song and the Visual*. Leiden: Brill. 217–237.

Tsagalis, C. 2004. *Epic Grief: Personal Laments in Homer's* Iliad. Berlin: De Gruyter.

Tsitsibakou-Vasalos, E. 1989. "The Homeric ἄφαρ in the Oedipus Myth and the Identity of the Lille Mother." *Glotta* 67: 60–88.

Tsolakidou, A. 2012. The Helix of Dionysus: Musical Imagery in Later Euripidean Drama. Dissertation. Princeton University.

Tzanetou, A. 1999–2000. "Almost Dying, Dying Twice: Ritual and Audience in Euripides' *Iphigenia in Tauris*." *Illinois Classical Studies* 24–25: 199–216.

Valakas, K. 1993. "The First Stasimon and the Chorus in Aeschylus' *Seven against Thebes*." *Studi Italiani di Filologia Classica* 11: 55–86.

Vellacott, P. 1975. *Ironic Drama: A Study of Euripides' Method and Meaning*. Cambridge: Cambridge University Press.

Vernant, J.-P. 1988. "Tensions and Ambiguities in Greek Tragedy." Trans. J. Lloyd. In Vernant, J.-P. and P. Vidal-Naquet, eds. *Myth and Tragedy in Ancient Greece*. New York: Zone Books. 29–48.

Verrall, A. W. 1905. *Essays on Four Plays of Euripides*. Cambridge: Cambridge University Press.

von Fritz, K. 2007. "The Character of Eteocles in Aeschylus' *Seven against Thebes*." In Lloys, M., ed. *Aeschylus*. Oxford Readings in Classical Studies. Oxford: Oxford University Press. 141–173.

Wassermann, F. M. 1940. "Divine Violence and Providence in Euripides' *Ion*." *Transactions of the American Philological Association* 71: 587–604.

Watson, S. B. 2015. "Mousikê and Mysteries: A Nietzschean Reading of Aeschylus' *Bassarides*." *Classical Quarterly* 65: 455–475.

Webster, T. B. L. 1967. *The Tragedies of Euripides*. London: Methuen.

Weiss, N. 2008. "A Psychoanalytical Reading of Euripides' *Ion*: Repetition, Development and Identity." *Bulletin of the Institute of Classical Studies* 51: 39–50.

2017. "Noise, Music, Speech: The Representation of Lament in Greek Tragedy." *American Journal of Philology* 138: 243–266.

2018a. *The Music of Tragedy: Performance and Imagination in Euripidean Theater*. Berkeley: University of California Press.

2018b. "Speaking Sights and Seen Sounds in Aeschylean Tragedy." In Telò, M. and M. Mueller, eds. *The Materialities of Greek Tragedy: Objects and Affect in Aeschylus, Sophocles, and Euripides*. London: Bloomsbury. 169–184.

2019. "Generic Hybridity in Athenian Tragedy." In Foster, M., L. Kurke, and N. Weiss, eds. *Genre in Archaic and Classical Greek Poetry: Theories and Models*. Leiden: Brill. 167–190.

West, M. L. 1971. "Stesichorus." *The Classical Quarterly* 21: 302–314.

1982. *Greek Metre*. Oxford: Oxford University Press.

1990. *Studies in Aeschylus*. Stuttgart: Teubner.

1992. *Ancient Greek Music*. Oxford: Oxford University Press.

2007 [1987]. *Euripides: Orestes*. Warminster: Aris & Phillips.

Wildberg, C. 1999–2000. "Piety As Service, Epiphany As Reciprocity: Two Observations on the Religious Meaning of the Gods in Euripides." *Illinois Classical Studies* 24–25: 235–256.

Wiles, D. 1993. "The Seven Gates of Aeschylus." In Slater, N. W. and B. Zimmerman, eds. *Intertextualität in der griechisch-römischen Komödie*. Stuttgart: M & P Verlag für Wissenschaft und Forschung. 180–194.

1997. *Tragedy in Athens: Performance Space and Theatrical Meaning*. Cambridge: Cambridge University Press.

Willetts, R. F. 1973. "Action and Character in the *Ion* of Euripides." *Journal of Hellenic Studies* 93: 201–209.

1996. *Euripides: Ion*. Chicago: University of Chicago Press.

Willink, C. W. 1986. *Euripides: Orestes*. Oxford: Oxford University Press.

Wilson, P. 1999. "The *Aulos* in Athens." In Goldhill, S. and R. Osborne, eds. *Performance Culture and Athenian Democracy*. Cambridge: Cambridge University Press. 58–95.

1999–2000. "Euripides' Tragic Muse." *Illinois Classical Studies* 24–25: 427–449.

2000. *The Athenian Institution of the Khoregia: The Chorus, the City and the Stage*. Cambridge: Cambridge University Press.

2008. "Costing the Dionysia." In Revermann, M. and P. Wilson, eds. *Performance, Iconography, Reception: Studies in Honour of Oliver Taplin*. Oxford: Oxford University Press. 88–127.

2009. "Thamyris the Thracian: The Archetypal Wandering Poet?" In Hunter, R. and I. Rutherford, eds. *Wandering Poets in Ancient Greek Culture: Travel, Locality, and Pan-Hellenism*. Cambridge: Cambridge University Press. 46–79.

Winkler, J. J. 1990. "The Ephebes' Song: *Tragoidia* and *Polis*." In Winkler, J. J. and F. Zeitlin, eds. *Nothing to Do with Dionysus: Athenian Drama in Its Social Context*. Princeton: Princeton University Press. 20–62.

Winkler, J. J. and F. Zeitlin, eds. 1990. *Nothing to Do with Dionysus: Athenian Drama in Its Social Context*. Princeton: Princeton University Press.

Winnington-Ingram, R. P. 1969. "Euripides: *Poietes Sophos*." *Arethusa* 2: 127–142.

Wohl, V. 2015. *Euripides and the Politics of Form*. Princeton: Princeton University Press.

Wolff, C. 1965. "The Design and Myth in Euripides' *Ion*." *Harvard Studies in Classical Philology* 69: 169–194.

　1992. "Euripides' *Iphigeneia among the Taurians*: Aetiology, Ritual, and Myth." *Classical Antiquity* 11: 308–334.

Worman, N. 2002. *The Cast of Character: Style in Greek Literature*. Austin: University of Texas Press.

Wright, M. 2005. *Euripides' Escape-Tragedies: A Study of* Helen, Andromeda, *and* Iphigenia among the Taurians. Oxford: Oxford University Press.

　2006. "*Orestes*: A Euripidean Sequel." *The Classical Quarterly* 56: 33–47.

　2008. *Euripides:* Orestes. London: Duckworth.

Yoon, F. 2012. *The Use of Anonymous Characters in Greek Tragedy: The Shaping of Heroes*. Leiden: Brill.

　2016. "Against a *Prometheia*: Rethinking the Connected Trilogy." *Transactions and Proceedings of the American Philological Association* 146: 257–280.

Youd, D. 2022. "Orestes – Polymorphously Per-Verse: On Queer Metrology." In Olsen, S. and M. Telò, eds. *Queer Euripides: Re-readings in Greek Tragedy*. London: Bloomsbury. 155–164.

Zacharia, K. 2003. *Converging Truths: Euripides'* Ion *and the Athenian Quest for Self-Definition*. Mnemosyne Suppl. 242. Leiden: Brill.

Zeitlin, F. 1980. "The Closet of Masks: Roleplaying and Myth-Making in the *Orestes* of Euripides." *Ramus* 9: 51–77.

　1986. "Thebes: Theater of Self and Society in Athenian Drama." In Euben, J. P., ed. *Greek Tragedy and Political Theory*. Berkeley: University of California Press. 101–141.

　1990. "Playing the Other: Theater, Theatricality, and the Feminine in Greek Drama." In Winkler, J. J. and F. I. Zeitlin, eds. *Nothing to Do with Dionysus? Athenian Drama in Its Social Context*. Princeton: Princeton University Press. 63–96.

　1993. "Staging Dionysus between Thebes and Athens." In Carpenter, T. H. and C. Faraone, eds. *Masks of Dionysus*. Ithaca: Cornell University Press. 147–182.

　1994. "The Artful Eye: Vision, Ecphrasis and Spectacle in Euripidean Theatre." In Goldhill, S. and R. Osborne, eds. *Art and Text in Ancient Greek Culture*. Cambridge: Cambridge University Press. 138–196.

　1996. *Playing the Other: Gender and Society in Classical Greek Literature*. Chicago: University of Chicago Press.

2006. "Redeeming Matricide? Euripides Rereads the *Oresteia*." In Pedrick, V. and S. Oberhelman, eds. *The Soul of Tragedy: Essays on Athenian Drama*. Chicago: University of Chicago Press. 199–206.

2009 [1982]. *Under the Sign of the Shield: Semiotics and Aeschylus' Seven against Thebes*. Lanham: Rowman & Littlefield.

2011. "Sacrifices Holy and Unholy in Euripides' *Iphigenia in Tauris*." In Prescendi, F. and Y. Volokhine, eds. *Dans le laboratoire de d'historien des religions: Mélanges offerts à Philippe Borgeaud*. Geneva: Labor et Fides. 459–466.

Index

Abrams, M. H., 184
actor's lyric, 16, 35
   in Aeschylus, 21, 23, 187
   in Euripides, 36, 39, 86, 117, 128, 138, 155, 188
   in Sophocles, 21, 23, 33, 36, 187
actors
   professionalization of, 12, 13, 113
Aeschylus
   actor's lyric in, 21, 23, 187
   as actor, 12
   death of, 11
   in *Frogs*, 8, 15
   monodies of, 2, 21–26
   music of, 13
Agamemnon (Aeschylus), 24, 164
   chorus in, 23
   dating of, 8
   herald in, 183
   parodos in, 9
Agathon (poet), 11
agōn, 2, 3, 8
   definition of, 42
   in *Ion*, 41–42, 61, 62, 66, 80
   in *Phoenician Women*, 113, 137, 141
Ajax (Sophocles), 30–33, 35–36, 107, 127
Alcestis (Euripides), 17
Alcmaeon in Corinth (Euripides), 37
Alexiou, Margaret, 89
amoibaion, 16, 113, 148, 159
anagnorisis, 77
anapestic meter, 25, 26
   Aristophanes' use of, 8
   in *Hecuba*, 33
   in *Helen*, 25
   in *Ion*, 46–49, 50, 53, 57, 58, 63
   in *Iphigenia among the Taurians*, 91
   in *Persians*, 27
   in *Phoenician Women*, 123, 138, 139
Andromache (Euripides), 17, 108
Andromeda (Euripides), 25, 37, 89
Antigone (Sophocles), 118, 124, 183
Antiope (Euripides), 25

Apollo, 21, 41, 81, 163, 186
   as god of light, 69
   as god of music, 43, 66, 69, 73
   as god of prophecy, 73
   as healing god, 68
   birth of, 74
   Helios and, 47, 48, 68
   Homeric Hymn to, 74
   lyre of, 55
   names of, 56, 76
   nature of, 41, 42, 63, 80
   paean to, 37, 45, 51, 63
aporia, 84, 107, 109, 145
arias, 10
Aristophanes, 7, 15, 19, 25, 142
Aristotle, 6
   on monody, 16
   on music, 19
   on pathos, 20
aulos players, 12, 13, 14, 55

Bacchae (Euripides), 17, 37
   messenger in, 163
   music in, 19
Bacchic dance, 140
Barlow, Shirley, 51, 160
Barrett, James, 7, 161, 162
Bassarides (Aeschylus), 24
Bauform, 6, 8, 37, 107, 158, 187
Birds (Aristophanes), 19
Booth, Wayne C., 184

character development, 3–4, 188
Choephoroi (Aeschylus), 23, 24
chorus size, 10
Cinesias (musician), 13
Cratinus (poet), 15
Csapo, Eric, 16–17
Cyclops (Euripides), 36

de Jong, Irene, 7, 161
deliberation speech, 82, 106, 107
Demetrius (literary critic), 55

desperation speech, 107
deus ex machina, 6
  in *Ion*, 43
  in *Iphigenia among the Taurians*, 110
  Plato on, 7
deuteragonist, 12
Dionysia, 11
dithyramb, 10, 13
dochmiac meter, 25
  in *Ajax*, 32
  in *Ion*, 64, 71
  in *Iphigenia among the Taurians*, 104, 105
  in *Phoenician Women*, 123, 128, 130, 139, 172
  in *Seven against Thebes*, 122, 123
dramatic form, 2, 6–10
dramatis personae, 3, 42

ekkyklema, 30, 164
Electra (Euripides), 17, 89
Electra (Sophocles), 183
emotion, 18–21
  Aristotle's definition of, 20
  cognition in, 20
enoplian meter, 105, 123
epirrhema, 16, 113, 117, 125, 156
Erinys, 142
Eumenides (Aeschylus), 7
Euripides
  actor's lyric in, 36, 39, 86, 117, 128, 138, 155, 188
  at Macedon court, 11
  dating plays of, 36
  in *Frogs*, 8, 15
  messenger speech in, 161, 163, 180
  monody in, 33–40
  prizes awarded to, 187
  Timotheus of Miletus and, 181

Fraenkel, Eduard, 6
Frogs (Aristophanes), 7, 15, 142
funeral rites, 22, 92
  in *Phoenician Women*, 141
  mourning robes of, 134

gender, 5, 115, 124
  laments and, 22, 33, 34, 149
  lyric and, 18
  monody and, 25, 39
  suicide and, 136
genre, 7
  hybrid, 6, 10, 81
ghosts, 8, 15, 33, 147

Hall, Edith, 17, 25, 33
  on Iphigenia, 83, 105
Hecuba (Euripides), 17, 18, 33–36, 108
Hegelochus (actor), 12
Helen (Euripides), 17, 25, 89
  dating of, 37, 90
  messenger in, 163
  nightingale in, 144
Helios, 47, 48, 68
Heracles (Euripides), 17
Hesiod, 19
Hippolytus (Euripides), 17, 18, 108
Homer, 73, 162
Homeric Hymn to Apollo, 74
honor (αἰδώς), 65
Horai (Cratinus), 15
hymns, 11, 45, 56, 67, 93, 98
Hypsipyle (Euripides), 26

Iliad (Homer), 89, 127, 176, 177
  teichoskopia in, 118, 119
Ion (Euripides), 17, 36, 41–44, 80–81, 187, 188
  agōn in, 41–42, 61, 62, 66, 80
  dating of, 37
  dochmiac meter in, 64, 71
  messenger in, 163
  monody in, 108, 169
  parodos in, 58
Iphigenia among the Taurians (Euripides), 17, 36, 82–85, 111, 187
  dating of, 37, 38, 82
  dochmiac meter in, 104, 105
  messenger, 163
  parodos in, 85, 88, 91, 98, 110
  rhesis in, 82, 86
  stichomythic exchange in, 99, 101
Iphigenia in Aulis (Euripides), 14, 17, 37, 84

Jens, W., 6

kithara players, 13, 24
kitharoidic song, 181–182, 185
Knox, Bernard, 25
kommos, 22
  in *Ajax*, 30, 32
  in *Iphigenia among the Taurians*, 88
  in *Persians*, 29

laments, 2, 11, 21–26, 91
  funeral rites and, 22
  gender and, 22, 33, 34, 149
  in *Iliad*, 89

laments (Cont.)
    in *Iphigenia among the Taurians*, 92
    in *Persians*, 26–30
    kommos as, 22
    language of, 91
    monody and, 22, 25
    structure of, 22
    threnos as, 22
lullabies, 11, 26
Lycurgus trilogy, 24
lyric
    choral, 10
    dramatic role of, 4
    emotionality of, 38
    gender and, 18
lyric dialogue, 16

magic spells, 11
Mastronarde, Donald, 7, 9, 146
Medea (Euripides), 7, 17, 107, 163, 166
Melanippes (musician), 13
melisma, 15
messenger speech, 3, 6, 8
    Bauform of, 158, 162, 165, 168
    in Euripides, 114, 153, 161, 163, 180
    monody as, 157–160, 185–186, 188
    scene-setting in, 175
monody, 37, 189
    aesthetic qualities of, 5
    Aristotle on, 16
    as "super-normal stimulus," 20
    as self-expression, 18
    Barlow on, 160
    coining of, 15
    definition of, 16
    dramatic form of, 6–10
    emergence of, 10–18
    etymology of, 10
    gender and, 25, 39
    in Aeschylus, 2, 21–26
    in Aristophanes, 8, 15
    in Euripides, 33–40
    in Sophocles, 2, 24
    innovation of, 2
    laments and, 22, 25
    music of, 187
    Plato on, 10
    polyphonic, 184, 185
    polyptoton in, 142
    role of, 5
    status markers in, 17

music, 4
    emotional power of, 18–21
    notation of, 14
    psychology of, 19

New Music, 13–14, 55
    Aristophanes on, 15
    composers of, 13
    critics of, 13
    definition of, 5
    Greek name for, 13
    imagery associated with, 132
    Timotheus of Miletus and, 181
nightingale, 144
nomos (astrophic narrative song), 181, 184
Nooter, Sarah, 24

ode, 2, 7, 11
Odyssey (Homer), 18, 177
Oedipus Tyrannus (Sophocles), 129
Olsen, Sarah, 18, 45, 63
    on dance, 132
    on Io's monody, 23
Oresteia (Aeschylus), 86
Orestes (Euripides), 12, 17, 36, 108, 157–160, 185–186, 188
    Agamemnon and, 172
    amoibaion in, 159
    dating of, 37, 39
    musical notation in, 14
    parodos in, 159, 160
    rhesis in, 39
    Wohl on, 176

paean, 51, 93
parodos, 6
    in *Agamemnon*, 9
    in *Ion*, 58
    in *Iphigenia among the Taurians*, 85, 88–91, 98, 110
    in *Orestes*, 159, 160
    in *Phoenician Women*, 114, 128–130
    in *Seven against Thebes*, 118, 121–123
pathos, 20
Persians (Aeschylus), 24, 26–30, 33, 35–36
Persians (Timotheus of Miletus), 181–182
Philoxenus (musician), 13
Phoenician Women, 155
Phoenician Women (Euripides), 17, 36, 112–115, 187, 189
    agōn in, 113, 137, 141
    amoibaion in, 113

Antigone's monody in, 138–145, 149
Bacchic dance in, 140
dating of, 37, 39, 112, 116
dochmiac meter in, 123, 128, 130, 139, 172
funeral rites in, 141
Jocasta's monody in, 130–137
messenger speech in, 114, 153
parodos in, 114, 128, 130
Seven against Thebes and, 116–117, 120–127
Sophocles' Antigone and, 118, 124
teichoskopia in, 113, 117–128, 145, 151, 156
Phrynis (musician), 13
Pindar, 122
Plato
  on *deus ex machina*, 7
  on monody, 10
  on music, 19
  on New Music, 14
Pliny the Elder, 144
polis, 3, 4, 135
polyphonic speech, 184, 185
polyptoton, 141, 153
prayers, 11
Prometheus Bound (Aeschylus?), 23, 44
Pronomos of Thebes (musician), 13
prosopa ("masks"), 3
psychagogic force, 2

recognition duet, 102, 104, 128
reunion duet, 100, 103, 105, 110
rhesis, 3, 8
  agonistic, 38
  Aristophanes on, 8
  in *Agamemnon*, 8
  in *Iphigenia among the Taurians*, 82, 86
  in *Orestes*, 39
Rhesus (Euripides?), 36
Rutherford, Richard, 7, 21

satyr-play, 13, 36
Segal, Charles, 35, 91
Semele (Aeschylus), 24
Seven against Thebes (Aeschylus), 117
  dating of, 116
  dochmiac meter in, 122, 123
  parodos in, 118, 123

Phoenician Women and, 116–117, 120–127
teichoskopia in, 118
Sophocles
  actor's lyric in, 21, 23, 33, 36, 187
  as *kithara* player, 24
  messengers in, 183
  monodies of, 2, 16, 24
Sphinx, 143, 144
Stesichorus, 172
stichomythic exchange, 3
  in Aeschylus, 7
  in *Agamemnon*, 9
  in *Ion*, 43
  in *Iphigenia among the Taurians*, 99, 101
strophic response, 11
subjectivity, 18–21
suicide, 108, 136, 150, 151
Suppliant Women (Aeschylus), 23
Suppliant Women (Euripides), 7, 17
Suter, Ann, 149

teichoskopia, 113
  in *Iliad*, 118, 119
  in *Phoenician Women*, 117–128, 145, 151, 156
  in *Seven against Thebes*, 118
Telestes (musician), 13
Thamyris (Sophocles), 24
Thesmophoriazousai (Aristophanes), 25
threnody, 139
threnos, 22
Timotheus of Miletus, 13, 181–182
Trachiniae (Sophocles), 183
tragedy
  development of, 11
  hybrid structure of, 6, 81
  innovations in, 12–14
  New Music and, 13
tragic style, 7
Trojan Women (Euripides), 17, 89, 127
  dating of, 37

Water Bearers (Aeschylus), 24
wedding songs, 11
Weiss, Naomi, 4, 70, 90, 92
Wohl, Victoria, 2, 77, 163, 176

Zeitlin, Froma, 86, 116, 158, 160

For EU product safety concerns, contact us at Calle de José Abascal, 56–1°,
28003 Madrid, Spain or eugpsr@cambridge.org.

www.ingramcontent.com/pod-product-compliance
Ingram Content Group UK Ltd.
Pitfield, Milton Keynes, MK11 3LW, UK
UKHW050428090925
462724UK00026B/1519